The Rules *of* Inheritance

The Rules *of* Inheritance

◆ *A Memoir* ◆

Claire Bidwell Smith

HUDSON
STREET
PRESS

HUDSON STREET PRESS
Published by Penguin Group
Penguin Group (USA) Inc., 375 Hudson Street, New York, New York 10014, U.S.A. • Penguin Group (Canada), 90 Eglinton Avenue East, Suite 700, Toronto, Ontario, Canada M4P 2Y3 (a division of Pearson Penguin Canada Inc.) • Penguin Books Ltd., 80 Strand, London WC2R 0RL, England • Penguin Ireland, 25 St. Stephen's Green, Dublin 2, Ireland (a division of Penguin Books Ltd.) • Penguin Group (Australia), 250 Camberwell Road, Camberwell, Victoria 3124, Australia (a division of Pearson Australia Group Pty. Ltd.) • Penguin Books India Pvt. Ltd., 11 Community Centre, Panchsheel Park, New Delhi – 110 017, India • Penguin Books (NZ), 67 Apollo Drive, Rosedale, Auckland 0632, New Zealand (a division of Pearson New Zealand Ltd.) • Penguin Books (South Africa) (Pty.) Ltd., 24 Sturdee Avenue, Rosebank, Johannesburg 2196, South Africa

Penguin Books Ltd., Registered Offices: 80 Strand, London WC2R 0RL, England

First published by Hudson Street Press, a member of Penguin Group (USA) Inc.

First Printing, February 2012
10 9 8 7 6 5 4 3 2 1

REGISTERED TRADEMARK—MARCA REGISTRADA

HUDSON
STREET
PRESS

LIBRARY OF CONGRESS CATALOGING-IN-PUBLICATION DATA

Smith, Claire Bidwell.
    The rules of inheritance : a memoir / Claire Bidwell Smith.
        p. cm.
    ISBN 978-1-59463-088-0 (alk. paper)
    1. Smith, Claire Bidwell. 2. Children of cancer patients—United States—Biography. 3. Daughters—United States—Biography. 4. Bereavement—Psychological aspects. 5. Psychotherapists—United States—Biography. 6. Women psychotherapists—United States—Biography. I. Title.
    RC265.6.S647 2012
    616.99'40092--dc23
    [B]
                                2011025136

Printed in the United States of America
Set in Adobe Garamond Pro

Penguin is committed to publishing works of quality and integrity.
In that spirit, we are proud to offer this book to our readers;
however, the story, the experiences, and the words
are the author's alone.

This book is printed on acid-free paper. ∞

To my mother and father—I have nothing but gratitude for all that I have inherited.

Part One

◆

Denial

There is a grace in denial. It is nature's way of letting in only as much as we can handle.

—*Elisabeth Kübler-Ross*

Chapter One

1996, I'm eighteen.

MY FATHER'S VOICE is tinny through the phone line. I am in the booth at the bottom of the stairs in Howland dorm. It is my freshman year of college.

Claire, he is saying, your mother is back in the hospital.

It is a Tuesday. My mother was just here two days ago, visiting for parents' weekend, and I am immediately confused as to why she is in the hospital.

Claire, are you listening to me?

I take a deep breath.

I'm here, Dad.

Listen. I don't know how to say this. The doctors, they don't think there is anything else they can do. The cancer is too far gone.

What do you mean?

I don't like the words "too far gone." They make me think of a ship lost at sea.

As I listen to my father run through the details of my mother's hospital visit, the previous weekend replays in my head on fast-forward, scenes flashing by in blurred succession.

My mother had arrived on Friday. We drove along the winding mountain roads together, Vermont like a foreign country to both of us, the autumn trees like bursts of flame—orange and gold and deep, deep red. There was a weird silence between us, a space that had never been there before.

The two months since I'd been at college were as long as we'd been apart in my whole life.

My mother worked hard to close the new distance, acting chipper, and I tried to fill the gap too, telling her about my classes and my roommate, Christine. That night we ate dinner at an Italian restaurant in town. She ordered two glasses of wine, let me have one. Around the room two or three other students sat at tables with their parents, and for no real reason I felt embarrassed for all of us.

On Saturday we strolled around campus, the white clapboard buildings and rolling green hills like a New England postcard. I pointed out my poetry teacher, an old hippie with a scruffy beard, and the boy I have a crush on, Christopher. From the steps of the dining hall we watched Christopher swing one leg over an old motorcycle, kick the thing to life.

He has a girlfriend, I told my mom.

Of course he does, she said. I watched her watch him, knowing that she already knew that kind of boy.

That afternoon we went shopping, and she bought me a shirt and a pair of hiking boots. In the coming months I'll cling to that shirt as though I'd cared about her that weekend, as though I'd actually been grateful for her visit. As though I hadn't wanted her gone already so that I could get back to my life.

As the weekend went on my mother grew too loose with me. She let me ignore her, let me smoke cigarettes in her rental car, and invited my friends out to dinner with us on the second night. She seemed desperate for me to let her in.

But I had only just discovered how to be without her. Why would I want to let her in?

On Sunday I watched her drive away, my lip between my teeth, blood on my tongue from the force of it.

That was two days ago.

I tune back in to what my father is saying on the phone. Something about hospice.

Wait, wait, I say. Back up.

She collapsed in the bedroom this morning, sweetie. There wasn't anything I could do.

I picture my mother in one of her long Yves Saint Laurent nightgowns in their bedroom in Atlanta. Picture my elderly father stooping to help her back to bed.

But she was just here, I say.

I know she was, sweetie. I know.

Months later, after she is gone, my father will tell me that he thinks she stored up that last burst of energy just to visit me. He will tell me that once she saw me safely ensconced in my life there, she was finally able to let go. When he says this, I will immediately wish that I had been more of a mess.

The doctors have recommended hospice, he says.

What's hospice?

My father is silent for a beat.

It's when you go home to die, he says finally.

It's here where everything becomes very still. Kids are laughing in the common room. The TV is on, and I hear glasses clinking. I pick at a flyer taped to the wall, pull at a corner of it until it tears away, watch it flutter to the floor.

My father calls several more times that week. First to tell me that my mom is home and that they have a nurse with her. Then to tell me that she's feeling better, not to worry. I should just keep going with school for now.

Can I talk to mom?

Not right now, sweetie. She's sleeping.

Both times he calls she is sleeping.

That weekend Christine and I go to New York with a couple of guys from our dorm. They're both named Dave. One of them has a rich dad, and drives a fancy, red Jeep. I cling to the roll bar as he swerves through Manhattan. The other Dave is an anarchist. He says things like "Fuck the Man," and I nod my head gently, afraid to agree but even more afraid to disagree.

Dave with the rich dad takes us to a jazz bar in the Village that night. It's a tiny, smoky place, and we all pile into a corner together. I've never done anything like this before—go to bars, run around a big city at night. I feel at once exhilarated and terrified.

Suddenly rich Dave leans in and whispers at us excitedly.

Holy shit. That's Cecil Taylor.

I look across the room at an old black man tapping his foot along with the music. Throughout the night my gaze will come back to him over and over, taking in his frail frame and deeply wrinkled hands. Even though we are in the same room it feels like we are in different universes.

Later that night we crash at someone's apartment just outside the city, and I end up in bed with anarchist Dave. He kisses me and paws at my shirt. He whispers gruffly in my ear that if I scratch his back, he'll scratch mine. I cringe inside and turn my back to him, falling asleep to his grunts of dissatisfaction. I vow that after tonight I'm done messing around with boys for a while. Anarchist Dave is the sixth or seventh guy I've made out with in the last couple of months and no good has come of any of it.

When I call home on Sunday night, my father finally hands the phone to my mom.

Her voice is hoarse. She says she is in bed.

I tell her about the trip to New York and she tells me that when she and her first husband, Gene, a jazz musician, moved to New York, they crashed on Cecil Taylor's couch for a month.

I don't tell her about sharing a bed with the anarchist the second night.

I HAVEN'T GOTTEN a package or a letter from my mother in two weeks. During the first couple of months of college there was something in my mailbox every time I checked, my mother insistent that we stay connected. She was nervous about me being so far away, even though she liked the college I chose.

Marlboro sits on a mountaintop in southern Vermont, far away from my hometown of Atlanta. There are only 250 students; most of them are writers or artists or musicians. They have fucked-up parents, scattered backgrounds, no idea of who they are.

I live in Howland, a squat, two-story, coed dorm that houses twenty students. Even the bathrooms are coed, and I shower late at night, tiptoeing down the hallway, flinching at the sound of the water hitting the cold plastic curtain. Christine is the only one on campus who is from the small town nearby, the only local among a lot of wealthy kids who hail from rich Connecticut suburbs and sprawling California subdivisions.

For the most part, I'm a good fit for Marlboro. I'm a little weird and a little eclectic, in that disgruntled-suburban-teen-girl kind of way. At my high school in Atlanta I was the school poet, spending hours writing long and angst-filled verses about my boyfriend or my mother's cancer. I smoke Camel Lights and I'm a little daring.

At eighteen, I'm tall and thin. My wardrobe consists of a collection of white V-neck T-shirts that I buy in packs in the men's section of the department store. I wear jeans and combat boots, black bras that show through the thin T-shirts. My hair hangs long past my shoulders, dyed a silky crimson that offsets my blue eyes. Two weeks before leaving for college I lay back on a tattoo artist's couch and let him put a needle through my nose. I now sport a tiny silver stud in the hole he created there. I think all these things will help me stand out at college, but really I fit right in.

So far I love being at Marlboro, love being away from the drama of my high school friends in Atlanta, away from my mother's cancer and my father's sad attempts to support our small family. I love the changing leaves and my trek up the hill to the library where I read twentieth-century poetry for long hours. And even though I am outwardly ashamed of it, I love my job washing dishes after dinner in the dining hall. I love the camaraderie with the other work-life students; I love how angry I can be. I try to impress them by drinking beer as I work, by smashing cans with my boot for the recycling bin.

I'm not fooling anyone though.

Another week goes by. My father calls every day to update me on my mother's condition.

Do you want me to come home? I ask him this every time.

Not yet, sweetie. Your mom and I have talked. We want you to stay in school for now.

I nod, and I try to ignore the pit of doubt unfurling in my stomach.

I go about my business at school, running forever late to my poetry class on Monday mornings, stomping cans outside the dining hall after dinner, drinking whiskey in the common room at night with whoever else is around. It has begun to grow cold and the leaves are falling, skating across campus in big drifts.

I try to focus on my classes but it's not easy. I'm having trouble with a paper for my cultural history class. I can't seem to form the paragraphs, can't seem to construct sentences to support my thesis. I write in circles, saying nothing. Finally one night I head over to the little building where the writing tutors work. Upstairs I sign in on a clipboard and print my name on the last available slot: 11:00 p.m.

I return to my dorm, to a note on the door that my father has called. Downstairs in the phone booth his voice is resigned.

She's not getting any better, my father says. The doctors here say there isn't anything else they can do.

There is a pause. Suddenly I hate this phone booth, hate the little metal stool I am sitting on, this stupid poster on the wall that I'm always picking at.

My father continues. I found a hospital in DC with a doctor who's willing to operate on her though. It's worth a shot, he says.

I listen, saying nothing. I don't know what to believe anymore. My mother has been sick for five years. Ever since she was first diagnosed with colon cancer, when I was fourteen, our lives have been a roller coaster of operations, chemo, and carefully researched alternative treatments.

I've changed your ticket to go to DC next week instead of coming home for Thanksgiving, my father says.

I listen for a while longer, my father's words rising and falling against me like waves.

When we hang up, I go back to my room and lie across the bed. I feel pinned there, like an insect.

After a while I look at the clock. It is almost eleven. I gather my books and head back to the writing center. A single light glows in the upstairs room. The stairs creak as I make my way up them.

The tutor is a senior named Michel. He's French Canadian and his name is pronounced *Me-SHELL*. I say it out loud a couple of times, and he looks at me quizzically.

We've never spoken, but I've seen him in the dining hall, observed his height, the angle of his jaw, his blue eyes. He is handsome but doesn't seem to know it. He wears an old coat with worn elbows. There's something about the coat. It's not like the ones the rich kids get from thrift stores. The coat is real; it's the best he can do.

I sit down opposite him and push my paper across the table. I am ashamed. I know it is badly written. I know that he has been reading papers all night and that he surely wants to go home.

I sit quietly while he reads, and I stare out the windows at the snow and parked cars. I think about my mother, about when I will see her next, about yet another hospital we will all become familiar with.

Suddenly I am crying.

Michel looks up from my paper and narrows his eyes. He says nothing.

My mother has cancer, I blurt out. She's going to a hospital in DC. I'm supposed to go there for Thanksgiving, instead of going home. My father says she is going to die.

I'm aware of my voice, young and husky. I don't know why I'm telling him all of this, but it feels good to say it out loud.

Michel sets my paper down on the table. It will remain there, forgotten. Somehow the following week I'll finish it, hand it in.

My father committed suicide a year ago, he says in response.

He just says it. Not without emotion, but as if he can't bear for me to go on without knowing this.

The sentence hangs there in the air between us.

The room is electric. It feels like we are touching, even though we aren't.

Michel says it again: My father committed suicide.

After that our conversation unspools like smoke. We sit at the table for the next couple of hours, long past the time the center is closed, talking, leaning forward in our seats. Michel tells me about his father. I tell him about my mother. In some moments we are shy, our eyes seeking out the corners of the room. In other moments we are brazen, the room charged with the strange energy we have created.

It's my father's birthday, Michel says. Right now, tonight. He tells me this at midnight, and then together we watch the second hand on the old clock on the wall sink over into a new date with an audible click.

Now it's my birthday, he says.

Our birthdays are one day apart, he continues. When we lived in different time zones, my father would call me when it was eleven here, midnight there. For that one hour, we shared a birthday.

I am dumb with awe. I can think of nothing to say.

Michel begins to cry, and I watch the tears drip down onto his sweater. This boy who is almost a man, who is almost a stranger, begins to cry.

He tells me that he's never told anyone all of this, that he's never cried for his father, not once in this whole last year.

I am silent, marveling at the power we have to unlock a person.

We stay up all night, talking. At some point we move to the empty dining hall. It is always left unlocked, giant cereal dispensers and milk available for students all night. We fill bowls with granola and sit across from each other, the food in front of us an afterthought.

Michel tells me all the things he wished he'd told his father. He is stern in his insistence that I not make this same mistake with my mother.

You have to tell her this stuff now. You might not get another chance. He leans forward, his blue eyes barreling into me.

Okay, I nod.

And sitting there across from Michel, I really think I will. I feel energized and empowered. I feel awake and alive and more determined than ever. Before tonight my mother's cancer just seemed like this thing that was just happening to all of us. But Michel has made me feel like I can actually play a part in what happens next.

Hours later, when dawn breaks, I am lying awake in my top bunk, replaying the evening. Michel's instructions, his careful and urgent sentences, float down over me until I am covered in them, breathing in lightly through my mouth.

But the thing I do not realize is that, no matter how I feel in this moment, I do not really think that my mother will die.

◆

FOR THE NEXT TWO WEEKS, Michel and I are inseparable. We have opened something, unlocked a door, crossed a threshold. But there are limits to where we go once inside.

I am determined to stick to my vow of celibacy following the disgust I felt with the anarchist, and I inform Michel of this on the second day that we hang out. I immediately regret this decision because all I want to do is bury my head in his neck, feel his hands in my hair.

One afternoon he invites me to visit his apartment in town. He is a senior and does not live on campus. He drives an old, beat-up car and picks me up in the late morning.

The drive to Brattleboro, the town at the base of the mountain, is about twenty minutes of hairpin curves, slowed by the occasional logging truck. We chatter idly in the front seat, the enclosed space presenting an unexpected intimacy.

Michel lives in a tall building in the town's center. At eighteen I don't know many people who live in apartment buildings. Michel's studio consists of a large room with an old, queen-size bed as the focal point. We stand in the center of the room, awkwardly, and I try to pick out something to remark on, but my gaze only falls on the muscles in Michel's neck, his jawline, and the way his hair waves slightly behind his ears. His eyes are sad, his lips full.

Let's go for a walk, he says.

We set out along Main Street and duck into the town's only bookstore, which sells a combination of new and used books. I run my fingers across the titles, hovering here and there, trying to decide on a book to pull out that will impress him.

Michel himself pulls out title after title without hesitation, and I make a list in a little notebook I carry around with me. Michel is a writer. He is almost finished with a novel. He has written dozens of short stories. He is meticulous about them, combing through the words like a surgeon afraid of leaving something behind.

E. Annie Proulx. He says the name with the same stern tone he used when he spoke about my mother. Years later I'll read a review of Michel's first published novel that compares him to Proulx, unknowingly bestowing on him the highest compliment he could have.

My mother becomes the silent chaperone of these afternoons with Michel, her threatened existence the reason we are spending time together. She is the subject we return to when the sexual tension between us rises. In a coffee shop Michel's hand stops on the small of my back, and both of us go rigid. He removes it. We breathe again.

So, when do you leave for DC, he asks?

After the coffee shop we go to the Price Chopper. Michel fills a basket with day-old bread, dented cans of soup. I've never been in a grocery store like this. It dawns on me that there is no one to pay his rent for him, no credit card with which to buy his groceries, like the one my father gave me.

We walk by the river, taking turns holding the bag of groceries. We are careful not to let our hands touch when we switch off. We stop under a bridge, sit next to each other on a concrete piling.

What do you want to do with your life?

I want to be a writer, he says.

You are a writer.

Not yet, he says.

He doesn't ask me what I want to do with my life. I want the same thing he does, but I don't tell him that.

Back in his apartment we eat our soup and bread, sitting on milk crates. When it's time for me to go, we stand near the door. A friend from school is giving me a ride back up the mountain and she is waiting.

Michel and I step carefully toward each other, and in one easy move he folds me into him. He is so tall and broad and warm. I want to crawl inside him and sleep there. We stand pressed together for a long time. I turn my face inward, breathing him in, my lips on his neck.

I kiss him there; I can't help it.

He pulls back slightly. I know he is looking for permission to kiss me.

But I gently push away and walk out the door.

I leave the next day for DC.

◆

THE FIRST NIGHT in the hospital I burn with Michel's words. I sit on the edge of my mother's bed. I haven't seen her since parents' weekend, and she looks worse than ever.

My mother was once a very beautiful woman, statuesque with a perfect sheath of white-blond hair that fell to her shoulders. She turned men's heads well into her fifties. But now her skin is gray, her cheeks sunken and sagging, and tubes snake their way from her nose, disappearing into the sheets. The skin hangs on her arms like threadbare towels on a laundry line.

She was operated on a little over a week ago. The doctor removed her colon entirely and created a colostomy bag by drawing part of her intestine through an opening in her abdomen. It provides a new path for the feces leaving her body.

The bag hangs from a hook on the side of the bed. I am careful not to kick it with my boot.

My mother reaches up and touches her hair.

You cut it, I say.

She nods, fingering its short length. Does it look awful, she asks? Her voice is slurred as though she is drunk.

No, just different, I say.

She drops her hand back to the sheets, closes her eyes.

With a sharp pang, I realize I miss her.

My mother was forty when I was born. She met my father in her late thirties, had already been married twice, but had never had kids. Even at eighteen I already know that she poured all her energy into raising me, as though by giving me so much of herself she could somehow erase the mistakes of her past.

Mom, I have to tell you some things.

She opens her eyes and slowly finds mine.

We've never talked about it. What it would be like if she died. She's been sick for four years and we've never talked about it. I don't know where to start.

Mom, I say, I just want you to know . . . I start but cannot finish.

What do I want her to know? Michel's words ring in my ears, but they are his to say, not mine.

I'm never going to stop, Mom. I say this finally, tears springing like little stars in the corners of my eyes.

I'm not sure what I mean, but I want her to know that this fervor I have for life—that it won't go away, that I won't let anything defeat it. I stare at the metal chain behind her bed that turns on the light.

I can't look at her.

She nods at me, her eyes bright with pain. I know, she says.

I ramble on for a bit, and when she is sure I am finished, she closes her eyes, leans back against the pillow.

I sit waiting, breathing through my mouth, as though I am out of breath.

She opens her eyes finally.

Claire.

I think she is going to soothe me, but what comes next isn't that.

Can you help me with this bedpan? She motions to a small plastic tub on the bedside table.

I blanch but nod.

It's awkward, trying to help her. She pulls the sheet away and lifts her bottom for me to shove the pan under. I don't know if I've done it right, but she's releasing anyway and I can hear urine hitting the plastic.

She moans as she pees, and the sound settles over me like a shiver.

The days come and go after that. I walk the corridors, memorizing the layout of the hospital. I'm good at this. I've been visiting hospitals since I was fourteen. There's a cold, dead garden that I stand in for long minutes, blowing plumes of cigarette smoke up into the air, stubbing the toe of my boot against a concrete planter.

I sit in her room for hours at a time, leaning back in my chair, careful not to disturb the colostomy bag. There is a tennis match on the television. My mother watches with limp concentration, her mouth open, her lips dry and cracked. She used to be fanatical about tennis. Every summer her arms grew stronger and more bronzed by the month. At night she would complain about her backhand, going over the details of the day's match at the country club.

My aunt Pam comes into the room suddenly, breaking my reverie. She is my mother's younger sister. Their relationship has always been a complicated one, fueled by competition, but for now they seem to have put that aside.

My mother smiles weakly at her.

Sally, Pam says with a bright smile. She treats my mother as though nothing has changed, and I am both jealous and resentful of this ability.

Oh, you're so dry, honey, she says. Let's get you all fixed up.

Pam grabs a little tube of Vaseline and rubs a smear of it across my mother's cracked lips. My mother presses her lips together, musters another smile.

Let's see these feet, Pam says, pulling back the sheet. Oh, I bet we can do better with these too.

She grabs a bottle of lotion and begins to gently rub my mother's feet. My mother closes her eyes.

I watch all of this silently from my chair. I wish I could do these things for her. But I can't. The truth is that my mother's body disgusts me. The truth is that I am terrified of it.

I can't shake the idea that she is rotting from the inside out, like a piece of fruit, bruised and swollen in places. I am afraid to touch her. I miss her beauty, miss her tanned, fit form. I am sick of the sutures and the colostomy bag. I don't like her cracked lips or her scaly feet. This creature is not my mother.

Later a nurse comes to bathe her. She helps my mother out of bed, spreads a towel over the floor for my mother to stand upon. The nurse unties my mother's hospital gown, tosses it into a corner.

My mother is naked, her form hunched over, her skin loose. I can see the bones in her spine, bumping down her back. The nurse runs a sponge over them. In my chair I pull my knees even tighter to my chest.

The nurse hands my mother a warm, wet washcloth, and my mother puts it between her legs. She looks over at me.

This is where we live, Claire.

I don't know what she means. I become perfectly still, trying to will this moment from happening.

I want to go home, but I don't know where that is anymore.

I want my mother back, but I know that she is already gone.

I don't want to remember any of this, but I know that I will.

◆

THE NEXT DAY my father and I join a few other families, in a windowless conference room off the cancer ward, for Thanksgiving dinner. I pick at the turkey on my paper plate as I listen to the other families talk about how grateful they are that their loved one is still alive.

I'm grateful for the doctors here, one of them says.

I'm grateful my father has lived two years past his diagnosis, another says.

Everyone is nodding at one another, tears brimming in their eyes.

Someone suggests we all hold hands and say a prayer.

Fuck this, I think.

I want to scream. I'm not grateful for any of it. Not for this pity dinner, not for my mother's colostomy bag or her extended prognosis. Not for Pam's sympathetic looks or my father's hand on my shoulder. Fuck it all.

I push away from the table abruptly and slam out of the room. I picture everyone around the table exchanging knowing glances. She's a teenager, I imagine them saying.

Poor thing.

Fuck them.

Fuck them all.

I suddenly hate everything: myself, my father, the doctors, this hospital, and all those families sitting around the Thanksgiving dinner table. I dig my fingernails into my palms until there are bright red little half-moons left there.

I find a pay phone in an empty hallway and I dial the number to Michel's apartment.

He picks up on the second ring.

Hi, I say.

Hi, he says.

He sounds relieved, excited to hear from me.

This is hard, I say.

I know, he says.

We are silent for a while then. All I can think about is what it would be like to kiss him.

I'll see you in a few days, he says.

Yeah, Sunday.

I hang up the phone and stand there for a while with my hand still on the warm receiver. I imagine Michel doing the same.

When I resurface later, Pam is swift to remind me that I should be grateful that we had Thanksgiving at all. I hate her.

Later I try to tell my mother about it. I've always been able to tell her everything, even terrible things, like when I was sixteen and thought I might be pregnant. I remind her now of the Thanksgivings we've had at home, of the funny feasts she prepared.

Do you remember the year you stuck Fourth of July sparklers in the turkey?

She stares back at me. Her face is blank and then breaks into the slightest curve of a smile.

I want things to go back to the way they used to be, I say.

The smile disappears. Her eyes fill with tears.

I bite my lip, look out the window. I am so angry. I hate her too.

I am relieved when Sunday comes; my father's figure receding behind security at the airport feels like freedom.

I CALL MICHEL that first night back, but he doesn't answer. I look for him the next day in the dining hall too, but he is nowhere to be seen.

He answers the phone the second night. I can hear music in the background, someone laughing.

Hello, he says.

Hi, I say. It's me.

Oh, hey. His tone is different. More casual, distant.

I'm back, I say.

Oh, right.

I wait for him to ask about my mom, but he doesn't. A beat passes and neither of us says anything.

Well, I say finally, you sound kind of busy.

Yeah, he says. Sorry. We'll talk soon.

I hang up the phone, feeling confused. Back in my room, I lie across the bed. I've never felt as lonely as I do right now.

I see Michel the next day in the dining hall. He is sitting with a girl named Kate. She is rich and from Manhattan. She has one of those pert noses that I've always envied. I can tell just by looking at them that they have slept together. In an instant shame seeps into me.

Right now I am simply confused and deeply hurt. It won't be until later that I will be able to recognize what it was like for Michel to walk into my world the way he did. Only then will I understand that my grief was too much for him. Right now the only thing I can think is how incredibly alone I am in all of this.

Michel comes to my room one afternoon, a week later, and asks me to return a short story he had written and given to me. In the story a man and a woman hike to opposite precipices of the same mountain. Taking turns, they each photograph the other.

I give it back to him. Almost immediately I wish I hadn't.

◆

FOR A WHILE, nothing changes with my mother. My father calls almost every day. He tells me what they watched on TV, if the doctors have anything new to report, that my mother says she misses me. I wonder if she really said that or if my father is making it up. He tells me that I will spend my Christmas break, a whole month, in DC.

I start hanging out with this girl named Katie. She has stars tattooed on the soles of her feet. So that she's always walking on stars, she says. She has a shock of thick, dyed, black hair that is startling against her pale skin, and because she's an RA, she has her own room. I start going there most nights after my dishwashing is done. We smoke cigarettes, listen to music.

Katie is friends with Christopher, the boy I've had a crush on since the first week of school, the one I pointed out to my mother over parents' weekend. He comes by most nights too, and the three of us sit there. I try not to look at him too often.

Christopher is the improbable choice. He is the boy all the girls follow with their eyes as he moves through the dining hall. He is handsome and, unlike Michel, he knows it. He is tall, with a mess of blond hair, bright eyes, quick fingers. He is a jazz musician. I like the way his pants hang from his hips.

Christopher's girlfriend has left campus for the rest of the semester, gone to Spain or South America or something, and suddenly he is everywhere: sprawled across a couch in Howland common room, cross-legged on rich Dave's bed and keeping time to Charlie Parker, leaning against a wall outside the post office when I go to check my mail.

It's impossible: me and him. I know this, but still I can't stay away. Our paths keep crossing. Sometimes I think it's just because of his friendships with Dave, who lives in my dorm, and Katie, but maybe it is more than that. Whatever it is, Christopher starts appearing at my door in the evenings. A bottle of whiskey hanging from his hand, a pack of cigarettes in his shirtsleeve.

I let him in and he takes a seat in the corner of the room. We don't talk much. We listen to music. We smoke cigarettes. Sometimes we go outside, stand in the snow, and look up at the night sky, at the stars there, their singular brightness seeming just as improbable as any of it: me and him, my mother's death, the future beyond them.

We don't talk about my mother at all, even though I'm pretty sure he knows. We don't touch either, even though I can't think of anything I want more. I don't even know why I want him so badly. Because I'm lonely? Because my mother is dying and touching boys feels like the opposite of that?

I don't know why Christopher keeps coming back to my room, but I don't dare ask him. Instead I just open the door and let him in, night after night. On one of those nights, after he is gone and I am alone again in the old armchair in the corner, I practice saying it aloud.

My mother is dead.

She is not dead yet. She is in her hospital bed in DC, but I want to know how it will feel to say it.

My mother is dead.

I say it several times.

My mother is dead.

My mother is dead.

The words become living things. They scuffle at the corners of the room, and I wrap my arms tight around me, trying to keep still so they will not notice me.

◆

CHRISTMAS BREAK FINALLY comes and with it a flurry of papers handed in, bags packed, and dorm rooms glanced over one last time before slamming the door, running out into the cold to catch a bus to a flight to a place I don't want to go.

DC is the same. My mother is the same: Gray. Slack. Tired. Not my mother.

She is out of the hospital now, and in a hospital bed in the study of my half sister's house, just outside DC. My father has three children from his first marriage, and one of them, Candace, lives with her husband and son in a suburb in Virginia.

My father and I sleep upstairs in guest rooms, and my mother occupies the downstairs, with nurses and hospital equipment, gently dripping IVs, and pink plastic bedpans.

I smoke cigarettes in my nephew Brian's room. He is only a few years younger than me, and we stay up late playing video games and drinking red wine that we have snuck from the kitchen after dinner.

On the first day I try to talk to my mom again, but it's like she isn't there, like she has already checked out of the world. I tell her about school and my last papers, about Christopher and the snow that finally blanketed the mountain. All these things she once would have cared about, but her gaze focuses in and out and she doesn't respond, other than to nod.

I sit upstairs in my room after that, sobbing into a pillow so that no one will hear me.

My father takes me for a drive a few days later.

Claire, he says, you know that the situation isn't good.

I stare out the window. My father is seventy-five years old. For most of my life people have thought he was my grandfather.

She's dying, he says. His voice is gentle.

I don't say anything. I want out of the car, out of this moment, away from all of this.

But there is nowhere to go.

After we get back to the house I stand in the doorway of the study, watching my mother sleep, missing her.

My father asks me to be on call that night and he gives me a baby monitor. He says he is tired, that he needs a break, but really I think he just wants me to spend more time with her.

She wakes up at least once a night, he says. All you have to do is sit next to her, comfort her until she goes back to sleep. She's just scared, he says.

That night, while we're playing video games and drinking wine, I swallow a little white pill that I've been carrying around in my pocket all day.

What's that? Brian asks.

Kind of like a quaalude, I answer.

Where'd you get it?

My dad, I say, washing the pill back with a swig of wine.

Brian shrugs and then unpauses the game we are playing. The tinkling sound of scoring resumes. I've already forgotten that it is my night to get up with my mom.

Hours later I stumble to bed in the guest room. My father has set up the baby monitor by my bedside and the little green light glows in the dark. It's the last thing I see before my eyes close.

I don't know what time it is, maybe three or four in the morning, when I open them again. I can hear my mother crying softly. I don't know how long she's been crying, but her soft mewling lights up the monitor with each intonation. My limbs feel like sandbags. I am warm and loose and so, so heavy. I push my way out from underneath the covers and make my way downstairs.

There is a tiny light on in the corner of my mother's room, and I stand for a moment looking at her. She is curled onto one side, her arms wrapped around her abdomen. She looks so small underneath the sheets.

I step forward finally and ease myself down onto the side of her bed. She doesn't seem to notice that I am there.

Mom?

She continues to cry. I reach out and begin to stroke her hair. The quaalude has left me feeling open and loose. I am not afraid of her.

Mom, I say again. It's okay. It's okay.

I murmur these words to her as I stroke her hair, smooth my hand in circles over her back.

It's okay. It's okay.

Her crying fades to a gentle whimper.

It's okay. It's okay.

My eyes are closed now too, and I lay my head down against her shoulder.

Mom, I miss you.

She is quiet now, her form gently rising and falling with each breath.

The memory of this moment will become the sole thing that prevents me from completely evaporating with guilt in the years to come.

Mom, Mom, Mom, I say quietly. The word like some kind of prayer.

We stay there for a long time like that, and when I wake up the next morning in my bed upstairs it will be hours before I remember any of it.

◆

OVER CHRISTMAS BREAK Christopher decides not to return to school. He tells me this over the phone. He is going to work for his uncle in New Jersey for a while, painting houses, saving money. Then he plans to move to San Francisco.

Don't you want to finish college? When he doesn't reply I immediately feel stupid for having asked. Naive and girlish.

The last time I see my mother is the day I drive back to school. She is in the passenger seat of my father's car. He has dragged her out of the hospital bed, wants to take her for a drive, to remind her of the world outside. He has wrapped her in blankets, and her skin is the same gray as the seats of the car.

I lean in through the open door, try to put my arms around her, but it's awkward and I just kind of press myself against her.

Her voice is hoarse, her hands claw at me just a little. I love you so much, honey.

I do not know that this is the last time I will ever see her.

Months later, years later, when I think back on this moment, I'll wish for so much more from it. In my head I'll scoop her up from the car seat like an infant. I'll hold her against me, burying my head into her. Mom, Mom, Mom. Years later I'll cry hard and loud, wishing I had done exactly this.

But instead I just give her that awkward hug and then I climb into my car. I let out a breath, light a cigarette, and put both hands on the wheel. I had insisted on leaving, on returning to school, but now that I'm actually doing it I feel uneasy.

It's a seven-hour drive back to Marlboro and already late afternoon when I leave. As I drive the last hundred miles through Massachusetts and into Vermont, a snowstorm sets in. I can hardly see the road, the world outside a blurry white eclipse. I drive thirty miles an hour, smoke cigarette after cigarette. I listen to the same songs on repeat.

I am frightened as I drive through the storm. It's not the snow or the road that I'm afraid of but the fact that I'm doing this alone. Just four months ago my parents were driving me to college, our cars laden down with flannel sheets and lamps that would clip to the headboard of my bunk bed.

On that three-day drive from Atlanta to Vermont my mother rode in my car with me, my father alone in the Acura, leading the way along the highway. On the last night of the trip I broke down crying at a restaurant in Massachusetts. My mother sat outside on the steps with me, rubbing my back.

Why did I pick a school so far away? I mumble through my sobs.

My mother smiles, leans into me. She wasn't sick again yet.

Because you're brave, she says. And ambitious and hungry for the world.

Tears ran down my cheeks, and I wanted to go home. I wanted to go back to Atlanta and to my bedroom in the basement. Back to curfews and dinner times, back to being a kid.

My mother rubbed my back, and we sat there until I stopped crying.

I think about this now as I drive through the snow, through Massachusetts in the middle of the night, my mother asleep in her hospital bed in DC.

As I finally make my way to campus it is a dark, dead place, and I instantly want to take everything back. I want to go home. I want my mother.

❖

TWO WEEKS GO BY. I trudge back and forth to my classes. Christine is gone all the time, busy with a new playwright boyfriend. Christopher is in New Jersey. Michel is nowhere to be seen, having holed up after his brief relationship with Kate fizzled out.

One afternoon toward the end of January, my father calls. I am sick of these calls. I hate the student who finds me, holding out a little Post-it note: Your dad called. I hate the little phone booth under the stairs in Howland where I go to return his calls.

Your mother is unconscious, he says.

I pick at the flyer on the wall. Rip another corner off and turn the bit of paper over in my fingers.

The doctors say she won't last more than a few more days.

I open my fingers, watch the piece of paper drift to the floor.

We talked about it, your mother and me. We decided that you should stay at school.

He takes a breath. He is waiting for me to say something.

I can't think of anything to say.

But look, kiddo, you're an adult now. You're eighteen. It's up to you.

I breathe through my mouth.

I'm coming, I say, and I hang up the phone.

It's already afternoon, but I figure I can be in DC by midnight. In my room I throw a few things in a bag: a book I'm reading, a pack of cigarettes, the shirt my mother bought me during parents' weekend. I leave a note for Christine.

It's one of those cold, overcast days where everything looks silvery and bright, just before it snows. I take my foot off the accelerator and let the car gather momentum as I wind down the mountain. I wonder how long it will be before I have to brake.

My mother is dying.

My mother is dying.

I say it louder.

MY MOTHER IS DYING.

The words mean nothing. I take a drag on my cigarette and steer the coasting car around a curve.

My mother is DYING.

Nothing.

Before long I'm crossing the border into Massachusetts, the road has leveled off. I think about how happy my father said my mother was when she returned home from parents' weekend. He said she was glowing, that she couldn't stop gushing about my life at school. I look at the little clock, calculate the hours, light another cigarette.

By 6:00 p.m. my body has adjusted to the constant hum of the engine. I've only stopped once, for gas and to pee. I've smoked too many cigarettes. My heart is pounding. I've made it through the endlessly boring stretch of Connecticut, but I've still got New York, New Jersey, and Maryland to go.

I cross the George Washington Bridge and watch Manhattan fade into the background. I think about my mother living there for all those years. I remind myself that she is dying.

DYING.

Claire, your mother is dying.

Nothing. I feel nothing.

I make my way onto the New Jersey turnpike and press my foot even harder against the accelerator. The light is ebbing from the sky and my chest feels tight. Maybe I'll get pulled over.

Do you know how fast you were going, young lady?

I do officer, but my mother is dying.

Dying?

DYING.

Right now?

Right now.

Go, go, he'll say, his eyes welling with sympathy and awe for this brave, young girl who is alone out in the world, her mother dying.

But I don't get pulled over. I just keep driving, the needle on the speedometer bobbing steadily at ninety-five miles per hour. My heart is pounding and I can't tell if the vibrating in my chest is from the engine or my own breathlessness. I've smoked too many cigarettes. *Pound, pound, skip.* I'm having heart palpitations. *Pound, pound, skip.* I squeeze my eyes tight for a moment, take deep breaths. *Pound, pound, skip.*

I start seeing signs for the town where Christopher is living. I want to stop. It's all I can think about.

After the third sign I let the car coast off the highway, down an exit ramp. I park at a gas station and stand in front of a pay phone.

I stand there for a long time, just breathing and watching the light fade from the sky. It's cold and my breath comes in plumes. Finally I pick up the phone and dial the numbers. Christopher's aunt answers.

Is Christopher there? My voice is whispery.

There is a long pause while I wait for him to come to the phone. I think about hanging up, about getting back in the car, about continuing on. But then he picks up. I tell him where I am, what I'm doing. He gives me the name of a coffee shop nearby, says he'll be there in ten minutes.

I'm shaking as I dial the next number, the one that will connect me to my father.

Dad? I'm in New Jersey.

I tell him I'm stopping for coffee with a friend, that I need a break.

I can't breathe, I say. But I'm only about three hours away. I'll be there soon.

My father tells me to take my time. He says that everything will be fine. He is at the hospital with my mom. She is still unconscious. He wants me to breathe. He wants me to rest. He wants me to be safe.

Can you stay the night, he asks?

You can see your mother in the morning, he says.

These are all the things I'm hoping he'll say.

Guilt reaches its fingers through my rib cage, massages my heart. *Pound, pound, skip.*

I stay in the coffee shop parking lot and lean against the hood of the car as I wait for Christopher. It's cold and I'm shivering.

I watch him pull up and park. I haven't seen him in a month, and he stands in front of me for a beat. Inside we sit across from each other in a booth, order cups of coffee. We don't talk about my mom at all.

I don't know what it is about Christopher. I am powerless around him. I feel like I'm constantly on the verge of scaring him off. I stay still, make no sudden movements; I am careful with my sentences. I am always amazed that he is still sitting there.

I like his hands, his mouth, the way his eyelashes curl up slightly, making his eyes that much brighter. He runs his fingers through his hair, shakes his head at me.

Clar, he calls me. It's at once diminutive and affectionate.

We talk about Marlboro and about his job painting houses with his uncle. I like the way he holds his cigarette, clipped between his thumb and forefinger. His eyes are steady on me as I talk. For whole moments, everything feels normal. I keep very still.

Our cups have been refilled twice and are empty now.

And then he says it: You can stay at my uncle's tonight if you want.

I want.

This is the moment that I will come back to for years to come. Over and over, this moment. Me and Christopher in a coffee shop in New Jersey. Late January. Cold night. Three hours from DC.

This moment. It will play over and over and over, rendering me more powerless than Christopher ever did. My insides will tumble out onto the floor around me, a slick, hot mess of hate and regret, this very moment, me and Christopher in a coffee shop in New Jersey, the epicenter of it all.

I'll heave into myself, pulling at my skin, wishing over and over that I had shaken my head, that I'd said, Thank you, but no. That I had just walked away from this stupid boy who didn't give a shit about me. I will offer up anything—limbs, friends, jobs, even my father—for the chance to do it over again, to be able to get in my car and go to her.

But instead I nod yes at Christopher and follow him home to his uncle's house.

In his uncle's kitchen, Christopher takes two glasses out of the cupboard, pours them tall with vodka. He unscrews the cap from a bottle of orange juice, pours a tiny bit into each glass.

For color, he says with a smirk.

We sit down at the kitchen table. I take my glass, drink my vodka, keep still.

It's late when we stumble upstairs. I am drunk. The stairs creak under our feet. At the top we lean against the banister. I am swaying lightly.

G'night, Clar, he says.

Goodnight, Christopher.

He goes to a room on the left. I go to a room on the right.

Years later when I lie in bed at night, helpless against these memories, I'll want to scream and thrash out at myself, standing there at the top of those stairs.

Don't go in that room, I scream at her in my head. Stop, I scream.

But she doesn't stop. I don't stop.

Instead I walk into that room, some plain guest room in an unfamiliar house in New Jersey, and I strip down to my underwear and a T-shirt. I crawl beneath the sheets and I close my eyes to the blackness, to the room spinning around me.

Hours later, when I wake up, the room is dark, but a swath of yellow light has cut its way across the floor.

Christopher's uncle is standing in the doorway, the light from the hallway glowing behind him.

He is handing me the phone.

It is three in the morning.

I am still drunk.

My father's voice is there. Faraway, quiet, resigned.

I'm so sorry, honey, he says.

She's gone, he says.

My mother is dead.

Chapter Two

I'M STANDING IN the cosmetics aisle of the local Kmart, holding two bottles of nail polish, trying to decide which one to steal. One is a bright berry color that makes the insides of my cheeks smart with flavor, and the other is a deep plum that makes me think of a pair of my mother's suede high heels.

I decide on the berry.

I take one more look around, at the empty aisles surrounding me, and then quickly tuck the bottle into the pocket of my jean shorts, feeling a soft thwack as it clicks against a matching tube of lipstick already hidden there.

I tug at the hem of my shirt, hoping it covers the bulge in my pocket, and my heart zings with a familiar burst I've grown to crave. Years later I'll recognize this thrill as the same one I receive upon the first drag of a longed-for cigarette or when that second drink takes me just over the edge from sobriety.

As I walk toward the entrance of the store I keep my head down. I'm hoping to appear disappointed, as if I haven't found what I'm looking for. Out of the corner of my eye I take note of the lone cashier, a bored-seeming woman in her twenties. She is picking at her fluorescent orange fingernails, oblivious to my presence.

I slip through the doors and as the warm, Florida air hits my air-conditioning-cooled skin, I feel an immediate sense of relief followed by another zing of excitement.

I've gotten away with it.

I walk back across the parking lot, to my parents' restaurant, thinking about this whole stealing thing. I'm not really sure how it started or how it's gotten so out of control. In the beginning it was just a pack of gum or a pen, but lately the items have been exclusively cosmetics, ten to fifteen dollars' worth at a time.

I slip through the door of my mother's catering shop, which has recently morphed into a café. It sits in a string of other shops, catty-corner from the Kmart. My mom is in the kitchen, her hands deep in a bowl of homemade pâté, and my father is in the office, perusing wine catalogs. The gamy scent of the goose liver my mother is working with is heady in the air.

I lean against the counter, next to my mother.

Hi, sweetie, she says with a smile. Did you finish your homework?

Yup.

This is a lie. I haven't even touched it. I am failing math and just this afternoon I had to stay after with Mr. Gorin. He smells like pimentos and cream cheese and some kind of musky aftershave, but he is kind and patient with me.

Did your dad help? My mother blows an errant wisp of hair out of her face as she asks this.

I nod again.

It's true, my dad did help. Or at least he tried. My dad is a former engineer, and math is a love of his. But he is not as patient as Mr. Gorin.

Now, come on, Claire, my father implored as we sat behind his desk in the back office. If $5x - 4 = 26$, what does x equal?

I have no idea.

I hate math.

I hate x.

That was when I dropped my pencil on the desk and pushed back my chair, the urge to go across to Kmart popping into my head. My father called after me halfheartedly as I headed for the door, but I knew that he wouldn't mention it to my mother for fear of her scolding him.

Great, my mother replies now. It makes your father feel good to be able to help you, you know?

I nod.

Sweetie, she says then, can you tuck my hair behind my ears?

I smile at her and lean forward. My mother holds her pâté-covered hands out to the sides, and I carefully push her thick, blond hair away from her face. She is a beautiful woman, tall and slender, with a curtain of naturally white-blond hair that hangs perfectly to her shoulders. She has an easy smile and sparkling green eyes. I sometimes think that she is like a grown-up Sweet Valley High twin. Except weirder.

My mother is a chef. Before she met my father she worked as a food stylist in New York, arranging platters of sandwiches and heaping bowls of pudding to look appealing for commercials and print advertisements. Her portfolio, which now leans against a wall in the garage, is full of photos of raw Sara Lee turkey breasts hand-painted to look cooked and shrimp cocktail arranged like little bouquets in cut-glass dishes. She throws lavish dinner parties on a regular basis and obsesses over restaurants and menus.

During my parents' honeymoon through Europe, my mother kept a diary—not of what it felt like to be a newlywed but, instead, of the meals she and my father consumed. She wrote about bottles of wine drunk in Italy, cheeses devoured in France, and hangover remedies in Ireland ("very runny eggs and a pint of Guinness").

About a year ago, at the urging of friends, she started a catering business. At first it was just kind of for fun, something my father and I helped with, each of us carefully removing trays of mini quiche and sautéed mushrooms from the backseat of the Volvo. But then she and my father rented a space, broke down some walls, ushered in the commercial appliances, and now our little family runs a full-blown restaurant. My father is in charge of the wine, my mother the food, and I usually stand behind the cash register fiddling with buttons and doodling in a notebook.

You know, my mother says, her hands back in the pâté, her hair tucked behind her ears, your father is going to be just fine.

I know, I say, nodding. I was hoping she wouldn't bring this up.

We are *all* going to be fine, she continues. Her voice is tight, measured. Even at fourteen I know it is not just me she is trying to convince.

Two weeks ago my parents told me that my father has cancer. They used their serious voices to explain what prostate cancer is, how he will have an operation and then some radiation. Then they made jokes I didn't get about my father getting heat flashes from hormone treatments.

He's going to be just fine, my mother said that day too.

She says it one more teeth-clenching time right now, and I just nod at her, idly fingering the bottle of nail polish in my pocket.

◆

MY FATHER IS SEVENTY-ONE years old.

Most people assume he is my grandfather, and I don't bother to correct them anymore. Sometimes he makes a game of it. When some old lady in a diner approaches us, asking, Oh, is that your granddaughter? my father will lean back in his chair and chuckle.

Nope, he'll say. She's my grandson's aunt.

We smirk at each other across the table as we watch her try to puzzle it out.

He was fifty-seven when I was born. My mother was forty.

My father, Gerald Robert Smith, was born in 1920 in Michigan. One of four children, he picked blackberries in the summer, delivered newspapers growing up, and enlisted in the air force the day after the attacks on Pearl Harbor.

He was trained as a fighter pilot, flew B-24s over Europe, dropping bombs on Germany. His plane was shot down in 1944 and my father was captured and taken to a German prison camp for the last six months of the war.

Although he likes to talk about the war, I find it impossible to follow along. War is a two-dimensional concept to me—a few pages in a history book read aloud in a class I don't want to be in.

There are more interesting parts to my dad's life, I think. Like his other family.

After the war, at age twenty-four, my father returned home to Michigan, to a wife he barely knew and to a son who'd been born while he was away. He finished college, went on to have a couple more children, and then moved his whole family to Southern California.

My father then delved into a career as a mechanical engineer. He began working with men like Wernher von Braun, a German rocket-science engineer, whose name I will come across for the rest of my life. And for the next two decades my father traveled the globe, leaving his family alone in their little house in Pasadena, while he sat in smoky conference rooms with men who were trying to change the world.

In my twenties my half siblings, who are all twice as old as I am, will tell me stories of the man they hardly knew, the one who came home late at night, the one who was gone first thing in the morning. The man with the temper, the guy who hardly knew his wife. This man they speak of, our same father, is one I never met, and sometimes I have to remind them of this when they question my devotion to him.

In the early seventies my father moved his family again, this time to Florida. It was there that he finally divorced his wife Helen, and that his children became old enough to go to college.

He married once more, this time for less than a year. I can never remember her name.

By the time 1975 rolled around my father was living in Atlanta. He had three grown children, two divorces under his belt, and a prosperous steel-manufacturing company that afforded him more money than he'd ever dreamed of.

1975 also found him wearing a funny blue suit he'd bought in Mexico as he rang my mother's buzzer in Manhattan one warm June morning. The suit was stitched to look like denim and embroidered with brightly colored flowers.

My parents had been set up on a blind date by mutual friends, but the night they were supposed to go out my mother stood him up. She'd gone to Long

Island that day, with a friend, to pick strawberries, and by the time she came home the last thing she felt like doing was going on a blind date with some older businessman from Atlanta.

My mother was thirty-seven years old and had lived in Manhattan for seventeen years by then. She had dozens of friends. She went to parties and art openings. She smoked pot in the Village and spent Tuesday nights in smoky jazz clubs, sipping martinis and recrossing her legs.

My mother was funny and quick-witted, and always up for an adventure. She was uncommonly pretty, with those green eyes and that blond hair, that symmetrical face and easy smile. When she went to sleep that night in early June, in her little one-bedroom apartment on Twenty-eighth Street, she had no idea that her life was about to change.

My father, at fifty-five years old, was just entering his prime. In spite of—or perhaps because of—the two divorces and three grown children, he was happier than he'd ever been.

He flew first-class wherever he went. He stayed at the Watergate Hotel when he was in DC and the Plaza in New York. He winked at stewardesses and drank tumblers of scotch on the rocks. He wore hats and suits and left big tips at fancy restaurants.

He wasn't used to being stood up, so the next morning he rang my mother's buzzer at 9:00 a.m. "Who dares call anyone before noon on a Sunday in New York?" my mother later wrote about that first encounter. "It had to be you, as they say, and I opened the door with wet hair asking if you wanted a Bloody Mary, which you did, thank God."

I try to imagine this moment between them. My mother in the doorway with her wet hair. My father on the threshold in his blue Mexican leisure suit. The moment of them not knowing each other eclipsed in one short breath.

They went to the Sign of the Dove: "A very un–New York restaurant because it's so pretty and light and which I hadn't been to in years," my mother wrote. "It couldn't have been more beautiful and sunlit and green and smelling of fresh flowers and the oysters and eggs Florentine and bottle of Montrachet are what must have made me say yes to an invitation to go swimming in your pool in Atlanta that very evening."

They flew to Atlanta that afternoon and made daiquiris with the strawberries my mother had picked on Long Island the day before. They swam in my father's pool and smoked Camels and talked into the night, their legs dangling into the water lit from below by the pool lights.

They were married three months later on Cape Cod. I was born two years after that.

The next ten years were a blissful time for our little family. My father whisked my mother away from New York and set her up in a big house in a nice neighborhood in Atlanta. He paid off all her debts, bought her a cream-colored Alfa Romeo, and opened an account in her name at every department store.

When I was growing up, we spent the winter holidays on Grand Cayman, the summers in Mexico or Europe. My parents threw lavish parties that were well attended by Atlanta's upper echelon. I went to private schools, carpooled with moms who drove Mercedes-Benzes and Saabs, and I posed for professional pictures year after year.

I don't think it ever occurred to any of us that it wouldn't last forever.

In 1987 the stock market crashed and so did the steel industry. My father's company went under and he declared bankruptcy. In an attempt to escape the shame of it all, we moved to a small town in Florida.

Destin is known to tourists as the World's Luckiest Fishing Village. It sits on an isthmus, its population of almost twelve thousand residing on a low-lying mass of land sandwiched between the Choctawhatchee Bay and the Gulf of Mexico.

At night little green tree frogs press their stomachs soft against my bedroom windows and Spanish moss filters down, almost audibly, through the trees. We live in a house on Indian Trail, a lonely street that stretches out long and flush against the bay. The homes are all on the bayside, our only neighbors across the street the dense and scraggly forest, a winding twist of dried-out trees and lichens, with lizards that snake underfoot and opossums hanging hidden in the harsh noon sun.

By the time I am fourteen and in middle school, our life in Atlanta seems like just that—another life.

ON THE WAY HOME from the restaurant I carefully pull the bottle of nail polish from my pocket and hold it down low, close to my leg, where neither of them will see it if they happen to turn around. I turn it over, admiring its shiny exterior, the full liquid contents inside. It's like a prize, this bottle of nail polish. But a prize for what, I'm not sure.

I slip it back into my pocket and tune in to what my parents are saying.

Your stomach still hurting? My dad turns to look at my mother as he asks this. She is pressing one hand into her side.

Mmmm, she says, not really my stomach, more my side. I keep thinking maybe I pulled something playing tennis last week.

Honey, she says then, twisting in her seat as she addresses me, what do you want for dinner?

I shrug at her, my heart racing with how close she came to seeing the bottle of nail polish.

You all set for school tomorrow? Any more homework?

Nope. All set, I say.

I am in the eighth grade at Max Bruner Junior Middle School. Each morning I bury myself in a book in the backseat of the school bus, lifting my head only as we cross over the Destin bridge, heading north into neighboring Fort Walton Beach. It is my favorite time of the day, this moment of suspension between home and school. To my left the Gulf of Mexico is choppy and sparkling in the morning sun, and to my right the bay, brown and shallow, is held softly by the land. The air, warm even so early in the morning, lifts the hair from my face, and I tilt my head to the sun. And then the gears shift, my back is pulled flush against the sticky seat, and we roll down the ramp and closer to school.

I hate school. Each morning I count the hours until I am back on the bus, heading home to my room and my books, to my walks under the dock. I am impossibly tall and awkward, with a lanky frame, braces, and relentless acne. The girls at school are vicious, and the boys think I am intense. I write copiously in my diary and complain to my mother about the girls in Home

Ec who make fun of me. She smoothes the hair away from my face and lifts my chin to meet her gaze.

Trust me, she says, it won't last forever.

I want to believe her. My mother can always make me feel better about myself. But in doing so, she often makes my life a little bit worse.

Sure, she says when I wonder aloud if I should wear one of her oversized sweaters. It has little scraps of fabric hanging all across it, in some misaligned early nineties attempt at fashion. At school the next day the kids call me "rag doll" and I skulk through the hallways, trying to make myself invisible.

No, she says another time, when I beg her to let my best friend Tonia's mom give me a perm. I have watched countless times as Tonia and her sisters sit dutifully at the messy kitchen table in their house, their mother carefully winding their locks into tight curls, then lathering on the chemicals.

That's tacky, my mom says.

That night at dinner she asks me about Tonia.

You haven't had her over in a while, she says. Everything okay?

Yeah. I shrug.

Actually, things aren't okay at all. Tonia has been hanging out with a different crowd lately. With girls who are more into going to the mall on the weekends than playing with Barbies. I have yet to completely relinquish the latter.

Tonia and I got in a fight a couple of weeks ago and things haven't been the same since. She has a crush on a guy named Regan. I was supposed to go home with Tonia after school one day, a few weeks ago, but at the last minute she told me she was going to meet Regan on the playground instead.

Regan is a grade older than us, and I've heard bad things about him. Mostly that he's kissed lots of girls and that he smokes some kind of sandweed or something. When Tonia told me she liked him, I got really mad.

You're never going to be president, I told her. And I know that hurt her feelings. Ever since we were in fourth grade Tonia has said she's going to be the first female president. And I think she really might be. She's the most organized person I know.

My mom comes to my room after dinner. We lie back across the bed together to have one of our talks. It's a ritual we have.

Is everything really okay with Tonia?

No.

Do you want to talk about it?

No.

Okay.

She's got a new best friend.

That must hurt. My mother leans up when she says this, propping herself on one elbow and training her gaze on me. I keep my eyes focused upward.

Yeah. Jamie and I used to be friends too, but now she doesn't talk to me either. The two of them act like I don't exist. There's, like, this whole group of them now that hates me.

My mother sighs.

It'll get better, sweetie.

When?

I'm not sure. But it will.

Tonia and I will be friends again? I look at my mother when I ask this.

Well, maybe not, but life won't always feel so . . . so . . . confusing. Okay?

I guess.

I lie back again, looking up at the ceiling.

Look at me, she says all of a sudden.

I turn my tear-filled gaze to her pretty face. She tucks an errant strand of blond hair behind her ear.

This won't last forever, she says.

The world is a much bigger place than Bruner middle school. Those kids who make you feel bad? They're never going to know that. They'll grow up here, stay here, get married here, and have kids here. They'll never find out anything more than the petty grievances they're learning to inflict now.

Her gaze is steady as she continues.

But you, kiddo? You have bigger fishes to fry. I predict great things for you.

I nod at her. I want to believe her.

My mother lies back again and we are quiet, both of us looking up at the ceiling. Our arms are touching and I feel sleepy.

I think about how, when I grow up, I want to be just like my mother. I'm going to have a daughter too, and we're going to lie in bed at night just like this.

◆

MY MOTHER WAS BORN in New Canaan, Connecticut, the second of four daughters. The first, Phyllis, was the most beautiful and the last, Pamela and Penelope, were fraternal twins. Sally Edith Chatterton, my mother, was set apart from her sisters by more than the first letter of her name.

She grew up in a big white house in a good neighborhood. My grandfather struggled with depression, and his wife was stern with desperation. The four girls, fueled by jealousy, driven by competition, tore at one another in their claim for parental approval.

The Thoroughbred, my grandfather called my mother.

Penny was pudgy, with red hair and freckles; Pammy was plain but perfect; and Phyllis, "Oh, Phyllis . . ."

My mother's sister Phyllis died at thirty. She died of a cat scratch, of blood poisoning. Phyllis was an alcoholic. Every story I've heard about her is the kind you forget immediately, the details at once jumbled even as you're crossing the threshold of the room you heard it in.

There's much I don't understand about my mother growing up, about the venom whispered after lights out, about the pinches, the dress stealing, the silent treatment, the lap claiming. I only saw the aftermath.

My mother left home early. She went to Endicott Junior College, several hours away from New Canaan. She cried herself homesick before she even got there, but once her trunk was unpacked she flung herself into the nearest pack of girls and did what she knew best: flashed her ready smile and charmed her way into this new existence. She was class queen; she was never without a date; she was blond and loudmouthed and everyone loved her.

She went straight from boarding school to Rhode Island School of Design. She and her roommate, Nancy, both of them painting majors, shared an apartment on Benefit Street. They flirted with the boys in the apartment across the alley, giggling as they sipped martinis and pretended not to look. Both of them met their husbands at RISD, my mother the first to date Bob, the man that Nancy would end up marrying.

It was 1958 when my mother met Gene, a painter, a jazz musician, Gene who drove a motorcycle and Gene who, without a moment's hesitation, swept my mother off her feet. I won't actually hear about Gene until I am in high school, and when she talks about him a look will come across her face that I have never seen before. She will tell me about how they eloped one night, just before she graduated, and moved to Manhattan several months after that. The first night there they crashed on jazz musician Cecil Taylor's couch.

Their marriage was over within five years, both of them too young, too stupid to see it through. My mother stayed on in Manhattan. She had become a New Yorker—it was where she was always meant to be, she felt. She married again in her early thirties. That one only lasted a year. She was thirty-seven, living month to month in a walk-up near Murray Hill, when my father rang her buzzer unexpectedly one warm June morning.

◆

THE NEXT DAY AT SCHOOL I am sitting in Home Ec when Tonia walks by. We met in fourth grade and became fast friends. Our families couldn't have been more different, but neither of us cared. As it turns out, Tonia will not be one of those girls who gets stuck in Destin. She'll go on to run an aviation company, be president of it even. Just like she always said.

Tonia pauses awkwardly and looks down at the bottle of berry nail polish that I have placed in front of me. It has become like a talisman, this bottle. A symbol of something bigger.

Where did you get that?

I stole it, I say, hoping to impress her.

She flinches and I feel a thread of excitement run through me.

I could get some for you too, I say. The words are out of my mouth before I can stop them.

Her eyes light up. Really? And then they darken again, remembering that we aren't friends anymore.

Sure, I say. I could get some for Jamie too.

Whatever, she says suddenly, trying to downplay her enthusiasm.

But it's too late. A plan has been formulated. This is how I'll win her back, I decide.

I have to get off the school bus every afternoon at an intersection with a Circle K convenience store. From there, I walk two blocks up, to where my parents are working. The kids on the bus tease me. They say my mom works at the Circle K. My cheeks burn as I make my way down the steps of the bus to the sidewalk.

They couldn't be further from the truth.

When we lived in Atlanta, my friends had been the children of ambassadors, of lawyers, doctors, wives who sat on the boards of museums and husbands with wine cellars that rivaled my father's.

Here in Florida, what friends I do have usually live with just one parent. They have four or five siblings. Their parents are young, work all day, and return home at night to drink six-packs of beer in front of the television. My parents aren't friends with any of them.

I actually love these families. I love how different they are from mine, and I am enchanted by the liveliness of a Saturday morning in one of their homes. But right now, walking up the street, the Circle K behind me, I hate them all.

They know nothing, I think.

As I walk up Route 28 I begin planning my heist. When I will go, what colors I will choose. I think about how Tonia and I will be friends again. About how maybe school won't be so torturous anymore.

By the time I get to the restaurant I'm burning with my plan.

As usual, my mother is in the kitchen and my father is in the office.

Hi, sweetie, my mother says, smiling softly at me as she sifts flour into a large metal bowl. How was school?

Fine.

Do you have homework?

Not really.

Why not?

I did most of it on the bus, I say.

This is a lie. I know it's only a matter of time before my mom finds out how behind I am in my classes, but for now I'm determined to keep up the illusion.

Do you want to help me with this cake?

Nah, I say, I'm think I'm going to Kmart. I want to see if they have any new Baby-Sitters Club books.

Okay, honey. Do you need any money?

Nah, I say again, and my mother nods absentmindedly as she scans a recipe book, drawing her finger down the page until she finds what she's looking for.

Inside Kmart I wander through the clothing section for a few minutes. I have specific ideas about what makes me look conspicuous and what doesn't. I think that pretending to browse for long periods of time in random parts of the store simply makes me look like an indecisive customer.

Finally I make my way over to the cosmetics section.

I spend a long time mulling over the different colors and combinations. After several more minutes I finally make a decision. A soft, classic pink for Tonia and a deep magenta for Jamie.

As I go over these choices I notice that a man has appeared behind me. He is looking over a display of fishing tackle boxes. I've already managed to slip the two lipsticks into my pocket, but I have yet to take the nail polishes that match.

I risk a glance at the man. He is in his midthirties, plainly dressed, expressionless. Maybe he is just a customer, I think. But something in my gut tells me otherwise. I briefly consider leaving, forgetting about the nail polishes for now. But then I think about Tonia and how much I want to be friends again.

Suddenly the most brilliant idea occurs to me. I'll just keep them in my hand and walk over to another section, like I'm still browsing. I mean, that's what I would do if I was going to buy them, right?

I do just that, and in the toy section, after taking a quick look around to make sure no one is watching me, I stuff the nail polishes into my pocket.

Thwack.

Thwack.

Done.

Perfect.

My heart is racing nonetheless and I know it's time for me to get out. At the front of the store I walk casually through an empty checkout line and am within feet of the doors when someone steps in front of me. It's the man.

Excuse me, I say, trying to make my way around him.

He doesn't move.

I realize that he's blocking my way on purpose.

What happened to those bottles of nail polish you had?

My cheeks burn. My heart explodes into tiny pieces and scatters across the linoleum. The bottles of nail polish in my pocket grow to enormous proportions, sucking all the air out of the store.

I left them in a different aisle, I stammer. I decided not to buy them.

Show me, he says.

Slowly I lead him back to the toy aisle where I had so confidently put the little bottles into my pocket.

I point to a shelf.

I left them here, I say, shrugging.

There is a moment in which I think he almost believes me, but then I see a glint in his eye. He has been waiting all day for this.

Empty your pockets, he says.

◆

WHEN MY PARENTS ARRIVE, I am sitting in the manager's office, the two bottles of nail polish and their perfectly matched lipsticks lined up in a neat row in plain view on the manager's desk. My mother immediately begins to cry.

The manager tells all of us that he could have called the cops but didn't. My parents nod and thank him. I stare at the floor. Then he says that I'm not allowed to enter the Kmart without parental supervision. I burn with shame. After that it seems like hours before we all walk out of the store, but the whole affair really only takes about twenty minutes.

My parents' reaction is more extreme than I imagined it would be. They close the restaurant early and the three of us get in the Volvo to go home. The drive is painfully quiet. My mother sniffles here and there in the front passenger seat and my father keeps both hands on the wheel.

At home my mother gently tells me to go to my room, which I do. I sit on the edge of my bed, with the door closed, my backpack still hooked over one shoulder, unsure of what to do with myself. I feel miserable. Heavy and undeserving. I drop my bag on the floor and curl into the pillows, crying.

Later that night, at dinner, my parents try to talk to me about it. We are sitting at the glass Eames table in the kitchen. Beyond the bay windows the backyard is a large square of green that promptly drops off into the bay. The sun is setting and two fat pelicans sit out on the end of the dock, carefully watching for their dinner.

This is my fault, my mother says. Her food sits untouched in front her. Is it Florida? Do you hate it here?

I am silent. I keep wondering what would have happened if I had just put the nail polishes down and walked out.

Gerry, my mom asks my dad, do you think it's the school system? I know the schools were better in Atlanta, but maybe Bruner is worse than we thought.

My father is silent.

Honey—she turns back to me again—is it your dad? Are you scared?

I groan inwardly. I knew she was going to bring up the cancer.

He's going to be fine, she says, and I have to stop myself from rolling my eyes.

She reaches across the table and takes my hand.

Honey, look at me.

I look up. My mother's face is lined with worry, her perfect hair tucked behind her ears.

It's the restaurant, isn't it? She sighs now, leaning back in her chair and covering her face with her hands.

How can I tell her that it has nothing to do with any of this? That it's something else entirely? That there's some kind of rage built up in me, a desperate loneliness brought on by simple adolescence and a sense of false immortality?

I can't.

So I lie.

I nod yes, when she asks if it's been hard for me to have her working so much, knowing, even at fourteen, that this will be a swift punch to her gut. But also knowing that it will be the only thing that will put a stop to her questions.

After dinner I am sent to my room again. I leave the door open this time and can hear them in the kitchen, talking in hushed tones at the table, long after they have finished eating.

I lie across my bed and stare at my math homework. The numbers shrink and grow, dancing across the page, mocking me. I have the urge to crumple up the work sheet, to throw it in the trash. So I do. But after a few minutes I dig it out again, smoothing the wrinkles away with my hand.

I am lying on my back, staring at the ceiling, when my mother appears. She taps on the doorframe before coming in.

Honey, can I talk to you?

I curl onto one side in response. I want to sink through the mattress and disappear.

Oh, sweetie, she says, lying down opposite me on the other side of the bed.

Do you know how much I love you? She smoothes the hair away from my face when she says this, but I keep my eyes down, staring at the pink bedspread.

Do you know that being your mom is the best thing that ever happened to me?

I don't look up.

Sometimes I think about how I almost didn't get to have you, she continues. I wanted to have a child all my life, but at a certain point I convinced myself that it wasn't going to happen.

I am listening to her carefully now.

When I met your father I was thirty-seven. My time was almost up. Besides, your dad was so much older and had raised three kids already.

Sally, he said to me one day, I don't want you to miss out on this experience.

I think I fell even more in love with him that day. We started trying soon after that, and I got pregnant surprisingly easily.

But a few weeks into it I miscarried.

I have never heard this part of the story before, and I lie very still, afraid that if I move she'll stop talking.

I was devastated. I don't think I got out of bed for a month. I didn't talk to your father for two weeks. That was when I realized how badly I wanted to be a mother.

But after a while your father convinced me to try again, and we did. I held my breath all the way through the pregnancy, so afraid that I was going to lose you. But I didn't.

She turns her head to me now and runs a hand down my cheek. I've adored being your mother, Claire. Sometimes I think it's the only thing I did right with my life.

She is crying now. I can tell by the way her voice has gone tighter. I still can't bring myself to look at her.

We'll get through this. Okay, sweetie? I promise.

I finally look up at her and nod the tiniest nod.

She turns on her side, pulling me into her like a comma, and we lie like that for a long time.

◆

THE NEXT DAY AT SCHOOL I avoid Tonia in the halls. I briefly consider hiding out in the bathroom, skipping Home Ec, but I can't afford to get in any more trouble.

Tonia walks by my desk at the start of class.

Hey, she says.

Hey, I say back.

I want to tell her what happened. She's still my best friend.

I got caught, I say. Stealing nail polish at Kmart.

She blinks. Something in her demeanor shifts. Wow, are you okay?

Not really, I say.

That sucks, she says, and I look down, grateful for her sympathy. I hope everything turns out okay, she says softly, before she turns toward Jamie, taking a seat next to her a few tables away.

After school I head home. My mother has decided that she doesn't want me going to the restaurant after school anymore, and that for a while at least she's going to take the afternoons off.

My sneakers crunch on the oyster-shell driveway and the math book in my book bag feels impossibly heavy. When I walk in through the front door, it is immediately clear that something is wrong.

My mother is sitting on one of the couches in the formal living room, the one that we never sit in. My father is sitting next to her, when he is supposed to be at work. My mother is crying, and my father has his arm around her shoulder, his head bent toward hers.

My insides harden together like cement. I shouldn't have lied to her. I should have just told the truth that I wasn't stealing because she was working all the time. That it was for Tonia, so we could be friends again.

I stand in the doorway a moment longer before they notice me. I have to tell her. I have to tell her how much I love her. How she is actually my best friend. How glad I am that she got to have me.

My dad looks up first.

Claire.

My mother looks up sharply then, her breath catching in a sob.

Claire, my dad says, come sit down.

My feet are heavy, shuffling across the rug.

My mother blots her tears, and when I try to sit on the couch opposite them, my mother reaches out for me.

Come sit with me, sweetie. She is choking on the words.

I drop my bag on the floor and sit down next to my mother, who pulls me into her. She is hot all over, and her body jags against me with each wave of crying. I am frightened now.

My father leans over, one arm around my mother, the other around me. I peer up at him from underneath my mother's embrace.

Claire, he says, we just found out that your mother has colon cancer.

Chapter Three

I'M STANDING OVER the cluttered desk of the West Coast editor of *Big Fancy Magazine*. Behind her Hollywood shimmers through the floor-to-ceiling windows of her spacious office.

How about some yogurt? I say gently. This suggestion is met with dramatic eye rolling and scoffing.

I try again. A smoothie?

West Coast Editor drops her head to her desk. She is nearing fifty, single, and surprisingly unkempt for someone who runs the LA office of *Big Fancy Magazine*. She is wearing jeans and an ill-fitting blouse. Her blond hair hangs limply past her shoulders and her face looks puffy from too many cocktails at whatever event she attended last night.

Nooooo, she moans.

It's important for you to eat, I remind her. I try to tamp down the rising sense of panic swelling in my sternum. This is not going well.

West Coast Editor offers no response. She doesn't even lift her head from the desk.

We could order something from that macrobiotic place, I say.

Or how about just a bar? I've got a box of raw-food bars at my desk.

All these suggestions are ones I have been instructed to use by the girl who had my job before me. Her last day was yesterday, and when she walked out of the office for the final time she had a look on her face like I've only seen on newly liberated kidnap victims in Lifetime movies: shattered and disbelieving, no longer able to recognize freedom. I know I should take this as a warning, but I'm too excited to actually be working at *Big Fancy Magazine* to care.

No, West Coast Editor says sulkily in reference to the raw-food bar.

She picks her head up and inspects her computer screen, scanning the new e-mail waiting there. Her hair is clearly unbrushed. One side of it is snarled. The other side stills retains some of yesterday's blowout from the salon.

A beat passes.

Fine, she says suddenly. A smoothie.

West Coast Editor swivels away from me, and I follow her gaze through the windows of her office. Buildings spread out against the backdrop of the distant mountain range that separates the city from the valley. The Hollywood sign is faintly visible in the background and palm trees dot the landscape.

I've been living in LA for three months. The city feels like the opposite of New York, where I lived for the past four years. The palm trees, the wide-open boulevards, the ocean air, and hazy sunsets all play with my head. I miss Manhattan. I miss the sidewalks and the throngs of people. I miss my walk-up apartment in the East Village. I miss my bartending job and my magazine internship.

It was a hard decision to leave New York. After my mother died I dropped out of my quaint Vermont college, with its white clapboard buildings and ruddy-cheeked students, and moved to Manhattan, where my first friend was the shirtless old man across the street who wore a pair of pearl earrings every day and had built a sixty-foot structure made of wood scraps in the community garden next door.

It had taken the better part of four years to feel like I actually belonged in New York. Not to mention that I had just been asked to apply for a job at *Time Out New York*, the magazine where I'd been interning during my final semester of college at the New School.

I cried that afternoon, walking home along Second Street, through the East Village, past the vintage clothing shops and little cafés, knowing that I would have to turn down the job. I had promised my father that I would move to California when I graduated. He'd been waiting patiently, storing up doctors' appointments for me to take him to, and planning day trips for just the two of us.

But then the *Big Fancy Magazine* thing happened and suddenly the move didn't seem so bad.

I think about this as I tap my high heel impatiently, waiting for the smoothie. I can't shake the gnawing feeling that taking this job was a mistake. I glance at my watch: 9:04 a.m. My father should just be arriving at the hospital for his third day of radiation treatment.

A month after moving to LA, my father found out that his cancer was back. Ten years ago my mother discovered she had stage 4 colon cancer in the very same month that my father was diagnosed with his. He was forced to choose radiation over the more successful prostatectomy since my mother was the one who needed immediate surgery.

The radiation has kept him cancer free for ten years, but last week, in the office of a tired-looking doctor at the VA hospital, we were informed that his tenure was up. We had been waiting patiently, tension building, as the doctor shuffled through a stack of files on his desk.

My dad was wearing one of his favorite no-iron shirts from Robinsons-May, and the white hair around his ears tufted out, gracing his collar. My father had always looked old, but never more so than in that moment.

Ah, here it is, the doctor finally said, pulling a file out from the stack.

Hmm, let me see. Biopsy results, right?

It was immediately clear that this guy had no recollection of my father. I watched the doctor scan the contents of the folder.

Well, he said, I have some disappointing news.

I felt a prickle in my spine. My father has had a small lump in his jaw and the biopsy was to determine if it was cancerous.

The results do indeed show a malignancy, the doctor said. And it's likely that the tumor in your mouth is a metastasis of the prostate cancer. Looks like it finally decided to spread. Impressive that you kept it off this long though.

My body began to cave in on itself. My father let out a breath.

So, what now? he asked through clenched teeth.

Well, the doctor said, because of your age and other health concerns, your options are somewhat limited. More radiation is probably your best bet.

I stopped paying attention. My whole body was tingling.

In the car on the way to this appointment my father had tried to prepare us both for this, but it obviously hadn't worked.

No matter what happens, Claire, he had said, we should feel grateful that I've had as long as I have. No one ever thought I'd outlive your mom, yet here I am.

I nodded at him.

Except the thing is that I'm not that grateful.

I'm sick of cancer, sick of hospitals and doctors, and I'm sick of fucking radiation.

I don't expect my father to live forever. I've already come to the conclusion that I will probably be parentless by the time I am thirty.

But not yet. I'm not ready.

◆

IN A BIZARRE COINCIDENCE my dad's radiation treatment starts the same day that I begin at *Big Fancy Magazine*. When we found this out, I immediately offered not to take the job. I'm going to just take care of you instead, Dad, I told him.

Are you kidding? Your mother would kill me if you didn't take this job.

It's true. My mother may have imagined great things for me, but a job at *Big Fancy Magazine*, one of her favorite glossies, would have blown her away.

We argued back and forth about it a bit longer, but by that time my father had already started carrying a copy of the magazine around with him, proudly showing it to anyone in his path.

My daughter works here, he would exclaim, flashing a recent issue featuring an Oscar-winning actress on the cover.

And so it was decided. Each morning, Monday through Friday, my father will drive to a hospital in Loma Linda, where the doctors will zap his mouth with radiation. And I will drive to work so that I can spend eight hours taking orders from a demanding magazine editor.

The day I completed all the paperwork in the *Big Fancy Magazine* HR offices I drove to the beach and put my toes in the great, swelling Pacific. I allowed myself to imagine some incredible life unfolding before me. For no particular reason I pictured myself living in Paris, traveling through Uganda; I saw myself penning insightful and meaningful journalism, stories that truly explore the unbounded humanity the world has to offer. Well, I could hear myself saying to some faceless biographer, I started working at *Big Fancy Magazine* when I was twenty-four and it all just unfolded from there.

I think about this as I wait in line for the smoothie. I bet West Coast Editor has already forgotten my last name.

Back upstairs, I step carefully into her office and set the smoothie down on her desk.

She takes a sip without looking at me. And then she coughs, choking on it.

Blueberry? Her eyes are narrow slits. I think it's the first time she's looked at me all day.

I wanted peanut butter, she says.

She pushes the smoothie away, swiveling back to her computer. I am officially dismissed. I deduce that I'm getting the silent treatment from her for the rest of the day since she e-mails me duties and tasks from behind her closed office door—curt little sentences written in lowercase letters.

As per her instructions, I spend the afternoon dropping off a sack of her high heels to be resoled, buying groceries, and delivering them to her house, carefully wedging a bottle of vodka into the freezer, just as she said to. I fret over the brands I choose at the grocery store, knowing that I could easily be reprimanded for buying the wrong kind of protein bars.

My dad calls in the middle of it all. I'm trying to let myself into her house, my arms full of grocery bags and an armload of West Coast Editor's dry cleaning.

Hey, kiddo, he says.

Hi, Dad, I respond breathlessly, trying to sound chipper.

How's Hollywood?

Oh, you know. Demanding.

He chuckles and tells me about his morning radiation session. He has been characteristically upbeat about it all, making friends with the nurses and preparing a new joke every day for his radiologist.

I wedge the phone between my shoulder and ear as I stuff West Coast Editor's groceries into her cupboards. Her dog yaps and dances around my ankles.

I'm sorry I'm not there with you, Dad.

Don't be, sweetie. I'm doing great. The doctor said today that he can already tell that the tumor is shrinking. I want to make sure you've got an old man to look after for a few more years.

He chuckles again and I smile into the phone. The dog is starting to paw at the dry cleaning that I tossed over a chair, and I shoo him away from it, nudging him gently with the toe of my high heel.

Dad, I've got to go. I'll call you later.

I hang up and take one last glance around the house. It's a small one bedroom, and even in the daytime there's not a lot of light. I try to imagine West Coast Editor at home here, lounging around in her pajamas, but three days into the job and I can tell that she's hardly ever here.

I go home after that, driving up Fairfax, turning right on Hollywood Boulevard and driving past Grauman's Chinese Theatre, past the bums sleeping on the stars on the sidewalks, past the sex shops and the palm trees, turning left on Ivar and up to the top of the hill where I share an apartment with my boyfriend, Colin.

◆

COLIN AND I HAVE BEEN together for six years. We lived together for the whole four years that I was in New York, and he's part of the reason I moved to LA. Colin is an actor and thinks he'll have better chances of finding work here.

Hey, I say, as I step through the entrance to our apartment. Colin is in the living room, smoking a cigarette, watching CNN. He's always watching CNN.

Hey, he calls back, without turning around. I kick off my heels, a pair of black Isaac Mizrahis that I shelled out for when I got the job. I'm hoping no one at work will notice that I've worn them every day.

How did it go today? Colin asks, still focused on the television.

I walk into the kitchen, where I remove a bottle of beer from the fridge.

It was okay, I sigh. I got her the wrong kind of smoothie.

So?

So, she didn't talk to me for the rest of the day.

Fuck her, Colin says.

Colin is good at saying things like that. He's always angry. I'll never know if his rage was there from birth or if it is a product of his sister's murder seven years ago.

I'm going outside, I say.

'K, Colin says without turning around.

I walk between the two columns that mark the entrance to the living room. The hardwood floors gleam in the late afternoon sun and the rushing sound of the freeway is a distant thrum through the French windows.

Outside I sink down onto an old set of wooden steps that lead to the little backyard. In the middle of the yard sits a tree, fat with waxy blossoms that fill the air with the scent of orange and vanilla. My neighbor told me that he's only seen trees like it in Hawaii, and this bit of information makes me like LA a tiny bit more.

My beer bottle drips condensation into the railing, and I gaze out across the cityscape of Los Angeles. I can see the Capitol Records Building, and beyond that Hollywood dips down into a maze of squat buildings crosshatched by palm trees. The early evening air is balmy, like a warm swimming pool.

I let out a sigh. Nothing in my life is the way I thought it would be. Not my relationship with Colin, not my dependent and elderly father. Not this strange city or the aching loneliness that keeps me from falling asleep at night, despite the warm body next to me.

I think about the morning we left New York, almost three months ago. It was a bright, hot Monday, and we drove through the Holland Tunnel and out of the city. For five days we streamed across the flat plains of the country, through cornfields and long, empty desert stretches. I curled against the passenger window as Colin drove, staring out at the road rushing past and trying to imagine what we were driving toward, unable to conjure up anything specific.

In Kansas we drove over a family of ducks, a mom and her fuzzy little ducklings crossing the two-lane highway. We were going too fast to stop, Colin explained, and even though I repeated that sentence over and over in my head I couldn't shake the queasy feeling that settled over me after that.

It's been three months though, and I can no longer deny that the feeling has less to do with the ducks and much more to do with me and Colin, and the swiftly growing distance between us.

Six years is too long for anyone our age to be together, I've determined. We met a few months after my mother died, when I was eighteen. I had just moved back to Atlanta, dropping temporarily out of college, and moving into my old room at home. My dad slept in the guest room upstairs, unable to bring himself to sleep in the bed he had once shared with my mom.

While my friends continued on with their normal college lives, I started waiting tables at a café. Colin was the bartender. One night some of my high school friends sat on the patio of the café. I ignored my tables and leaned against the backs of my friends' chairs, chatting idly.

Holly leaned forward suddenly. Hey, she said, isn't that the guy who killed his sister?

I turned around to follow her gaze. She was watching Colin.

Tall with thick blond hair and dark eyes, Colin was the person at the café I'd talked to the least. He was always there at the end of the night, hanging around the bar with the rest of the staff, drinking beer and counting cash until we locked the doors and headed across the street to a corny piano bar that stayed open late and never carded us.

Colin? I said in response to Holly's question.

That's the guy who killed his sister, she repeated.

Oh yeah, Laura said, squinting at him. I recognize him from the newspaper.

Their faces were serious, watching Colin intently as he moved behind the bar, pouring drinks, wiping down the counter with a rag. I looked at my friends blankly.

It was all over the news, Laura said.

I think you were out of town, Holly finally said.

I had gone to Europe for six weeks with my friend Liz right after my mom died, and I suppose that was enough time for a big local news story like this to escape my attention.

Then they told me the story:

Colin had an older sister named Christine. She was twenty-one and home from college on spring break. About six weeks ago, while I was in Europe, Christine was home alone in the affluent suburban house where Colin and her parents lived. At three in the afternoon someone entered the house and stabbed her multiple times. Her younger brother, Colin, came home within the hour, found her there, covered in blood, no longer breathing.

Colin was immediately a suspect. His dark eyes, his penchant for driving too fast, for drinking too much, his timely arrival at his sister's murder scene—all these things earned him a photo in the paper, a caption that read something like: "Brother Suspected in Local Girl's Slaying."

Within a week Colin's name was cleared, his sister's murder linked instead to a string of stabbings across Atlanta that spring. A new suspect was caught, charged, featured in the paper.

The more of the story my friends revealed, the more I fixated on Colin. Laura and Holly went on talking, dissecting the details of the case, but I had stopped listening. I watched Colin with a newfound interest.

He was tidying up the bar, moving with a kind of deliberateness that I liked. He wiped down bottles, rinsed the sinks, emptied the ice bin. He frowned as he worked, his eyes growing darker.

I was utterly transfixed by him, captivated by our shared experience of loss. He knew what it was like to lie awake at night, wishing someone weren't gone.

I didn't think much about the murder, about the violence. Those things were too far out of my scope of experience. I only saw someone who lived in the same solitary world that I inhabited.

Things moved swiftly after that. We spent the summer leaning into each other in darkened bars, downing drink after drink until neither of us could feel anything anymore. We spent those nights tangled in bed, never having to explain to the other what it felt like to grieve with every pore in our being. In the fall we ran away to New Orleans in the middle of the night. We fell in love there, stumbling drunkenly down alleys littered with beads and bottles, sitting on wrought-iron balconies as dawn broke across the city.

When it was time to part ways a few months later, for me to go back to school in Vermont and for him to move to New York, we did so wistfully. But I hardly put in a semester in Vermont before I dropped out and moved to New York to join Colin in the East Village.

Now, almost six years later, the things that drew us together in the first place are the very things driving us apart. What remains of our relationship is splintered and brittle, a dry, dead thing. I'm sick of grieving. I'm sick of drinking. I'm sick of darkness and isolation. All of them the very glue of us.

◆

Colin is still asleep when I get up the next morning.

A few weeks into living in Hollywood, Colin found a doorman job at a club nearby and also enrolled in classes at a well-reputed acting studio. He studies during the day, works late at night. His dark eyes and full lips would lead you to believe that he would find success, but his air of confidence and superiority is off-putting. All my friends think he's an asshole.

I get dressed carefully, fiddling with the clasp on my slacks and twisting my hair up off my neck. Sometimes I try to imagine what my mother would think if she could see me now. I doubt that she would even recognize the college freshman she last saw, with the nose ring, dyed crimson hair, and combat boots.

I talk to my dad on my way to work. We are both in the car. He is on his way to radiation treatment, and I am bound for what is sure to be another exacting day.

When I arrive, I see that West Coast Editor is in her office, shuffling through papers and throwing things in a bag. I'm surprised to see her there so early.

Can I help with anything?

I'm going to New York tomorrow, she snaps. You can help with *everything*.

I completely forgot that this was the day West Coast Editor leaves for a month of editorial meetings in the New York office.

At my desk I nod at the other assistant, Sophie, who has clearly been in since at least 6:00 a.m., and start going through my e-mail. Sophie is on hold with the airline, trying to get West Coast Editor's ticket upgraded to business class. We both know that if she doesn't, she's going to be in trouble.

Sophie is blond and French, both things that I am not. She is also far more competent at this job than I am. I like her, but I am intimidated by her.

We spend the day preparing for West Coast Editor's travels. The airline comes through with the upgrade, and I manage to get her a last-minute mani/pedi appointment. I am emboldened by the thought of her being gone for several weeks and attack my duties with fervor. Sophie and I will be left in charge of the office.

At the end of the day West Coast Editor looms over our cubicle. She drops a handful of lavishly printed invitations on my desk.

These are the ones I want you to go to while I'm gone. The rest are up to you, she says, gesturing to a thick binder full of even more invites to all manner of upcoming Hollywood parties, screenings, and openings.

We must maintain the *Big Fancy Magazine* presence, she says, taking a rare moment to look me in the eye.

I gaze down at the fat stack of cards before me. There are easily several events for each night of the week.

If you can't make them all, West Coast Editor says, Sophie can go to some of them.

I'm still not clear why I am first assistant and Sophie is second, but I just nod and stack the invitations carefully.

West Coast Editor finally leaves in a flurry of last-minute instructions, barking orders at us even as she is stepping into the elevator. Once she is safely out of the building Sophie and I begin to pore over the glittering invitations, divvying them up, and doubling up on some.

Sophie calls in our RSVPs, her accent sounding haughty and commanding.

Yes, hellooo, she purrs, I'm calling to RSVP from *Big Fancy Magazine.* Yes, thank you, we *will* be in attendance.

The rest of the week goes by in a happy blur. The office is so much more relaxed with West Coast Editor gone. Even her bleating phone calls from New York don't faze me. Sophie and I order in lunch every day, play music at our desks, and even take cigarette breaks together, rolling the office calls to our cell phones, just in case.

On Friday night I drag Colin out to my first invite: an art opening for someone named Gottfried Helnwein, hosted by the actor Jason Lee. The gallery is in a warehousy part of town, and we walk nervously from the car to the entrance. A woman at the door scans her list for my name.

Oh yes, right here. *Big Fancy Magazine.* She smiles at me brightly when she says this and ushers us in.

We make a beeline for the bar, across the cavernous, exposed-brick room. Neither of us is sure what to expect from this event. How exactly am I supposed to make my presence known?

By getting drunk, Colin quips, ordering us two double vodkas from the bartender.

We wander the room, sipping our cocktails and taking in the scene. Heln-wein's images are disturbing. People with bandaged heads and children ly-ing immobile on the floor. We see Jason Lee standing in a corner talking to a group of people.

Colin nudges me after a minute and nods his head in the direction of a man sitting on one of the benches in the center of the room. He looks incredibly drunk and decidedly unshowered.

I realize it's Nick Nolte. He'll be arrested for DUI that same month, his mug shot displaying the same frazzled hair I'm seeing now.

We stay for the better part of an hour, talking to no one, downing more drinks, and eventually giving up on figuring out Helnwein's work.

With each event I grow a little more confident, and a lot more drunk. These parties become the saving grace of my relationship with Colin, the alcohol-infused evenings the only time we connect anymore. I catch glimpses of who we used to be as we lean into each other, feeling like the only two people in the world who get it.

We go to a party with Sophie and her boyfriend on the rooftop of the Stan-dard. It's a soiree to celebrate the kickoff of Mercedes-Benz Fashion Week, and the director talks our ears off about all the amazing kinds of couture we'll be seeing. I nod along drunkenly, pretending like I know what he's talking about and trying hard to hide my scuffed heels under the tablecloth.

Another night we attend a Frederick's of Hollywood fashion show at a trendy restaurant on Sunset Boulevard. I sway from the vodka running through my veins and stare up at the scantily clad women parading down a catwalk inches from my head. David Spade stumbles boozily into me on my way back from the bathroom, and I just nod at him. He seems to be at every party we go to.

I take advantage of every movie screening I can, thrilled to be sitting in these darkened theaters on studio lots, in the middle of the afternoon, see-ing films months before they come out in the theaters.

We go to a party to celebrate the opening of a mobile phone boutique on Rodeo Drive. The cell phone service reputedly costs twenty thousand dol-lars and comes with a special button you can press that will connect you directly to your own private concierge so that you can, say, have your favorite Nars lip gloss delivered to your bungalow in the Seychelles within hours.

I watch as Christian Slater inspects one of the phones, peering into the crystal display case. Oh, and there's David Spade again.

Claire Smith, *Big Fancy Magazine*, I say to the faceless girls who stand at the door of each of these events with their clipboards and headsets. Colin and I are ushered in every time. We sip mojitos and martinis; we pluck sashimi off silver platters. We brush elbows with Benicio del Toro, Keira Knightley, Annie Leibovitz, countless writers and producers, Hollywood wannabes, and more glitz and money than I ever realized existed.

All the stuff I'd always heard about LA is true: the movie stars, the Botox, the cars, the smog, the traffic, and the lavish parties. It's all there. There's more to it than that, of course, but right now, working this job, my days are filled with an undiluted version of Hollywood, something I never thought I'd be privy to.

But there's always a moment when I find myself standing against the rooftop railing of some hotel, a drink in my hand, and I think of my father alone in his condo, forty-five minutes away, clicking through movie channels, a glass of watery scotch puddling on the table next to him. I know he wants me to be here, out in the world, living my life, but this version of living just doesn't feel worth it.

I drive down to see him the next morning, vowing to start spending more time with him, but between the demands of the job and the distance of his condo it has become increasingly hard to see him outside of the weekends.

I insist on spending every Sunday with him. We go for long drives through the San Bernardino Mountains or the hills of Pasadena. My dad points out places where he worked in the 1950s and homes he lived in with his other family decades ago.

I find myself holding my breath on these drives, knowing that the time I have left with this man, with my only parent, is running out. He spins the wheel lazily with one hand as we snake down hairpin mountain curves, unspooling story after story about his life. I have begun to carry a tape recorder whenever I am with him, recording hours' worth of his voice.

Sometimes my father wants to go over technical things with me on our visits together. He wants to add my name to his bank account, help me understand how a living will works, double-check that I have the extra key to his safe-deposit box.

Dad, I moan, you're being so morbid.

Not morbid, sweetie. I'm just trying to prepare you.

But you're not going to die yet, I say.

Hopefully not anytime soon, he says. But when I do you're going to have to be on top of this stuff.

The radiation has been wearing him down. His taste buds have stopped working, and my heart sinks each time I watch him push a plate away, complaining that everything tastes like cardboard. For his birthday in October, I make him a little coupon book of all his favorite meals, something he can redeem when his taste buds return. Neither of us realizes that this is never going to happen.

I think about him late at night, as I try to fall asleep. About how I'm going to be completely alone when my father is gone. There is a screaming, gaping chasm that opens up inside me when I try to imagine it.

I still miss my mother, but it is my father whom I have come to depend on now. My deep, dark secret is that I am glad that she died first. Had she not, I may have never known him.

My father has mellowed and sweetened in his old age. He moves slowly, like a turtle, carefully planning each move in order to make the most of it. He cooks recipes from the *New York Times* and he cans peaches like his mother used to when he was growing up in Michigan.

He is friendly with all the young neighbors in his condominium complex, and he enlists my help in planting flowers around the perimeter of his front stoop. He inherited this condominium after his sister died, and he has since done away with her seventies avocado-green furniture and heavy draperies. He has outfitted the living room with black leather couches and black-lacquered credenzas. He acquired an absurd collection of lava lamps that he proudly displays on a shelf in the living room, and he hangs photos of my mother in every single room.

Most weekends we just watch movies together. Whatever is on HBO: *The Thomas Crown Affair*, *The Bourne Identity*, *Tin Cup*. I know that after four years of living alone he is unspeakably grateful for companionship.

I get that breathlessness again when I think about it though. The feeling of time spilling across the floor. Of my father ebbing away from me. Of not being able to do anything about it.

Now and then I offer to quit my job. I could move in with you, I say. But even as I offer I am torn. It's not Colin I'm afraid of leaving; it's my twenties. I'm afraid of giving up who I am.

Each radiation treatment depletes him a little more. He has lost weight and his skin has turned an unappealing shade of gray. The doctors want to start radiating his hips too, suspecting that the cancer may have spread there as well. My father sets his jaw and raises his eyebrows at me.

What other options do we have, kiddo?

On Sunday nights, when I drive the hour back to Hollywood, it is with a sinking feeling, a dreadful confusion that does not abate. I listen to Radiohead and I blow my cigarette smoke up through the moonroof into the balmy Southern California night air.

◆

WEST COAST EDITOR RETURNS from New York in a flurry of activity, with multiple orders to be carried out immediately. She even ships a giant box of her dirty laundry to the office a few days before her return, and Sophie and I stand in the center of the room, surveying the contents.

I cannot believe she mailed this stuff to us, I say.

I can, Sophie replies.

I tell Colin about it that night when I get home. I even try to explain to him that apparently this is standard Hollywood behavior. It seems no one would get their jobs done if they didn't have assistants to do this stuff for them, I tell him.

Fuck her, he replies, without looking up from the TV.

I can't even bring myself to respond to him. Our relationship has been deteriorating by the day. We are hardly speaking to each other. I can tell that we both want out but that neither of us knows how to make the first move.

The next day, when I go into the office, West Coast Editor is in a huff. She's only been back for two days but I'm already not sure I can do this.

West Coast Editor has been assigned a cover story on Sultry Movie Star and she is completely stressed. I have no sympathy for her. On top of the thousands of dollars she'll likely receive in addition to her salary for the piece, she actually gets to write, something I've been dying to do since I started the job.

But I don't have time to muse on all of this. West Coast Editor is in rare form. She walks in and out of her office, slamming the door, barking out orders at me and Sophie.

On top of the interview with Sultry Movie Star, West Coast Editor is scheduled to fly home this weekend, and we need to help her pack. While Sophie stays in the office manning the phones, I am sent out to Blockbuster to rent as many of Sultry Movie Star's movies as I can get my hands on.

I bring a stack of seven back to the office. One of the most popular ones was checked out already, and West Coast Editor seems pissed. I place the stack of DVDs on her desk.

What are you giving these to me for? You think I'm going to pack them in my suitcase? She briskly recites her father's address. FedEx them. I want them there by tomorrow morning.

I get back to my desk and glance at the clock as I pack the DVDs. My father should be finishing up his radiation for the morning, heading home to his condo. I wish I were with him.

Suddenly West Coast Editor is looming over my desk. She's got her message book in her hands. Her finger is digging a hole into a name written out in my handwriting under yesterday's date, the date when she should have returned the call.

Do you see this name? I hear her voice as loud, screeching.

I risk a quick glance around at the other cubicles, all full of advertising ex-
ecs. They stare at their computer screens, act as though nothing is happening.

Do you *know* who this is?

I sigh, shake my head.

I don't know who it is. All the names have started to blur together. Actors,
agents, producers. I need an encyclopedia to keep everything straight.

Do you *understand* your job, Claire?

I keep my eyes down. I am afraid to look at her. I hate the way she says my
name. When someone only uses your name when they're mad at you, you
wish they wouldn't use it at all.

I'm not going to cry, I tell myself. I'm not going to cry.

How *stupid* can you be?

With this question she throws the message book at the floor behind my
desk.

This is *fucking* ridiculous, she says, and walks into her office, slamming the
door behind her.

Tears smart in my eyes, and I keep my gaze trained on my keyboard so that
no one around me can see that I'm crying.

I wait until West Coast Editor storms out of her office again, and I cower
as she heads for the elevator. She has a lunch date and is heading home after
that. I won't see her again until tomorrow. The moment the elevator doors
close I let out a long-held breath of air. I motion to Sophie that I'm going
outside for a cigarette and she nods.

Outside I lean against the building and watch the cars going by. Mercedes-
Benzes, BMWs, Audis. Their shiny paint jobs flash in the morning sun as
they whiz down the palm-tree-lined street. I think about how it would feel
to push away from the wall, to just walk away from this job, to never see
West Coast Editor again. I take a long drag on my cigarette and think about
what I want for my life.

It's not this.

I call my Dad. His voice is barely audible. Dad, what's wrong?

Oh, I'm just wiped out, honey. This stuff really gets you.

My heart is bursting. I picture him alone in his condo, heating up some soup, watching television with the doors open to let the warm air in.

I suddenly make up my mind.

Back upstairs I phone HR from my desk. The woman who hired me is really nice and I ask her if she has a minute to talk.

Five minutes later I'm sitting across from her on a little couch. She has welcomed me in, smiling warmly.

My hands are shaking. My voice trembles.

Um, I begin. I'm not really sure this job is for me.

Oh?

You know, when I got hired I thought I would be more involved with . . . with the editorial side of things, but that isn't really what I've been doing.

Tell me more, she says.

With this prompt, I just pour it all out.

I tell her how West Coast Editor yells at me, how I'm made to spend my days doing her personal errands. I describe the giant box of dirty laundry. I tell her about having to walk West Coast Editor's dog and about how mad she seems if I get her the wrong breakfast.

When I finally stop, I sink backward against the sofa cushions, the air deflated out of me.

The HR lady crosses her legs, leans forward, and pauses.

I am expecting her to be shocked. I imagine that no one has had the bravado yet to rat on West Coast Editor like this. Maybe they'll fire West Coast Editor and give me her job. Sophie can be my assistant, and I'll never make her drop off my dry cleaning or stock my freezer with vodka.

She looks at me, her gaze steady, her tone decidedly changed from the friendly one I know. She says the next sentence slowly.

Do you know how many girls would want your position?

It feels like a scene in a movie. It feels like being underwater. My limbs get heavy, my responses slow.

The rest of the conversation deteriorates from there. She gives me the standard excuse about how my doing West Coast Editor's personal errands frees her up to do her job here. I can't even bring myself to respond.

By the time I'm back at my desk, after another tensely smoked cigarette outside, West Coast Editor has already been alerted of my betrayal. I'm forced to speak to her on the phone. Since she's out, I sit in her office, at her desk, and close the door for privacy.

I didn't realize you were so very unhappy. I picture a sneer on her face as she says this.

I stammer and am unable to respond.

I've made HR aware of your transgressions, she tells me.

My *transgressions*? What is she talking about?

West Coast Editor proceeds to run through a list of petty grievances, including not coming in early enough and failing to keep her phone messages in order.

I don't know how on earth you expect me to do my job, she says. But I've kindly asked HR to give you thirty days. You have until the end of the month to prove that you can shape up.

I'm shaking when I finally hang up the phone. Sophie comes into the office and together we stand at the windows, staring out at the city before us.

Fuck the thirty days, I say. I'm just going to quit.

Are you kidding? You can't *quit* a job at *Big Fancy Magazine*.

Why not?

Claire, she says, her voice stern and clipped. Every single assistant in Hollywood gets the exact same treatment you're getting right now. It's just the way it is. If you ever want to make it in this town—if you want to make it anywhere really—you have to pay your dues.

I don't believe that, I say. Not like this. Not this way.

If there's anything I've learned from losing my mother, it's that there are more important things in life than situations like this. And standing there in West Coast Editor's office, my dreams of Paris and Uganda fizzling in the distance, that's exactly what I say.

Fuck it. There are more important things in life.

I leave Sophie standing there as I go to inform HR that Friday will be my last day.

I head home after that, a wild feeling of freedom coming over me as I roll the windows down to let in the silky, Southern California air. It's the middle of the day and no one knows where I am.

I park in the driveway and let myself into the apartment. For a moment I just stand there, feeling like I'm suddenly privy to one of the apartment's private moments. Then I strip off my clothes and walk to the bathroom, where I stand underneath the hot water.

I turn up the heat until my skin begins to turn red and I start to cry.

I think about how my father won't get to carry that copy of *Big Fancy Magazine* around with him anymore. But then I think about how it doesn't seem like my father is going to be able to carry much of anything around with him anymore.

I think about Colin and the distance between us, and I think about what my life would be like if my father were gone. I sink down to the tiles and let the water pour over me. I have this feeling that I've fucked everything up, that all I've done in my life is make a series of wrong decisions.

I want to go home.

I want my mother back.

All this time, through all these things I've worked so hard on—graduating from college, moving to California, taking care of my father, getting this job at *Big Fancy Magazine*—somehow all along I've let myself believe that if I did all these things and did them well, maybe I would get her back.

MY FATHER TRIES to hide his relief when I tell him that I've quit. The radiation to his hips has been harder on him than the doctors anticipated.

He can hardly walk.

Everything is falling apart for real.

On my last day at *Big Fancy Magazine* I roll into the office a little late. West Coast Editor has gone for the weekend, and the office should be calm. But as I walk in Sophie looks up at me, sheer panic in her eyes.

What? What's happening, I ask.

Editor in Chief. He's on a flight right now, due to land at LAX within the hour.

Editor in Chief is the king of *Big Fancy Magazine*. He is the one to fear above all else at the magazine.

He's staying at the Beverly Hilton, Sophie says. And he needs three things to be there when he arrives.

I roll my eyes. It's my last day. I could give a fuck about Editor in Chief and his three things.

I *need* you to help me, Claire.

Okay, okay, I say. As much as I don't care about Editor in Chief, I don't want to fuck Sophie over.

I sigh. What are the three things?

I just got off the phone with his assistant in New York, Sophie says, and this stuff *has* to be behind the reception desk at the Hilton by the time he checks in. Sophie glances down at a notepad before her.

Okay, she says, and I hear an imaginary drumroll.

Editor in Chief needs: the largest box of Advil you can find; the largest, strongest box of nicotine patches available; and five hundred dollars in cash.

Jesus Christ, I say. Seriously?

I can't leave the office, Claire. You're going to have to do it. You have forty-five minutes.

I'm throwing my bag over my shoulder and heading to the elevator when Sophie screeches my name. I turn around and she hands me a stiff paper shopping bag with a *Big Fancy Magazine* label carefully adhered to the front of it.

Put it all in here and give it to reception, she says. Oh, and here. She hands me two black clips.

No staples, she says. Editor in Chief *hates* staples.

I spend the next forty-five minutes racing around town, running from the drugstore to the bank, where I have to make a hasty phone call back to Sophie, who in turn calls Editor in Chief's assistant, when I realize that I don't know what denomination Editor in Chief wants his cash in.

Oh, fuck, fuck, fuck, Sophie says.

The assistant has to make a guess since Editor in Chief is still on the plane.

Let's go with five twenties, two fifties, and three hundred-dollar bills, Sophie repeats to me.

I roll my eyes again and stuff the cash into a crisp *Big Fancy Magazine* envelope.

Outside the front entrance to the Hilton I throw the car in park and tell the valet guys I'll only be a moment. It's down to the last minute and even though it's my final day and I shouldn't care, I'm still worried that I haven't arrived in time. I expect to find Editor in Chief standing at the front desk, fuming over his missing bag of three things.

But the lobby is quiet and I simply hand over the paper bag. Can you please make sure Editor in Chief receives this when he arrives? He's due any minute. The receptionist nods, peering down her nose at my sweaty figure.

I walk outside and get in my car.

It's over.

A heaviness comes over me, like the feeling of being pulled back in your seat as an airplane ascends to the sky. I know that I won't be working again for a while. I know that the foreseeable months will be spent caring for my father.

I know these things, but I also don't know them. I cannot really imagine what is coming.

As I drive away from the Hilton I wonder what my life would be like if my parents had never gotten sick, if my mother wasn't dead, if my father's cancer wasn't back, if I was just a normal twenty-four-year-old with regular things like a stressful job and a distant boyfriend to worry about.

I realize that I'll never know. I realize that this is who I am.

◆

RATHER THAN SPEND the weekend celebrating the end of my dreadful job, I go down to Garden Grove to take care of my father. Colin and I had spent the previous evening talking about things.

What are you going to do now?

I don't know. Just take care of my dad for a while, I guess.

There was nothing left to say after that. We would have had to shout to hear each other across the ravine that had cracked open between us.

When I arrive at my dad's condo on Saturday, close to noon, he's still in bed.

Dad, I say, unable to mask the surprise in my voice, it's almost noon. What are you still doing in bed?

Ah, kiddo, these legs of mine aren't working so well. He smoothes out the sheets covering his lower body. His voice is hoarse, tired.

Next to the bed is an old plastic milk jug. I realize that it's half full of dark-yellow urine.

Dad, how long have you been in bed?

Oh, just since yesterday or so.

Dad, are you okay? Panic sucks at my breath.

Yeah, yeah, I'm fine, kiddo. I just need to rest up a bit, get my strength back.

I hesitate for a minute and then I pick up the jug of urine and take it into the bathroom, where I pour it carefully into the toilet. I hold my breath so I don't have to smell it, but my chest grows tight and as I back out of the bathroom, holding the empty canister, I take a swift, necessary inhalation. The smell of my father's urine, sharp and pungent, fills my nostrils and I gag.

Okay Dad, I say, we've got to get you out of bed.

I lean over and help to pull him forward. Then I swing one of his legs over the side of the bed. Then the other. He sits there after that, breathing heavily.

You ready?

Wait just a minute, he says. He massages the tops of his thighs, closes his eyes for moment.

I stand in front of him, swaying lightly. I can't shake the feeling that there should be someone else here. I can't help feeling as though some adult, someone more qualified and responsible than me, should show up and take over.

But there is no one.

You ready now?

He opens his eyes and I take one of his hands in each of mine.

One, two, three. I pull up with all my strength.

My father comes halfway off the bed, halfway into a standing position.

Ohhhh, he says then and lets go, dropping back to the mattress.

What's wrong, Dad?

I can't do it, sweetie.

What do you mean?

It hurts too much.

What hurts?

My hips.

I can feel pricks of fear rising under my skin. My father can't stand up.

My father can't stand up.

My father can't stand up.

Well, sweetie, just let me lie here for now.

But, Dad, this isn't good.

Well, it isn't bad either, he says. Somehow I can't argue with him.

We spend the rest of the day watching television. I lie on the other half of the king-size bed, and we flip through the movie channels. I make us bowls of soup and pour myself a glass of wine.

That night I sleep in the guest room, which I should really call my room. A year or so ago, when I flew out from New York, my father surprised me by redoing the room just for me. The month before I'd e-mailed him some stupid personal essay I'd written for a class, about losing my mother and not having a room to go home to anymore, and when I came out to visit next he'd hung a sign on the door that said "Claire's Room."

Inside he'd replaced the drab guest room sheets with a pretty comforter and curtain set. He'd dug out all my old stuffed animals from storage and piled them up in the chair in the corner. He put framed pictures of me and my mom on the dresser and bought a little box for me to keep jewelry in. I cried when I saw it all.

This is the room in which I go to sleep the weekend after I quit *Big Fancy Magazine*, the weekend my father's legs stop working.

The next morning I try again to get my father out of bed, but his legs still hurt too much. It's Sunday and there is no one to call, nowhere to go. We repeat the day before, watching movies, eating soup.

On Monday morning I empty the milk jug again, this time taking care to hold my breath as long as possible after leaving the bathroom.

I sit on the edge of the bed after that.

Well, Dad. What should we do? You can't stay here. We need to get you to the doctor.

Well, sweetie, there's no way in hell I'm going to make it to the car. I think our only option is to call an ambulance.

Really? My eyes are wide. Can't we just call the doctor?

Well, what good is that if I can't even get in the car to go see him?

My father reaches for the phone on the nightstand, hands it to me.

I don't think to call nonemergency. I just dial 911.

Within five minutes what seems like an army of paramedics has filled the room.

My father and I try to explain that it's not really an emergency, that his legs just aren't working.

Ma'am, please step out of the way, one of the paramedics says as he wraps a blood-pressure cuff around my father's arm. Another one places an oxygen mask over my father's face. He is saying something but I can't hear him through the mask.

I back toward the bathroom, watching the whole thing unfold, tears dripping down my face.

I've had enough of this, I think. I don't want to do this anymore.

I want my mom.

I want anyone.

Someone help me, please.

I try to follow the ambulance to the hospital but I lose them on the highway.

When I finally get there, I park as quickly as I can and enter through a door labeled "Emergency Services."

My father was just admitted, I say. He came in an ambulance.

The woman behind the counter takes my name, tells me to take a seat.

By the time I am led through the swinging doors, it is to an old, familiar scene.

My father lies in a hospital bed. Tubes snake their way from his nose. Machines beep softly around the bedside. A curtain is pulled loosely around the bed, barely hiding another patient on the other side.

Dad?

His eyes are closed.

Dad?

He opens them, gives me a watery grin.

You found me.

I sit down on the edge of his bed. I'm crying. I've sat on the edge of my father's bed like this a hundred times.

It's going to be okay, sweetie. I just need to get back on my feet.

You're not going to die, are you, Dad?

No, sweetie. Not yet, I don't think.

Promise?

I can't promise that, sweetheart.

Promise, I say again anyway.

He squeezes my hand and says nothing.

Part Two

◆

Anger

Anger surfaces once you are feeling safe enough to know you
will probably survive whatever comes.

—*Elisabeth Kübler-Ross*

Chapter Four

1997, I'M EIGHTEEN.

I'M LYING IN BED in my old room in Atlanta. I listen to a car drive slowly down the street. A lawn mower whirs in the distance. My mother is dead.

It will be months and months, possibly even years, before this isn't the first thing I think about when I wake up.

My mother is dead.

She has been dead for three days.

My mother has been dead for three days.

I say it out loud over and over as I lie there.

My body feels warm and heavy, and I lie still beneath the comforter, replaying the last three days in my head, trying to decipher if any of it's real.

After my father's 3:00 a.m. phone call to Christopher's uncle's house in New Jersey, announcing that my mother was gone, I had stumbled back to bed, curling beneath the covers like a wounded animal.

Christopher stood in the doorway for a moment. The house was quiet again. It was still dark out. He crossed the room then and climbed into bed, pulling me to him like a child. My shoulder blades jutted out like little wings, pressing into his chest, and I was conscious of the thin T-shirt I was wearing, of my bare legs.

Tell me about her, he said.

And I did.

I told him about her blond hair and her laugh. I told him bits and pieces of what I knew about her life in New York. I told him about the day she met my father, about the funny blue suit he was wearing.

After a while I could tell that Christopher had fallen asleep. His breathing was soft and shallow, his arms limp and heavy around me. I watched the light creep into the sky beyond the windows. My mother was dead.

Minutes passed, maybe an hour. Then Christopher jerked, his whole body flinching, startling me, and waking him.

I dreamed about a dead fish, he said thickly. Rotting and putrid.

I pushed out of his embrace, sat up on the side of the bed.

I'm sorry, I said without turning around. And I was.

I apologized one more time on my way out the door, this time to Christopher's uncle, who looked at me with such pity that I felt guilty for burdening him with it, and then I got in my car and drove the last few hours to DC.

When I got there, my father handed me a sleeping pill, the first of many during the next few weeks, and I fell into a muddied sleep in the guest room upstairs.

My mother was dead.

Hers was not the kind of death that threw people into frenzied action. This was not an emergency. It was not unexpected. Those of us involved moved with measured intention. No one looked at their watch or busied themselves with forms or urgent phone calls.

The thing was done.

My father and I left the next day for Atlanta.

Yesterday. Could that really have been yesterday?

At a gas station in North Carolina my father quietly asked me to go inside and get two cups of ice. Back at the car he opened the trunk and filled each cup from a bottle of scotch he had hidden there, amidst the suitcases and the plastic bags filled with my mother's things from the hospital.

In the car he handed me one of the cups, and then we eased back onto the highway. We drove like that, each of us sipping carefully. I'd never had scotch, and the taste was strong and bitter. Each swallow left me breathless.

By the time we got to Atlanta it was late. As we pulled up the steep, cracked driveway I stared at the old, white house on the hill. We'd only lived here for a few years. It was a rental, the best we could do after we moved back from Florida, my parents' medical bills taking priority over long-term housing.

My dad parked in the carport, and after he switched off the ignition both of us remained in our seats for a moment longer, listening to the ticks of the cooling engine. Finally one of us moved, maybe him, and we eased our way out of the car and up the steps to the back door. Neither of us had been in the house in months.

My mother's purse sat on her desk, from the last time she had set it down. I let my fingers brush its leather as I passed by, floating into the house like a ghost.

I moved slowly through room after room. Each one more still than the last.

In the kitchen I stood staring at my reflection in the window above the sink. Ghost.

A plant on the windowsill was dry, and I ran the little pot under the tap. I opened the refrigerator and stared into its mostly empty contents. Half-drunk bottles of juice and condiments with crusted caps were scattered across the shelves. I opened the freezer door too, peering in at the sauces and stocks my mother kept stored there. Sheets of cold, like apparitions, wafted down at me.

I could hear my father in another part of the house, opening and closing doors. A muffled hush had fallen over everything.

Goodnight stars. Goodnight air. Goodnight noises everywhere.

I made my way to the back of the house and stood in her bedroom, the light from the hallway casting a glow into the darkness there. A nightgown lay draped over a little couch by the window. A book sat propped open on her nightstand. I touched each object lightly, my ghost fingerprints leaving a trail of dampened, white smudges behind me.

Eventually we found our way to the living room, both of us sinking down onto the couch cushions. My father lit a cigarette, and I stared at him in shock—my mother never would have let us smoke in the house—and then I realized that it didn't matter anymore, and I lit one too.

We exhaled long, thin streams toward the ceiling. There was nothing to say. There would be nothing to say for a long time.

At the top of the stairs, before going to bed, my father pressed a little blue pill into my hand.

To help you sleep, he said.

I swallowed it without water and went downstairs to my old room in the basement. Slept that dreamless sleep.

My first three days without a mother.

And now, day four. I make my way upstairs.

My father has kept the coffee pot hot for me and it ticks in the corner. I stand at the kitchen window and inspect the plant I watered last night. It shows little improvement.

I pour a cup of coffee and join my father at the coffee table in the living room. He is holding the phone in one hand and slowly turning the pages of my mother's address book with the other.

I watch as he dials a number.

Gail? Hi, this is Gerry Smith.

There is a pause as the woman on the other end says something.

No, no, that's why I'm calling. Sally . . . she . . . she . . .

His voice stops, starts, cracks. He shakes his head and thrusts the phone at me.

Hello? I say into the receiver.

There is crying on the other end. Then a woman clears her throat. I can't remember a Gail. Maybe it's someone from my mother's art group.

Hi, I say. This is Sally's daughter.

She passed away two days ago.

The words come easily. They have no taste at all.

After that I make all the calls. My father runs his finger down the pages of the address book and dials the number before handing me the phone. I marvel at how easy it is.

Hi, Ann? This is Claire, Sally Smith's daughter.

Sometimes they begin crying before I even tell them. They have been waiting for this call.

Sometimes I have to say it.

This is Claire, Sally Smith's daughter. I'm calling to tell you that she passed away two days ago.

My mother is gone. She died two days ago. My mother died on Tuesday. My mother passed away this week. She died on Tuesday. My mother is dead.

Oh, Claire.

They say this over and over. Oh, Claire.

They tell me what an incredible woman she was. They tell me what a good friend she was. How beautiful she was. How much she loved me. How proud of me she was.

I feel nothing.

My mother is dead. My mother died.

◆

MY BEST FRIEND, LIZ, arrives from Spain the next day. She's been studying abroad for the last few months and we've been friends since we went to

Montessori. The very length of our shared history makes her the closest thing I have to a sister.

Over Christmas break the previous month, Liz flew all the way to DC to say good-bye to my mother. I envied the way they were with each other, Liz seemingly able to ignore my mother's gray skin and IV tubes. They hugged for a long time, both of them sinking into the hospital bed together.

One night that week Liz and I decided to shave our heads. We stood in my nephew's bathroom chopping at each other's hair until there was hardly anything left. I went first after that, running clippers over my scalp like I had seen on TV.

Afterward we stood back, marveling at each other in the mirror. Liz is beautiful and even a shaved head couldn't detract from her smooth, olive skin and warm brown eyes. On the other hand, my face had taken on a sallow look. At least my outside was matching how I felt inside.

The next day my mother looked at me blankly from her hospital bed.

My cheeks flushed with shame, just like they do again now, thinking about how I will have to attend her memorial service with my shaved head.

It's been a month since that winter night when we shaved our heads, and when I open the door the first thing I do is inspect Liz's hair. It's growing out softer and prettier than mine. I run my hand across my head self-consciously, the hair there like rough velvet.

That afternoon my father gives me a wad of cash. He instructs Liz to help me find something to wear to my mother's memorial service. At the mall we wander the shops aimlessly. I tell her about New Jersey, about Christopher and the rotting fish. She holds my hand, says nothing.

What do you think about this one? I ask holding up a colorful shift dress at Ann Taylor.

Liz shakes her head, and we both stand back and look at my reflection in the mirror. Although it makes my eyes pop, the silky blue material is too bright.

I already know that everyone will wear black because this is a sad death. It is not one of those deaths where the person was old and had a good run and you wear something bright and cheery and talk about how it's really a celebration of life.

A salesgirl approaches. Can I help you with anything?

We both shake our heads, trying not to make eye contact.

She pushes on: Are you looking for anything in particular? Something for spring formal maybe?

Nope, Liz says. I keep my mouth shut. We shuffle to another rack, trying to put some distance between us and the salesgirl.

We've got some really cute dresses over here, she says, pointing in the opposite direction.

We're fine, I say, turning my back to her. She doesn't give up though, and follows us over to the next rack. I'm starting to burn a little inside. I wish she would just go away.

I'm really happy to help you if you would just tell me what you're shopping for, she says.

Something inside of me snaps.

I'm shopping for a dress for my mother's funeral, I say, turning to face her. The words are hard, sharp things. They fall to the floor around us with a clatter.

I watch the salesgirl's face go flat, and then crumple just a bit. She is young, trying to do her job. Her mouth opens and then closes. I wait to feel remorse, but it doesn't come.

I'm . . . I'm sorry, she mumbles finally before turning away and slinking back to the cash register.

I feel something spreading inside me, slick and black. Like tar. Like anger.

I settle on a dress shortly after that, a simple black wool thing. At the cash register the salesgirl keeps her eyes trained on her hands. She takes my money, folds the dress, opens a bag. I silently dare her to look up.

She doesn't.

I don't know it now, but this won't be the last time I force someone else to try on my pain just so I can see how it looks.

◆

THE SERVICE IS A BIG, stupid affair. Everything is stupid now. Most of all me, with my shaved head, walking down the aisle of this church, holding my father's hand.

The scent of flowers is thick and nauseating. My dress turns out to be shorter than I thought, and I tug at it, feeling like an utter disaster, like I have failed my beautiful mother in every way possible.

I walk down the aisle with my father as though it is my wedding.

I try to keep my eyes on the floor, but I can't help looking at the people around me.

There is my math teacher Ms. Cusak. Why is she here? I never liked her and almost failed math. Standing next to her is the principal of my tiny high school. Even though I always liked him, I can't help but hate them both for being here.

There are my mother's two best friends, both named Ann. They react with shock at my appearance—the shaved head and the too-short black dress coupled with my rapidly decreasing weight and under-eye circles. I give them credit for not bothering to hide it.

My friends sit together in a cluster. They are wearing cobbled-together outfits. Church shirts with black skirts, tights, wrinkled jackets that have been hiding in the back of a closet somewhere.

After the service I stand outside with them in a haze of cigarette smoke.

I'm going to move to San Francisco, I tell them.

They nod gravely.

◆

THE DAYS BLUR together after that.

My father and I go to Cape Cod for a second service with my mother's family. I take a detour to Vermont to pack up my things from my dorm room.

I retch into a trash can as I carefully sort through the letters my mother sent me during those first few weeks of school, and then I drive to a tattoo parlor in town, where I instruct the artist to ink a perfect black circle on my shoulder.

A few days later, on Cape Cod, I peel up the bandage and pick at the black scab that has formed there. The blood beading up feels deserving, and I press my fingernail into it even harder.

There is a hatred forming inside me that grows deeper and darker everyday.

I curl into a corner of my aunt's house on Cape Cod, thinking about my mother. It is January and the wind whips around the eaves, masking the scent of the sea with one of quiet cold.

My mother and I traveled to the Cape every summer, staying at my grandmother's house for two weeks, sharing the queen-size guest bed in the back room, and falling asleep to the salty smell of the ocean filtering through the screens at night. My mother's relationships with her sisters and her mother were complicated, and as I grew older she leaned into me like a friend during these trips.

One night she dragged me on a walk with her to the beach. She was crying. It had something to do with her mom. We sat in the curve of a sand dune, the wind whistling through the reeds around us, and we shared a cigarette. I'd never seen my mother smoke and was surprised to see her do so with such ease.

Years later that moment, that shared cigarette and my mother's crying, will become the only hint I have of the kind of relationship we might have had as adults.

On our last day on Cape Cod, as I am walking through an upstairs bedroom, I see my father through the window. He is standing in the driveway, in front of the open trunk of the car. I squint my eyes, but I can't tell what he is doing.

I hurry down the stairs, calling his name as I approach. He looks up, sighs, and straightens his shoulders.

You might not like this, he says.

I round the corner of the car and look into the trunk. A thick plastic bag of my mother's ashes sits there. My father is using one of my aunt's wooden serving spoons to transfer some of them into a smaller ziplock bag.

Dad, what are you doing?

I watch in horror as he digs in for another scoop. A gust of wind blows a layer of ash off the top. It scatters across the interior of the trunk and even beyond, onto the gravel driveway.

I want to take some of these up to Nauset Beach, he says. His voice is tired, resigned.

I look down into the bag of ashes. They are darker than I expect, with grainy bits and tiny shards of what must be bone.

I watch him finish filling the ziplock bag and then I wait as he goes inside to get his hat.

I'm coming with you, I say.

We drive to Nauset Beach, the place where my father asked my mother to marry him.

After only two months of dating, my father had whisked my mother down to Atlanta, away from her life in New York, literally sweeping her off her feet. At the end of that summer he surprised her with a trip to Cape Cod, where he proposed.

About that day my mother wrote this in a letter to my father:

You announced on Monday, August 4, that we were driving to Cape Cod to see my mother. Into the car we poured, with a full bar in the backseat, and immediately to the Watergate Hotel and the last decent bed we'd have until our return trip here. Then the champagne corks flew as we bubbled our way into New York, me passing out just before the Holland Tunnel as you subtly asked me where Tiffany's was.

Oh God, an engagement ring from Tiffany's, and I had never been properly engaged before and had made that request also and here you were filling it. I felt alternately like a spoiled brat and like a woman who knew it was finally okay to want the things I'd always wanted.

You went to New Jersey the next day, for a meeting, and said you'd be back by three, and you weren't and I knew where you were and what you were doing, and I was having heart failure but tried to be very cool.

Friday morning we left for Cape Cod and you asked my mom for my hand and she was as nervous as I was and almost followed me to the bathroom when I excused myself after I heard you getting serious. I was so proud of you and moved beyond belief by what goodness was happening for both of us, and we spread it that evening with everyone, knowing that we were committed to one another, and we were more awed and in love than ever.

So, darling, it's Saturday, August 9, 1975, and the ring is in Boston at some obscure airport and we are on Cape Cod, two hours away, and the place closes at 1:00 p.m. and no one seems to know anything about anything, and we are in the car tearing up there, you driving superbly, me with plans of outracing any cop who dares try to stop us.

I love you, Massachusetts police force, because you all must have stayed home. We made it, threw the box in the trunk, and then drove two more hours to Nauset Beach, where I'd hinted I wanted to become engaged. It's a place that held indescribable magic for me as a kid, a place I'd always return to as an adult, and a place I'll always remember because you asked me to marry you there.

And I said yes, more out of nervousness than anything else, and you told me to be quiet and you started and finished this time and almost left me speechless for the first time in my life. And I said yes again, and you gave me the now famous box and the most beautiful diamond ring that is so flawless and full of fire and fit so perfectly and I LOVE IT.

It is here, on this same beach, where I watch my father wade out into the soft sand dunes by himself. After a while I can see only the top of his head bobbing through the sea grasses, and I realize, for the first time, how alone we are in our grief.

◆

MY FATHER AND I spend the next two months back in Atlanta, sitting around in the living room, until one day he decides that I should to go to Europe to meet Liz.

We can't just sit around here smoking and looking at each other, he says.

I know he's right, but I'm afraid to him leave alone.

Don't worry about me, he says, as if reading my mind.

Liz lives in a small city called Santander on the northern coast of Spain. She's supposed to be attending university and taking a year off before college. But really she just spends her days lounging around her Spanish family's house, skipping class, and fucking their oldest son.

I fly to Madrid and Liz meets me at the airport. As the plane touches down something inside of me snaps. I have been unmoored, set adrift in the world. It's the first time that my grief has made sense.

Grief is like another country, I realize. It's a place.

Liz and I only spend an afternoon in Madrid. We are thrilled to be together. The world is ours for the taking. We hop a midnight train to Paris, smoke cigarettes in the couplings between cars. We meet a handsome young Spanish boy our age, and the three of us lean back against the wall of the coach, averting our eyes as we try awkwardly to bridge the language barrier.

Paris and then Basel, Brussels, and Amsterdam, Rome for a week, and then into Barcelona. We pass ourselves from family friends to bunk-bedded hostels and then back to family friends again. We sit in bar after bar, smoke a thousand cigarettes, huddle over crumpled maps, flirt with boy after boy. We fight too, grow sick and tired of each other, and walk silently down empty, echo-filled streets.

I have nightmares most nights, my mother in a bathtub of blood, my mother like a zombie, my mother, my mother, dead over and over again.

Liz strokes my hair as I dial the numbers that reach my father's voice back at home. I sob into the phone, and his voice is metallic through the line, in between my halting breaths. I am worried about him. Is he lonely, is he sad too?

Yes, Claire, I am.

FROM Barcelona, we go up to Bilbao, where we take a bus to Santander. I lean my head against the window and my tank top clings to the sweat on my lower back. We've been traveling for a month now. My life back at home seems incredibly far away.

In Santander we spend our days at the beach, giggling, as we lie topless on the sand. At night we sit in dismal bars and smoke Ducados because they are the harshest, smelliest cigarettes we can find. My trip is coming to an end. In a few days we will travel back to Madrid together. I will fly home, to Atlanta, to my father, to that gloomy and hushed house.

I shudder when I think about going home. It's easy here in Spain to forget about my life in Atlanta. These foreign streets have quelled the blackness gnawing inside me.

But it is still there. I feel it at night when I lie in bed next to Liz, trying to fall asleep as I listen to her quiet nighttime breathing.

I hate myself.

I dig my fingernails into my palm.

I actually hate myself.

Fat, hot tears roll down my cheeks, and I lie still so that I don't wake Liz.

We spend the last few afternoons seated on the patio of a little café, sipping espresso and beer and writing postcards. I write a few to Christopher and think about those cards traveling halfway across the world to the PO box on Haight Street.

Sitting there at the café, my skin feels lonely and tight. I miss being touched. I tilt my neck, stretching the muscles from my collarbone up through my jaw, and I catch the eye of a young man a few tables over. I look away and out at the ocean. I can feel his eyes on me, traveling through my red tank top, across my breastbone, over my lips. I look back and he looks down, marks a page in his book, and gets up from his seat.

As he walks toward our table, his coffee cup in one hand, I reach into my bag and withdraw my camera. In Spanish I ask if he will take a picture of us. Liz looks up from her book. She's been lost in reading, has no idea of the careful dance that has gone on between us. He answers me in English, takes the camera, and stands back a few feet. Liz and I lean into each other. We've done this a hundred times in the last month.

His name is Alvaro. He is Spanish, has been studying at Oxford. He comes from a wealthy family, is home on break, just out for the afternoon, enjoying a coffee, the sunshine. His hair is thick and lustrous and his dark eyes sparkle in the afternoon light.

Do we want to meet him for drinks later that evening?

We do.

Years later I won't remember anything about the landscape of Santander. The layout of the city, the size of it, the streets will escape me completely. But I will remember the bar where we meet Alvaro. The three of us sit upstairs at a little table, and I do all the things I always do for boys. I match him drink for drink. I talk about Vonnegut and Hesse. I quote Kerouac and I French-inhale my cigarettes. I lean forward so that the shallow curves of my clavicles become deeper, and I look away when he looks at me.

The moment Liz leaves for the bathroom he is kissing me.

I already know I will sleep with him. I knew it the moment I reached into my bag at the café, my fingers closing around the sturdy weight of my camera. Knew, as I handed it to him, my fingers brushing his, that this was the final piece of the trip. I will sleep with a perfect stranger.

Do I want to see his family home, he asks between kisses. I do.

Liz is worried and I am drunk.

I'll be home by dawn, I reassure her as I climb into Alvaro's convertible.

I wave to her, my gaze fastening on her frame for just a moment before I swing back around in my seat, lifting my face to the wind that whips down over the windshield.

If Alvaro and I talk during the drive, it's only about trivial things. Mostly there is the road, dark and rushing before us. Despite the alcohol swirling in my veins, I feel incredibly present to this moment. I am distinctly aware of what I am doing. I know that I am eighteen years old and that my mother is dead. I know that I am in the passenger seat of a strange boy's car, that we are winding along a nighttime road, that there is a town glimmering with little lights below us, that I am somewhere in Spain.

It's one of those moments that will be easy to return to, for years to come.

The house is impressive: beautiful stonework makes up the exterior, landscaped pathways lead to various entrances, and the whole property is perched on a cliff overlooking the Bay of Biscay. We stumble through the rooms under the pretense of a tour. I am never scared of him. He is young and clumsy. It is obvious that he comes from a good family, that he is trying to impress me.

His hands are on my lower back. I focus my eyes on a suit of armor. He points out the family emblem emblazoned on a shield. In another room I fall back onto a bed, Alvaro on top of me. It is over within minutes. I open my eyes for just a moment before it ends though. His are closed tight.

Remember this moment, I tell myself and I know that I will.

Afterward, we lie still, the thing done. A sheen of sweat glimmers across his neck and shoulders. I close my eyes again.

After a few minutes I get up to the use the bathroom and I realize that the condom must have broken. I return to the room and his eyes narrow in fear when I tell him.

We are suddenly young again. Whoever we were both pretending to be, those people are gone in an instant, replaced by two teenagers, half-dressed and nervous with each other.

Moments can be so simple sometimes. In this one I realize that I have convinced myself that nothing could ever hurt as much as my mother's death, but in fact the opposite is true.

Everything hurts.

Tears well up in my eyes. It occurs to me that I have been pretending, that I thought I deserved this. For the first time, I feel the knife slide in just a little.

I turn my head to one side to hide my tears and I feel Alvaro's heavy silence.

I've never done this, he whispers.

I turn back to him, searching his face.

A few days ago his girlfriend of two years—his first love—left him. His voice is a whisper as he tells me this. She already has a new boyfriend.

I knew, Alvaro says, the moment my fingers closed around your camera that I would sleep with you.

My mother is dead, I say in response. She died a couple of months ago.

I knew I would sleep with you too, I say.

We spend the rest of the night talking, face-to-face, our legs crossed Indian-style on the bed, and then perched on stools at the kitchen counter, drinking cold juice, and later, back in his car, the stars are high and clear above us.

It doesn't occur to me until later how much this night is like the one I spent with Michel, but when it does, I will again marvel at the power people have to unlock each other.

On the drive back to the apartment where Liz lives I lean back into the leather bucket seats of the convertible and gaze out at the first vestiges of dawn rising pink and rosy over the bay. We pull over, not wanting to return just yet. There is still more to say. The little town lies sleeping before us, the tiny lights twinkling in the early morning twilight.

I RETURN HOME to Atlanta different somehow. I'm not afraid anymore.

I'm going to San Francisco, I tell my dad.

I think you should stay here and get a job instead, he says.

I will, I say. I promise. But first I have to go to San Francisco.

And I do. I need to know if it is where I should be. Not just the city, but Christopher too.

I take a Greyhound bus, to prove that I'm not afraid. My father drives me to the station, in a grimy part of Atlanta that I've never visited.

Are you sure you want to do this, kiddo?

I'm sure.

Even though I'd spent most of the night before sobbing, I have inherited my father's stubborn streak.

Last night I cried about nothing, about everything. I cried until I went upstairs and woke up my dad. He rubbed my back until I slowly began to calm down. He told me stories after that, ones that took place in the years before I remember—stories about my mom, tiny details and images I'd never heard. He talked until his voice was hoarse, and his eyes closed.

I look at him now from my window inside the bus, and realize that I'm going to miss him. I'm going to miss my father, whom I don't think I've ever missed before.

The bus ride from Atlanta to San Francisco takes fifty-six hours, straight across the country. I stare at my reflection in the tall, smudged windows. I notice that my hair is getting longer and curling softly around the edges of my face; it actually doesn't look so bad anymore.

I change buses in the middle of the night in places like Salina, Kansas, and Stovepipe Wells, California. I smoke cigarettes and tighten my arms around me against the 3:00 a.m. frost. The people who ride the bus are like none I've ever met before. Young, pregnant women toting toddlers and beat-up suitcases, transvestites and weathered young men with prison tattoos.

I carry a tiny, silver flask of whiskey and a copy of Milan Kundera's *The Unbearable Lightness of Being*. There's nothing new about this girl I've chosen to be, except the act of choosing itself.

Christopher picks me up at a bus station in San Francisco, and I am immediately in love. With him. With the windswept and whitewashed city. We stand across from each other for a long minute before we embrace. I haven't seen him since the night my mother died.

Four months ago.

Christopher takes me back to an apartment he shares with several other people. It's an old, sprawling place with high ceilings and hardwood floors, just a block off the Haight. We share a bed because there is nowhere else for me to sleep. We are careful with the space between us.

During the day, when he goes to work, I wander the streets of San Francisco, enchanted with every inch of it. I pass through clouds of patchouli and marijuana, past homeless kids on the sidewalk and musicians busking for money. The shadows are cool, the sun is scalding.

I feel like I can breathe here.

At night Christopher and I go out for drinks and I marvel at this new world. The one in which I am a girl without a mother, the one in which I sit in grown-up bars in San Francisco.

I almost wish she could see me.

All through my visit I throw myself at Christopher. I even tell him that I am in love with him. He smiles mysteriously. Pats my head. Calls me "Clar."

We sleep together one night.

It is a detached, ugly thing. We are watching television in bed. He puts his hand between my legs. I scissor them open. I want so badly for him to love me.

It is something I regret before it is even over. I am someone I hate before the thing is even done.

I take a walk the next morning by myself. I know what I must do.

Back at Christopher's apartment I gather my things and find him in the kitchen.

I'm leaving, I say.

He just nods.

With that I walk out the door and into San Francisco. I spend the next three days in the dismal room of a youth hostel, drinking whiskey and reading Italo Calvino. If I have felt alone in my life, it has never been like this.

My mother is gone. My father is seventy-eight years old. This is it. I am on my own.

I take out my camera and set it up to capture the profundity of the moment. In the grainy black-and-white, I am leaning back against the wall, one knee pulled to my chest, a cigarette between my fingers. My head is turned to one side, my hair is short around my ears, and my tattoo is showing.

I'll come across this photo for years to come and it will never cease to give me pause, instantly transporting me to the first time I realized that no one was ever going to save me.

I leave for Atlanta the next day, fifty-six hours straight on the bus.

Christopher will call once in the new year, late at night, long after I have gotten over it. (Do I ever get over it? I was with him the night my mother died.)

I'm sorry, he'll say into the phone.

Don't be, I'll say. I asked for it.

Chapter Five

2000, I AM TWENTY-TWO YEARS OLD.

I AM AT WORK when the call comes.

I see one of the hostesses walking toward me, an intent look on her face. It's a Monday night, which means it's slow. There are empty tables scattered around the cavernous restaurant, and I've been standing behind the bar, idly surveying my customers, and glancing at the clock on occasion to calculate how many hours until we close.

Republic is a chic pan-Asian restaurant on Union Square, and I've worked here as long as I've lived in New York, a total of three years. My little locker downstairs, the other veteran staffers, and the tiresome familiarity of it all make it feel like home.

I glance away from the approaching hostess, still not quite realizing that she is headed my way, and gaze out the windows at the end of the bar. It is late January and snow is falling softly on the square. Cars stream by in a blur of lights, and I can hear the wet spray of frozen sludge as they pass.

My mother's three-year death anniversary was two days ago and it's stayed with me like an unsettling dream. I curl my arms around myself, and I flinch when the hostess taps my arm.

Phone's for you, she says.

I walk out from behind the bar, nodding at a waiter to watch over things, and I cross the room to the granite hostess stand where the phones are located. I won't have a cell phone for another year, but even so, I'm not used to getting calls at work and something about this call tugs at me ominously.

I pick up the receiver and hold it to my ear.

Hello?

Colin's voice is tight, not like I've ever heard before.

He's dead. He fucking killed himself.

Who's dead? Panic floods my sternum.

Darren. He fucking hung himself in jail.

I'm on my way, I say.

◈

I TAKE THE STAIRS down to the locker room two at a time and spin the combination on my lock until I hear a subtle click. I pop open the metal door and grab my coat. I share the locker with a waitress named Angel, and in a throwback to our middle school years we have decorated the inside of the door with pictures of Patrick Swayze, Johnny Depp, and Kirk Cameron. The photos ruffle as I slam the door closed again.

My heart is racing. My fingers fumble with the lock as I try to replace it and eventually I give up, dropping it to the floor, turning on my heel to jog back upstairs.

I can't tamp the panic I'm feeling. A torrent of thoughts plunges through my head. I need to get home to Colin. I don't know how he is going to react to Darren's death.

On Fourteenth Street a cab skids to a stop in front of me, and I clamber awkwardly into the backseat, lugging my heavy bag with me. I was at school before work, and haven't been home since this morning.

Avenue B and Fifth Street, I say to the driver, flopping back against the seat and biting my lip. We fly down Fourteenth, swerving onto Second Avenue.

The tires sing on the wet asphalt and Manhattan flashes by in a stream of twinkling lights outside the window.

When I open the door of our apartment, Colin is sitting at the table, a cigarette in his hand, his face like stone.

I drop my bag on the hardwood floor and cross the room to him, then snake my arms around his torso, burying my face in his neck. I stay there waiting.

Darren fucking killed himself, Colin mumbles into my hair.

I don't know what to say. My gut reaction is that this is a good thing.

Darren is a thirty-year-old prisoner in Atlanta, awaiting trial for the murder of several people, including Colin's sister.

◆

I TURNED TWENTY the week I moved to New York City. I wore a pale blue dress on my birthday and I was young and skinny and much more beautiful than I realized.

New York was instantly everything.

It was sudden and disarming and utterly consuming. Before a week had passed I couldn't imagine ever leaving.

In those early days I swayed under the weight of the buildings towering above me. The ribbons of people on the sidewalk pulled me to and fro, and I learned quickly to just give myself over to it all.

Colin had been living here for two months when I arrived. I told myself that it would just be for the summer, that I'd go back to Vermont and college in September, but even then I knew I wasn't going anywhere. The second I stepped foot in Manhattan I had no intentions of ever leaving. In the fall I applied at the last minute to the New School, the university where I would finish my last few years of college.

I had insomnia that first summer and stayed up watching as dawn rose lazily outside the window, quietly extinguishing the city lights until the skyline was something solid and dusky. Right away I knew I shouldn't have moved in with Colin, that we were too young and too damaged to see the thing through.

On those nights I thought about my mother, about her living here for all those years, and I wondered what she would think about me being here. Each street I walked down I wondered if she had done the same. Every bar or shop I went into I tried to picture her there too. I imagined my timid footsteps leaving dusty prints on top of hers.

My mother wouldn't have approved of me being here, that much I knew. New York was too big, too gritty for the daughter she had known.

The night I moved to New York I drove down FDR Drive, alongside the rushing brown river, past the high-rises and the Domino Sugar factory. My cat mewled quietly in her carrier in the passenger seat beside me and the Lower East Side loomed in the foreground. I couldn't shake the sinking feeling that this was not the girl I was supposed to be.

No, the girl I was supposed to be would still be at college in Vermont. I would have some sweet and apologetic hippie boyfriend who I would spend the summer with before starting my sophomore year. We would drink coffee all the time and take walks in the woods. He'd have those stupid poetry magnets on his fridge and would write me little messages that would make me blush with both gratitude and embarrassment.

But, gripping the steering wheel as I made my way into the East Village that night, I knew that girl was lost forever.

She disappeared the night my mother died, and I was never going to see her again.

Three years passed. Three years without a mother. Now I am irrevocably this girl: the one who has tattoos and drinks too much, the girl who rushes from her noontime writing classes in Greenwich Village to her bartending job in Union Square, the one who is sometimes afraid of her alcoholic boyfriend.

In three years my grief has grown to enormous proportions. Where in the very beginning I often felt nothing at all, grief is now a giant, sad whale that I drag along with me wherever I go.

It topples buildings and overturns cars.

It leaves long, furrowed trenches in its wake.

My grief fills rooms. It takes up space and it sucks out the air. It leaves no room for anyone else.

Grief and I are left alone a lot. We smoke cigarettes and we cry. We stare out the window at the Chrysler Building twinkling in the distance, and we trudge through the cavernous rooms of the apartment like miners aimlessly searching for a way out.

Grief holds my hand as I walk down the sidewalk, and grief doesn't mind when I cry because it's raining and I cannot find a taxi. Grief wraps itself around me in the morning when I wake from a dream of my mother, and grief holds me back when I lean too far over the edge of the roof at night, a drink in my hand.

Grief acts like a jealous friend, reminding me that no one else will ever love me as much as it does.

Grief whispers in my ear that no one understands me.

Grief is possessive and doesn't let me go anywhere without it.

I drag my grief out to restaurants and bars, where we sit together sullenly in the corner, watching everyone carry on around us. I take grief shopping with me, and we troll up and down the aisles of the supermarket, both of us too empty to buy much. Grief takes showers with me, our tears mingling with the soapy water, and grief sleeps next to me, its warm embrace like a sedative keeping me under for long, unnecessary hours.

Grief is a force and I am swept up in it.

◆

THE ONLY THING that anchors me is Colin. And he does so fiercely.

When we fell in love it was exactly like that: falling. Deep and dreamless, love was like an opiate, rendering each of us powerless against the other. It was like we were the only two people in the world who spoke the same language. It was like we had no choice about falling in love.

But there's always a choice, isn't there?

Three years later we are at the bottom of a very deep abyss, each of us quietly looking for a way out.

Colin is moody and intense. He is confident and confrontational. He moves with purpose. He is aggressive in a quiet way. He is suspicious of everyone, and about this he is not apologetic.

Colin is never apologetic.

He is demanding and intimidating and he rarely compromises.

If Colin discovers a weakness in a person, he cannot help but confront it. His eyes will glow and a small smile will edge the corners of his mouth.

He once told me a story about taking acid with a group of friends in high school. It was the middle of the night and they were hanging out on the banks of a river, tripping on the moonlit scenery and the rushing water. One of the girls was having a bad trip and had chosen to cling desperately to a plastic water bottle as her talisman.

After an hour or so Colin ripped the bottle away from her and threw it in the river. Even as he tells me the story, his mouth curls into a little smile.

Colin tells me what to wear and, more specifically, what not to wear. He is critical of my friends and suspicious of their intentions. He is withholding in his affections, and often I have to barter for hugs or comfort. Colin drinks too much and when he drinks he becomes explosive.

I am often scared of Colin.

Yet it is these qualities that also draw me to him.

Colin loves me the way you love a child: ferociously and with a sense of propriety.

A decade from now I'll be a psychotherapist in a little clinic in Los Angeles. I'll take on a client one day who lost her father when she was a teenager. Her mother deteriorated after that and my client and her sisters scattered into the arms of whoever happened to be nearby.

When I come to know this client, she will be in her early twenties, living in a sparsely decorated townhome with an abusive boyfriend who closes his hands around her throat on a nightly basis. He follows her every move, seething with anger when she does not obey his instructions about who to be friends with, where to work, what to wear, when to come home. Every week she says she is going to leave him. She never does.

I'll immediately recognize in her that same need I had at age twenty-two. The need, not just to be loved, but to be owned.

◆

COLIN DOESN'T WANT to talk about Darren. In fact he doesn't want to talk at all. He pours himself another drink, vodka with just a splash of soda water, and he pulls a chair in front of the stereo.

These are the nights that frighten me the most. There is a rage building quietly inside him, like logs in a fire that have been lit from within. I curl into the futon in the living room, bracing myself for whatever is coming next.

Sometimes Colin simply sits there until he is too drunk to do anything else, eventually heaving himself up and into bed.

Other nights he becomes explosive.

One night he slammed his fist into the plywood door of the living room, leaving a dent there for our remaining time in the apartment, a constant reminder of the darkness that lives with us. Another night he hurled a tumbler so forcefully that it lodged itself right there in the drywall, Colin falling to the floor with the effort of it.

Sometimes he has night terrors, jumping out of bed in a daze, terrifying us both, yelling, and hitting out at the room around him, at the phantom intruder in our midst.

Other times he just makes broad and cryptic declarations about his mortality. In the beginning I used to argue with him, sometimes even try to soothe him.

Now I just do my best not to antagonize him.

On milder nights he lines up the evening's empty bottles in front of the door—a homemade alarm system built to alert us to intruders—and stumbles to bed. Colin is fanatical about locking doors, about safety. For years, after we are no longer together, I will leave every door open and unlocked, just because I finally can.

Tonight could be any of these nights.

Colin appears suddenly, swaying in the doorway.

I'll never fully understand what it was like for him to lose his sister. I may know grief, but not the kind he knows. Not the kind brought on by finding a sibling drowning in a pool of blood in your parents' living room.

I wish I could have killed him myself, Colin says about Darren, his voice slurred.

I believe him.

◆

I WANT TO COMFORT Colin, but I know he won't have it.

On nights like this I feel trapped here, not that I have anywhere to go. Colin discourages me from making friends but I do anyway, being sure only to see them when he is working. I know he is afraid my friends will try to take me away from him.

He should be afraid. My friends try to do exactly that. Always at the end of some evening one of my girlfriends will lean forward in her seat.

Claire, she will implore, hapless concern in her eyes, can't you just leave him?

I shake my head. She doesn't understand. None of them do.

I don't understand either.

The truth is that I am afraid of staying with Colin, but I am more afraid of leaving him.

In a way Colin is all I have. After my mother died it wasn't just the house we packed up, her things that we got rid of. It was everything. For days I sifted through her clothes, beautiful designer dresses she had worn to elegant events with my father, scarves she bought in Paris, sweaters from Ireland. I opened and closed drawers, my hands roaming over the contents, breathing in the essence of my mother while the piles of her discarded belongings grew in heaps behind me.

We even had to find new homes for our two dogs, Welsh corgis named Russell and Rosie. They were nine and ten years old when my mother died, near the end of their own lives, but neither my father nor I could keep them after the way everything was dismantled.

I think about the dogs late at night, after Colin has fallen into a drunken, dreamless sleep. I remember when Tonia and I held a wedding ceremony for them when I was in fourth grade, and I weep to have abandoned them, weep because I have been abandoned too.

My father lives in California now, and not a day goes by when we don't connect in some way. Mostly we talk late at night, when I am on my way home from work, when it is still early on the West Coast. He is watching movies, drinking scotch, missing me and my mother.

He tells me about his appointments, about the neighbor kids who stop by in the afternoon to say hi to him. He tells me that he planted some flowers on his patio, that he hopes I'll come out to visit him soon.

I feel a twisting in my stomach when he says this. I know that I should be in California with him. I promise that I'll move there when I graduate. Two more years, I say.

He came to visit me once, the first summer I moved to New York. We had to pause on each landing as we made our way up the five flights to my apartment. Afterward he sat in the kitchen, breathing heavily, his face flushed with exertion. He was diagnosed with emphysema shortly after that, putting a stop to any more traveling.

On that one visit to New York he showed me around the city, taking me to places he used to go with my mom. We ate béarnaise burgers at P. J. Clarke's, and my dad pointed out the table where they were sitting the day Jackie Onassis came in. We stood in front of my mother's old apartment building on Twenty-eighth, and I tried to imagine him that morning, twenty-five years earlier, wearing the funny blue suit as he rang my mother's buzzer for the first time.

The plan is to move to California when I graduate.

It's where Colin wants to go too. He is a doorman at a club in Chelsea. He has been taking acting classes but hasn't found any parts. He thinks all that will change in California.

I think I will finally escape once we get to California.

For now, I just find freedom in little ways.

One of them is school. Colin couldn't care less about my writing, scoffing at me when I hesitantly ask if I might read something aloud to him, but I will have the same writing teacher for my entire four years at the New School. Joan and I meet in coffee shops for my independent study sessions, and I write furiously for her, reading aloud in my soft, breathy voice.

My real escape, though, is at work.

I will work at Republic for four years, hostessing, waitressing, and eventually bartending. I will memorize the menu, and those pale, sleek dining tables will imprint themselves into my psyche. I will make friends that I will keep in touch with for decades. And years later, even when I find myself dining in elegant four-star restaurants, some part of me will always wish I were on the other side of the table, forever nostalgic for the camaraderie of waitstaff.

The moment I walk through the doors of Republic I feel a softening through my whole body, a palpable sense of relief. Sure, it's like any restaurant job. The customers are annoying, our managers are idiots, and the drama among the staff is more interesting than any TV show, but it's also home.

Most of the other waiters have worked here as long as I have. We spend the slow hours leaning against the counter, talking about our lives. Even if we're not the kind of people who ever would have been friends, we know one another intimately.

The cast of waiters, bartenders, hostesses, and busboys is a fluctuating hierarchy of anorexic models, hopeful actors, ambitious screenwriters, and flaky fashion students. There are scandals and affairs and there is theft and betrayal. Friendships are formed and dissolved and all of it is discussed over cigarettes on the back stoop.

I have a crush on a waiter named Haynes. He's part of my secret life. He's an actor too. He went to Juilliard, or somewhere impressive, and he acts in plays on a regular basis. He is gruff and disgruntled and bitingly funny. He has a crush on me too.

We go as far as to match our schedules, both of us arriving early for our shifts, lingering in a little hallway downstairs, as we smoke cigarettes and flirt shamelessly. In these moments I feel like a girl again, not the fearful and drained young woman I have become in the last few years.

I think about Haynes late at night when I'm trying to fall asleep. About what it would be like to go on a real date. About what it would be like to be a real girl again, to feel free to smile and laugh and move through the world unchained by grief and all that it's led me to.

My heart races when I think about what Colin would do if he ever found out. He came in once when I wasn't expecting him and found me behind the counter, doubled over in laughter with a waiter named Eric, whom I adore. Colin stormed out before I could even wipe the smile from my face.

I was careful about work after that.

◆

SOMETIMES I TRY to tell someone at Republic about my mom. I don't know how to explain myself without the context of her death.

It's late afternoon and the tables are empty. I lean against the bar, next to another waitress, and we chat idly. Boyfriends, school, who on staff has a coke problem, hostess Melissa's crazy outfit behind the cash register.

Sometimes the talk runs deeper. Where we grew up, who we live with, where we're going.

My mom died a couple of years ago, I'll say tentatively.

I've learned quickly, though, that this is a conversation stopper. Unless the person I'm talking to has been through something equally terrible or sad, they don't know what to say. They usually mumble some kind of awkward apology, and it's not long before they push off from the bar, walking purposefully toward a customer.

I stay there a minute longer, resting my back against grief's chest.

I don't know who to be without my mother. More important, I don't know *how* to be.

One day I wait on a mother and her daughter out to lunch together. After they have paid their check I sit outside, by the dumpsters in the alley, sobbing.

I miss her so much sometimes that I can't breathe.

I obsess over the last year of her life. What I said and didn't say. What I did and didn't do. Over and over I replay that particular afternoon in the hospital when my aunt Pam rubbed lotion into my mother's legs and feet, smoothed Vaseline across her lips.

Why couldn't I have done those things for her myself? If I could go back to that moment, I would crawl right into bed with her. I would put my arms around her, tell her how much I love her, and I would stay there forever, just me and my mom.

I curl over into myself as I think these things. It is afternoon and I am alone in the apartment. My sobs bounce off the walls and I tear at the skin on my arms. I want her back.

I want any tiny moment of it back.

I am drowning a little every day. There is a chasm inside me, a lake of grief so deep and so wide that I fear I'll never be able to swim to shore.

As I go about my days, trudging up Ninth Street to class, hailing a cab home from work late at night, I am drowning. The light at the surface is growing farther away; my chest is tightening; my whole body is a lead weight sinking slowly toward the bottom.

I would do anything to have my mother back.

One day I walk to Twenty-eighth Street after work. The building isn't anything interesting. A simple, ten-floor brick number with a little awning out front. I stand in front of the door for a long time and then push my way through the entrance. A tired-looking doorman stands sentry at a desk, an old fan blowing a stale breeze.

Can I help you?

I make eye contact with him.

Um, no. I just . . . I trail off.

I just want a minute here, I want to say. One minute to close my eyes and be in this place where my mother was so many times. Every day I walk through Manhattan and wonder if she walked down this street or once ducked into this bodega, but here—I know she was here. The doorman eyes me suspiciously though, and finally I back away and push out the door.

On the sidewalk grief takes my hand, leading me home so that I can cry myself to sleep, flushed and sweaty, like a little girl.

◆

BARELY A COUPLE of days go by and there is another phone call. Nothing ever came of the night Darren died. Colin stumbled drunkenly to bed like usual, and I stayed up until dawn, smoking and scribbling in my journal.

There is a cycle occurring, one I won't fully recognize until later, but one that is there all the same. There is a softening after each of these nights, a honeymoon period. Colin's steel grip releases just a bit, and I find myself unable to remember why I am so desperate to leave him.

We go to a movie the night the second call comes, and afterward we trudge home through the frozen streets of the East Village. It's one of those late January nights in Manhattan when the whole world seems frozen over. There was a big snow a few days ago and the once soft, fragrant heaps have hardened into great crystalline mountains streaked through with sludge and grime from the passing cars.

Walking home, we take each step on the icy sidewalks carefully, reaching out now and then to steady ourselves with the coarse fabric of each other's wool peacoats and slipping anyway. We make our way down Avenue B until we reach the heavy door of our apartment building.

Over the course of the four years that we'll live here gentrification will slowly spread its way east until Avenue C is where all the hippest boutiques and bars are. But right now, in 2000, Avenue B is still a little sketchy.

There is an abandoned building full of squatters next to ours. Sometimes we have to step over homeless people sleeping under tarps on the sidewalk and we crane our necks upward, listening to the fights filtering out of windows.

Our building is of the solid brick sort and we live at the very top, on the fifth floor. I will trip on these stairs over and over, sometimes drunk, sometimes carrying bags of groceries, other times for no reason at all. In the base of the building is a little deli where we go to buy cigarettes and six-packs of Bass Ale and pints of Häagen-Dazs in the summer when our little window unit air conditioner isn't enough to combat the sweltering heat.

An older Puerto Rican couple lives next door to us. The wife never emerges from the apartment, and all day long the husband travels up and down the stairs carrying enormous plastic bags filled with empty bottles and cans for recycling money. For years, I'll say that this is how they pay their rent, and then one summer when they finally go out of town I'll sneak a peek at the rent slip when I see it wedged in their door.

Because of New York's rent-control laws, and because they have lived there so long, their rent is only $65. Ours, for the same size apartment, is $1,450.

As we trudge up the stairs, to our little apartment on the top floor, I can hear the phone ringing from halfway down the hall.

Colin fumbles with the keys, his fingers cold. The phone bleats just inside. We push through the door finally, and into the darkened kitchen. Colin is the first to reach the phone. A cursory hello, then silence. He hands it to me.

It's Julie, he says.

I'm still tugging off my gloves, unwinding my scarf from my neck. Why is Julie calling? We spoke two days ago.

Julie is one of my best friends. She is twenty-two years old, a student at the University of Georgia. We went to high school in Atlanta together and despite the disparate landscapes of London, Vermont, New York, and Athens that pepper our post-high-school life, we have remained close.

But still we only talk every few weeks, filling the interim with fat, handwritten letters and the occasional e-mail. Why is she calling only two days after such a catch-up session?

I hold the phone to my ear.

Julie?

Colin rolls his eyes and disappears into the living room.

Claire?

Her voice is soft, like the freshly fallen snow that drifted across the window-sill two nights ago. She continues without pause.

Claire, I have something to tell you.

And then she just says it:

I'm in the hospital and I have leukemia.

Her voice breaks here, her breathing cascading into rough whispers across the phone line and into my ear.

Everything stops.

What do you mean?

It's all I can manage.

Her explanation unfolds like an instruction pamphlet: backward, forward, upside down, all of it connected, all of it unavoidable. My brain turns her words over and over, trying to fit them together in a way that makes sense, but it's impossible to fold it all back together into a neat package, into something palatable.

Yesterday, at her medical science internship, she blacked out while peering into a microscope. She was taken to the hospital, where blood tests imme-diately revealed an invasion of white blood cells. More than she would ever need. Millions. Trillions. Filling her up, destroying everything in their path.

Leukemia.

It was a simple diagnosis. The news was delivered with one brutal blow, everything shifting in an instant. Chemo, radiation, radical tests and treat-ments, a college semester dropped out of, a life completely changed.

I sit on the couch with Colin after I hang up the phone. We each light a cigarette.

I have to go to her, I think to myself. One night, a few months ago, Julie and I stayed up late, talking on the phone. Colin was at work and I had the house to myself. He had been particularly sullen, particularly controlling that week. I was crying to Julie. She was one of the few people with whom I actually talked about my relationship.

Let's make a pact, she said.

I nodded, sniffling into the phone.

If one of us ever breaks up, we'll drop everything and be there. That way it won't be so scary.

I nodded again. Okay. Yes. Definitely. Drop everything.

I think about that phone call as I sit on the couch next to Colin, Julie's news sinking into me.

She's going to die, I say.

The words are out of my mouth before I can stop them.

In the months ahead I will retract this prophecy. I will remain positive, along with the rest of our friends, that Julie will in fact not die.

But she does. Of course she does.

Of course Julie dies.

◆

OVER THE NEXT YEAR I fly to Atlanta on five separate occasions to be with Julie as she undergoes chemo, radiation, and an experimental stem cell transplant.

I sit with our friends for long hours in waiting rooms as we while away the time before we are allotted a brief and plastic-gloved visit to our beautiful friend who has lost all of her hair.

Julie lies pale in her hospital bed, and I hold one of her hands in mine. It is near the end, January again, and the stem cell transplant did not work.

I don't know anyone who's died, she says.

I am crying, but Julie is calm. There is a sense of wonder in her voice.

The next day when I return to her room she is unconscious, her breath raspy and shallow.

She dies the next night.

Her death leaves me both depleted and emboldened. That's what tragedy does to you, I am learning. The sadness and the wild freedom of it all impart a strange durability. I feel weathered and detached, tucking my head against the winds and trudging forward into life.

After Julie's death I return to New York with an empty feeling, and I go about my days with dead eyes.

Work and school, then home again to the apartment with Colin. Julie's illness had provided a brief respite from my relationship woes. In the face of so much fragility I once again felt grateful for Colin's firm grip.

But now she is gone and nothing seems to matter. Winter slides into spring and then into summer again. I am on break from my classes, picking up extra shifts at Republic and tilting my head to the soft breeze that pushes through the screens in the living room windows.

◆

THE MONTHS SLIP by and nothing changes. Not the East Village apartment I inhabit. Not my job at Republic or my classes at the New School. Not Julie's absence or my fear of Colin.

At night he thrashes in his sleep. Some nights he flings himself out of bed, attacking phantoms rushing forth in the darkness, destroying the alarm clock, knocking over a lamp.

Other nights are more predictable. He puts on Bob Dylan and just sits in front of the stereo for hours, a glass in his hand, his body rigid.

Sometimes there is nothing. Sometimes there is punching, kicking, breaking.

He never hits me. Not once.

But I am still afraid.

Daytime always brings peace. We wake close to noon, sunshine skimming across the hardwood floors, lighting all the darkest corners and warming the bottles by the door.

I start going to Cape Cod regularly. I take the Peter Pan bus from Port Authority, through Connecticut and Rhode Island and into Massachusetts, where it crosses the Sagamore Bridge onto the Cape.

My aunt picks me up at the bus station, my grandmother sitting up front in the car, and they drive me back home with them to the old Victorian house on the beach in Harwichport. I've learned how to be close with them, even though in the beginning it felt like a betrayal of my mother.

I sleep for long hours upstairs, under the cranberry quilt, the salty ocean air soft on my skin. At night I sit next to my grandmother in her reclining chair, and we watch *Jeopardy!* and hold hands.

I've been thinking about you, she says, and pats my arm. Her hands are cool and dry, the skin soft like paper.

I take long walks out on the jetty, stepping carefully over the rocks, and remember when I used to do this with my mother.

Mom, can you see me?

I wish I could talk to her about Colin. I know she would help me leave him.

Back in New York I sit up late trying to figure it out. Colin is at work, and I think about what it would be like to just leave, to disappear out the door and never come back.

But then I think about my cat and my trunk full of journals and letters from my mom. I think about the streets of the East Village at two in the morning and about my bank account, which is almost always empty.

I think about just telling him that I want to leave, and then I shudder with the thought. I imagine him throwing my belongings out the window; picture him hurling my cat against a wall.

I'm not sure he would really do these things, but I'm also not sure he wouldn't.

One night I dream that it was really him who killed his sister. I wake up, sobbing, gasping, and, before I can reconsider, I tell him about the dream.

He is quiet for days after that, but I'll never again be able to shake the tiny seed of doubt about his innocence.

I call my aunt on Cape Cod one afternoon, and when she answers the phone I break down crying. I want to tell her about Colin, want to ask her to help me, but I don't know what to say.

School is overwhelming this year, I say instead.

Oh, she says, I wish I could crawl through the phone line and put my arms around you.

When she says this, I am struck dumb with the memory of my mother saying the same thing to me once when I was seventeen and on an overnight trip, with some friends, visiting colleges. I had called her, sick and tired and wishing I was home.

Oh, she had said, I wish I could crawl through the phone line and put my arms around you.

A FEW NIGHTS LATER I come home from work. I have stayed out later than usual, drinking with my coworkers after Republic has closed, something that Colin usually disapproves of, but I've been pushing the limits lately.

Haynes had been part of the group, and it was the first time we were ever together outside of work. We sat next to each other in the booth, our knees touching, and I greedily consumed the thrill of it, not realizing how thirsty I was for something so sweet.

I am tipsy when I stumble out of the cab on Fifth Street and clomp my way up the stairs. I fumble with my keys, struggling drunkenly to fit them into the proper locks. My efforts make a scraping sound, metallic and grating. Finally the lock turns and I begin to push the door open.

Before I can even cross the threshold the door is slammed back in my face. A man yells loudly, flooding me with fear.

I'M GOING TO KILL YOU! The words are garbled, forceful things.

Someone is inside. Someone has broken into our apartment.

I start to back away down the hall, the fluorescent lights illuminating the grimy walls, the filthy staircase.

I'm panicking. Where should I go?

In a split second I run through different scenarios, all with the same ending: I see myself stumbling down the stairs, being slain halfway down by whoever is in our apartment right now. I see my body slumping to the floor.

Before I can take another step, the door opens. Colin steps out, rubbing his eyes.

I am frozen, halfway down the hallway. The yellow light bathes us both in the sad place we are in.

He was the one yelling. He was drunk and asleep. He thought I was an intruder.

I am the phantom.

◆

A WEEK LATER I curl up on a friend's bed, crying myself to sleep. I am house-sitting while she is away and I have been spending long hours in her apartment, trying to figure out a way to leave Colin.

I write a long letter to an unborn, imaginary daughter.

Don't ever find yourself in this place, I write, tears streaming down my face. Even if I am gone and you are alone, be a stronger woman than I am.

I go home and sit on the couch, waiting for Colin to get out of the shower. I am finally going to do it.

I am going to leave him.

I am shaking as I stare out at the Chrysler Building.

He walks through the kitchen on the way to his closet.

Colin, I call out. We need to talk.

He stands in the doorway, pulling on pants, a shirt.

I'm leaving, I say.

I pause, bracing myself. But nothing comes.

Colin buttons his pants and goes back into the kitchen, where I hear him open a bottle of beer.

He reappears in the doorway.

Well, he says, let's talk.

He listens calmly as I explain all the reasons I want to leave. I tell him how sick I am of him telling me what I can and can't do, can and can't wear, who I can and can't be friends with. I tell him that he scares me. I tell him that I am sad. So very sad.

He listens and he smokes, and we talk and after a while none of it seems so terrible and I can't remember why I've been so upset about it in the first place.

And just like that, things go back to normal for a while.

A few weeks later I am up early one morning so that I can catch a bus to the Cape. Colin is still asleep, and when I get out of the shower all our phones are blinking with messages. I scroll through the call history on my cell phone and see that it was Colin's father calling.

My heart drops. I imagine that his mother has been in an accident. Or worse, that my father is dead.

I push the buttons to call him back, but there is something wrong with the phone and the call won't go through. I try again and again until finally I hear ringing, then Colin's father's voice on the other end.

Are you okay?

What do you mean?

Turn on the television, he says.

In the living room I fumble with the remote, pushing the buttons until the screen pops into life.

The second tower has just been hit. Two great plumes of smoke pour upward into the sky.

Chapter Six

I AM SITTING IN the back of Ms. Cusak's tenth-grade algebra class when I meet Zoe. Technically it's not the back since all the tables are arranged in a circle, but it's as far as I can get from the center of the room.

Ms. Cusak is the only thing I dislike about my new high school. Well, her and Algebra I. Sarah Cusak is in her midthirties, single, and overly tanned, with stringy hair. She is the basketball coach and the math teacher, and she constantly tries to impress upon us how cool it is to be thirty. She tells us stories about her apartment complex and the bars that she hangs out in on the weekends. She favors athletes over the weirder of us.

Ms. Cusak will attend my mother's funeral in two years, and the pity her presence evokes for me will somehow be worse than my shaved head and too-short dress.

It is my first month and I'm still trying to figure out where I fit in. It's a small school—there are only thirty-seven of us in the tenth grade—and the philosophy is one that encourages individualism and creativity. There are town meetings, independent studies, tons of art classes. There are kids with blue hair and some who wear pajamas to school every day. When I graduate, three years from now, I'll do so barefoot, with flowers in my hair.

My mother was immediately enchanted by the school, and even if I am intimidated at first, I will look back on my experience here with wonder and gratitude for years to come.

Zoe and I end up sitting next to each other in Ms. Cusak's class. Although our friendship builds slowly, it doesn't take long to discover that we both hate sports and math and, in turn, Ms. Cusak.

Zoe has just moved back to the States from Paris, where she's lived for the last five years because her stepfather works for the UN. She has a magnificent tangle of inky black hair and amber-colored eyes. At fifteen, Zoe is not what kids my age usually think is beautiful, but I think she is anyway.

She is exotic too, with her flared jeans and ratty cardigans. She is the first in our class to own a pair of Doc Martens, and she got them in Europe no less. Zoe has smoked a cigarette and she's been drunk before.

Zoe's parents are divorced. She hates her stepdad and misses her own all-too-absent father. She is full of rage and self-loathing and she speaks in a quiet whisper most of the time. All of these things I find out later, not in those first few weeks of school.

But they are things I can tell about her already, things that aren't surprising to hear come out of her heart-shaped lips.

Zoe is shy, and our friendship starts out slowly. I've always made friends easily, but with Zoe it is different. There are rules to abide by. She has to be handled gently. I have to be careful not to push her too hard, too quickly.

Otherwise she just turns off.

Her lips close and a lock of hair falls over her face and suddenly she's gone. I am intrigued and eventually obsessed. Something about Zoe blinds me to everything else. I feel about her the way I've never felt about a friend before: impatient and possessive, needy and desperate.

Although I have arrived at school already attached—Liz transferring in the same year—I drop her immediately for Zoe. I don't take the time to acknowledge how much this hurts her.

I can't.

In the last two years, since my parents' cancer diagnoses, something about me has changed. There is a rip inside me, a tiny tear in my fabric, a darkness waiting there, and everything about Zoe threatens to help me make sense of it.

We are living in Atlanta again, having given up on Florida offering our small family anything but misfortune. My mother has spent the last two years seeing shrinks, taking shark-cartilage capsules, and doing some kind of weird art therapy.

She spends hours in the basement, working tirelessly on a disturbing collection of decoupage masks, carefully laying them out to dry at the end of each day. At night she drinks red wine on the couch until she is sloppy, and my father sits at the dining room table, bills and papers spread out around him, trying to figure out how to support our family.

Although my father has been in remission since his radiation treatment, he is now seventy-three years old. His hair wisps around his ears in white tufts and he is slow to push himself up out of chairs. He leaves the house most mornings in a suit and tie, returns from each job interview defeated and deflated. Empty-handed.

I hide in my room, trying to just disappear from it all.

◆

THIS IS THE YEAR that everything changes between me and my mother. One day I shift from wanting to be her, to wanting to be anything *but* her. It's not as conscious as that, of course, but we both feel it in the ways I begin to withdraw.

Later it will be hard for either of us to tell whether this individuation was a result of my mother's cancer or simply my perfectly timed teen angst. Whatever the case, I begin keeping secrets from her. Just little things, mostly omissions.

How was school today, sweetie?

Fine.

It was actually great, but I don't want her to know that. I don't want her to have the satisfaction.

Are you making new friends?

Uh-huh.

I'd love to hear about them sometime.

Maybe later.

I don't consider whether these responses might be hurtful to her. I only know that if I say more than a few words, the anger simmering just beneath my skin might gush forth. The rage living inside me is new. It's not something I've ever felt before and I don't know where it came from. I don't know enough to connect it to the most obvious source.

The first day I saw my mother in the hospital, a year and a half ago, it felt like something was being taken away. I walked down the long, sterile corridor, my hand in my father's, as we approached her room.

The room was washed in a soft, gray light and my mother's eyes were closed, her hair limp and shapeless against the pillow behind her head.

When she opened her eyes and spoke to me, it was in a voice that wasn't hers.

Hi, sweetie.

There were tears in her eyes and she reached out for me.

My father nudged me from behind, and I moved forward to embrace this woman who wasn't my mother.

A year and a half later and I'm still not sure that I trust her.

◆

ZOE IS AN ARTIST. Her pencil never stops moving over a page. With just a flick of her oval-shaped fingernails against a no. 2, I'm looking into a mirror, a perfect portrait of myself, shaded in Zoe's lead, staring back at me while fractions and decimals swim by.

It's hypnotic to watch, and I am often left feeling kind of helpless.

We meet that first week of tenth grade, and by Halloween we are inseparable. Zoe spends almost every weekend at my house. We hole up in my basement room, and my mother makes occasional appearances, bringing offerings of brownies or pretzels. She likes that Zoe is an artist, but it only annoys me that they have a shared connection. I want Zoe for myself.

Zoe and I each have a boy at school that we are in love with. Hers is Ethan. He is a transfer too. Divorced parents; long, scraggly blond hair; a painter. He is mocking and cruel, and none of us can get enough of it.

Mine is Henry. Shy, sweet Henry, who likes to draw and has a permanent bump on his forehead.

Coincidentally, Henry and Ethan are best friends. I run cross-country with them after school. Zoe has third-period art class with them. We compare notes every night on the phone.

Neither I nor Zoe has any real experience with boys. I've kissed a couple of them, but they were awkward, fumbling experiences that weren't at all what I was expecting.

When it comes to boys, I've always been the same. I've always been the girl who gives too much too easily and expects the same in return. I don't remember which boy was first. In the beginning they were all the same: smooth and hairless and vulnerable, emulating or disobeying their fathers— there was nothing original about them yet.

Maybe there never is.

Suddenly—maybe it was the first week of sixth grade, I don't really remember—suddenly, I loved them all, their soft eyelashes and downy cheeks, the slight swelling in their biceps, the way their hair clung with sweat to their smooth, tan foreheads.

Then, back then, I could never be as beautiful as they were.

And suddenly an ache, this *ache*, filled me up so fast. And suddenly—it was all so sudden back then—I could not remember the time before the ache and I could see no way past the ache. So I followed the boys with my eyes, my skin warming as they walked past, sweaty and musky from gym class. I followed them at night when I closed my eyes and lay in my canopied bed, cicadas ringing at the windows.

I followed them like this, silently, throughout three torturous years of middle school and into the fringes of high school. Sometimes they seemed to notice my footsteps behind but I never spoke up. I was never sure where it was they were going, what I was following them toward.

Some part of me understood though, I know that now. I know that because the first time I reached the end of that path I knew exactly where we were.

The body has memories that begin before we do, I think.

My body knew Henry before I did.

◈

I LOOK FORWARD to cross-country practice every day after school, and not just because of Henry.

I love running. After a day folded behind desks and dry-erase boards, sack lunches and confusing friendships, running feels like screaming.

I can feel my whole body open up, the muscles harden and sing with meaning. I love the feeling of sweat sliding down the new curve of my breasts, the hard pavement beneath my feet. I can't even describe what it feels like to run behind, and not just follow, Henry.

It is his calves that captivate me first. They are muscled and covered in a coarse bristle of hair. Running behind him, I watch as the muscles tense and resolve, swell and soften. Eventually my eyes travel up to his forearms with their smooth, pale underbellies, his Adam's apple and unruly brown hair, his limpid brown eyes and wide forehead. I want to mother him. I want to smother him.

I want to do things to him that I won't know how to do until I am doing them.

But we're not quite there yet. Right now it's still the very beginning of the thing.

It all begins innocently enough, but it's here where Zoe and I begin to divide. Where she is content to cast secret glances at Ethan in art class, I have seen something I want and I cannot shake the idea that I can have it.

I devise a plan.

I notice that Henry is always at school by the time I get there. His father has to drop him off early on his way in to work. So I ask my mother to drop me off early as well. On these early mornings I lean my back up against my locker, pull my knees to my chest, and cast furtive glances at Henry. If I time the thing right, there is usually no one around for at least fifteen minutes.

When you're in tenth grade, that's a long time.

By the second week I've worked up the courage to ask him a homework question, and I can tell he has inched a little closer to me—not close enough so that we are sitting together, but close enough so that we can keep our voices soft.

By the third week we begin to talk about our lives. His parents are divorced. He lives in a two-bedroom condo with his father on the opposite side of town. His mother lives nearby. He has two older brothers, one of whom introduced him to the Velvet Underground and neither of which lives at home anymore.

I tell him about the quiet triangle of my family, always isosceles, never equilateral. Not that I even understand those terms yet. I won't take geometry until the next year and even then I won't begin to comprehend the knife-sharp angles that come with equidistance.

Before long, Henry and I have created a secret friendship—the fragile kind we pretend doesn't exist when we pass each other in the hall between classes. At some point, later that fall, close to winter, we move our friendship to the telephone. It is safer there, our whispers encased in the snakelike black cords that wind their way through Sandy Springs, across town, and into a small two-bedroom condo in Smyrna.

But on the nights that I fall asleep thinking about Henry, I dream about Zoe. The dreams are black and white, her amber eyes the only color.

◆

ZOE AND I STILL spend every weekend together. We speak every night on the phone and match our footsteps on the path to English class. We hate the same people and turn our scorn, our slitted eyes, toward them at the same moment.

We hate everyone really. No one can do right. Why do they wear that outfit, drive that car, stop to pick up that person's book? We sneak my father's big black Lincoln Town Car out in the middle of the night and coast up and down the darkened streets of Atlanta, knowing that there is more somewhere but not knowing which direction to turn.

Zoe lives in a crumbling, charming kind of house. It is messy there, the floors warped in some places, both Zoe's and her mother's hair tending to frizz in the humidity that traps itself under the eaves. We don't spend a lot of time there, always preferring the anonymity of my basement, the ease of sneaking out in the middle of the night. Sometimes we walk out to the middle of the road in my quiet neighborhood and just lie down on the still-warm asphalt, the night air cool on our bare skin.

Sometimes I talk to her about my parents. But as resentful as I feel about the doctors and the hospitals, about my father's age and my mother's stupid shark-cartilage capsules, my venting doesn't seem justified. Is having parents with cancer really that much worse than having parents who are divorced?

I tell Zoe bits and pieces about my tentative relationship with Henry, but not everything. I can feel her tense when I talk about him, can see her lips begin to close if I go too far. So I keep most of my secrets secret. Although I yearn for a girlfriend with whom I can share these things, I don't tell her that Henry has admitted that he thinks about me late at night. I don't tell her that this knowledge, this confession, thrills me, that I can feel myself opening in places I didn't know were closed.

Instead Zoe and I talk about ourselves, about the kind of women we think we'll be, about the places we'll live and the sound our footsteps will make one day on the hardwood floors of our studio apartments in some big, nameless city.

We talk about this future as though it is one single existence, not hers or mine, but just this single collective vision of the grown-up us we will become.

◆

ONE WEEKEND I sacrifice my standing Saturday date with Zoe for one with Henry.

He and I go to a music store together and wander up and down the aisles, our bodies gently bumping and pushing again back off each other's.

At this point he is still unsure of the thing. He wants to be friends, just friends. I want him so much I can't breathe.

Some of the most erotic moments I'll ever experience happen in those early days, in those moments after we've swung shut the car door and realized that we are alone together in the silent, heavy air.

The next weekend he invites me to his house, wants me to meet his father, to see his room. I am nervous as we stand in that small space, his bed the focal point. I gently touch each of his drawings hanging on the walls, take in the soft, plaid comforter pulled boy-neat at the corners, the books stacked on the nightstand, the dresser and the blinds on the window.

So this is where Henry is alone, I think, and I can feel myself opening.

We walk out into the woods behind his house. There is a train track running through the kudzu-covered oak trees. Cicadas hum in the warm spring air and we place pennies on the railroad lines and then step over them, going deeper into the woods.

We find a fallen tree and sit down side by side, our breath practically the only sound. At first we just put our arms around each other, but it isn't enough. When his mouth finally finds mine, I feel the ache shift for the first time in my life. It is as though there is a warm lake inside me.

By the time the train roars by we are on the ground, in the leaves and damp soil, Henry above me, my fingers kneading into the warm skin of his back. It will still be another month before I lose my virginity but I can feel him come against me, his face buried in my neck, the sunlight filtering through the trees above me.

Babes in the woods. We are lost, all right.

It's here where Zoe exits stage right. She and I still spend our days together at school, and she still spends the night on the weekends, but all I can think about is Henry.

At school it becomes difficult, yet thrilling, to pass Henry in the halls or to sit across from him in English class and pretend not to know what the soft curve of his abdomen feels like against my palm.

We see each other every weekend now and our rendezvous often take place outside.

Georgia in the springtime is magnificent, everything lush and green, magnolia trees and daffodils, weeping willows and thickly hanging wisteria. I feel the crush of my hips against a bed of tulips one day, and the thick thrust of sharp pain, signaling the very moment of my deflowering, my legs spread, taut under the quilt in Henry's bed one warm afternoon.

When I am with him, I think of nothing else. Not the look on my father's face when he returns home from another dejected job interview, not the sound of my mother retching into the toilet after chemo. I don't think about Ms. Cusak's class or the shadows that fall across Zoe's face.

Henry and I stand in the rain after cross-country one day, water streaming, gleaming down our pressed-together bodies. Another afternoon we wait in Ethan's yard for him to return home. We sit on the grass by a honeysuckle bush, and I show Henry how to find the honey, that careful pulling out of the stamen, that golden drop heavy and translucent on the tip of your tongue. Soon the sweet taste mingles back and forth between our mouths.

The spring goes on like this, each week like its own year.

One night I come home from a date with Henry and find my mother in the living room, white wine on her breath.

Sit down, she says.

She looks at me for a long moment, and I know that she is trying to see into me.

Are you having sex with Henry?

My first impulse is to lie.

No, I stutter, my cheeks burning.

Are you lying to me?

I shake my head. No.

Although lying to her has become a familiar thing, a sick feeling comes over me.

But these things I've discovered about my body? They are mine. Not hers.

All I know, she hisses, is that I hope you are still a virgin.

I stand and, without looking at her, walk away.

We are tense for days after that.

If only we had known how near the end was. It arrives swiftly, taking all of us by surprise.

◆

ALL I KNOW is that there is a coming to, a waking up, as though I've been asleep or dazed. I have been, I suppose.

When I come to I am standing in the bathroom at school.

I have just walked in on Zoe. She is hunched in a stall, the sleeve of her sweater pulled up to reveal a smooth, pale forearm. She sees me and instantly hides whatever she is gripping in her other hand. I can't be sure, but I think it's a razor. I grab her hand and pull her toward me, my heart pounding, breaking, but she shoves me off, her eyes those angry slits, and she bangs her way out of the stall and past me.

She is closed. No matter what I say, no matter how hard I try, she has closed herself off to me.

At night we sit silently on the phone.

It isn't hard to see that during these last months with Henry, while I was losing myself in my body and in his, she was drowning. I picture her underneath the water, the slick green weeds reaching up to her ankles, her ebony hair spreading out around her face.

I have failed her.

I instantly turn my anger and my frustration onto Henry.

Suddenly I hate the way he stares at me in class, hate the way he presses himself into me so pliantly. I ignore him completely at school, trying to prove to Zoe how much I love her, how far I am willing to go for her.

I turn cruel in my desperation.

Henry is suffering now too. His eyes grow wider, more pleading by the day. I let his phone calls to my basement room go unanswered. We said that we loved each other, and now I want to take it back.

I want to take everything back.

◆

School is almost over for the year. Summer has come and with it, Georgia's intense humidity. My skirt clings to the backs of my legs now as I follow Zoe down the path to English class.

Henry and I see each other a few more times. We walk out in the middle of an English class one day and drive to the park. Into the woods a ways we fuck on the ground, dead leaves and twigs digging into my back, leaving little red indents along my spine, scratches against my shoulder blades, and bruises on the insides of my thighs.

It is one of the last times I will see him. School lets out for the summer a few weeks later.

A month into the summer break I go to Michigan with Zoe and her family. We had arranged this trip long before she started the cutting, long before Henry and everything that followed.

I am determined to follow through with it even though Zoe is hardly speaking to me.

We'd had big plans for Michigan. We'd plotted to sneak out in the middle of the night, to go into the town, to meet boys, to drink. We'd planned to lie by the lakeside day after day, our feet in the warm brown water, our necks long and girlish, turned to the sun. But Zoe still hasn't come around completely; she still hasn't opened back up, and I don't know what to expect.

I officially break up with Henry a few weeks before the lake trip. We go to the park, near the same place where we have so recently fucked. It is too much, I tell him. I'm drowning, I say.

I can see the tears in his eyes. His throat moves up and down. I feel empty inside.

At home my mother is sympathetic when I tell her the news, but I can sense the relief in her voice. She finds me in my room later that night. I can smell wine on her breath, but her tone is soft and she is loose.

Can we look at the stars?

I have covered my bedroom ceiling with glow-in-the-dark stars, and I push my homework to the side and turn off the light. My mother lies down beside me.

We have been doing this for as long as I can remember.

You are so much wiser than I was at your age, she says to me.

I don't look at her.

I look at you and I can hardly see the little baby I held in my arms all those years ago. You've become a young woman before my eyes.

I can hear the tears in her voice.

There is so much more to come, kiddo. Trust me.

She takes my hand, and I let her. We lie there looking up at the stars, and I cannot decide if I want to be like her when I grow up.

❧

HENRY CALLS EVERY DAY after I break up with him. I scoff at the whispered messages he leaves, push my finger hard against the delete button. He leaves letters in my mailbox, hand delivered, filled with drawings, dried flowers. I make fun of him to Zoe. A small smile starts to crack the corners of her mouth.

The night before we go to Michigan, Zoe and I stay up late in her room. I want things to be the same as before, I tell her. She turns her eyes away. The wind blows outside and branches scratch at the window.

Our talk turns to Henry. He is so weak, we say. Why can't he see that I don't love him anymore?

We devise a plan.

It has been a couple of weeks since I've spoken to Henry. With Zoe listening on one phone, I call him on another. His voice is soft, careful about revealing its surprise at hearing from me.

I tell him I still love him. I tell him that I am going to Michigan in the morning but that when I return we will press into each other as though there had never been any space there at all.

I can almost hear the tears of relief slipping down his cheeks.

Zoe grins at me from across the room, and I gently replace the handset.

It is a three-day drive to Michigan. Zoe and I sit in the back of the van. We feed her little half brother Dramamine in a Coke bottle so he'll stop bothering us, and we roll our eyes at her parents, who are listening to a book on tape. We stare out the back window, at the road disappearing away from us, and I can feel her arm, soft and warm against mine. We stretch our feet out, and she puts her head on my shoulder.

When we finally arrive at the lake house, Zoe leads me upstairs to her grandparents' bedroom. She hands me the phone. The numbers come easily; I have dialed them so many times.

It was a joke, I say when he answers. Henry doesn't understand.

I can feel my throat swelling as I repeat the sentence.

I don't want to be with you anymore, I say.

Leave me alone, I say.

I hand the phone back to Zoe, and she clicks off the connection. We walk downstairs and out to the lake. I lift my face to the sun and can feel Zoe beside me doing the same.

Shortly after I return home from the Michigan trip I realize that my period is late. I panic and count the days, backward and forward, coming up with the same terrible number over and over.

I sit, knees pulled to my chest, on the edge of my bed, rocking back and forth. I hate myself. I hate how cruel I've been, how desperate and confused and self-centered I've acted. I want to take it all back.

But I don't know how.

Finally I go upstairs and find my mother on the couch. I'm crying so hard I can hardly get the words out.

I think I'm pregnant.

Instead of meeting me with the fury I expect, her whole body softens. She folds me against her and lets me sob for long minutes, whispering over and over into my ear that it will be okay.

When I am done, she takes me into the kitchen and I stand there next to her desk as she calls the doctor to make an appointment.

Everything will be okay. We'll figure this out, she says, and sends me downstairs for a nap.

When I wake up, the world is warm and hazy. Summer is almost over. School will be starting again soon. I lie on my bed, staring up at the ceiling thinking about Zoe and Henry. When I finally get up and go to the bathroom, I realize that I have gotten my period.

Upstairs, when I tell her, it is my mother's turn to cry, and when she is done I lean back into her on the couch and we watch afternoon television like that, neither of us speaking for a long time.

◆

By the time school starts again, in the fall, that day feels far away. The months with Henry are like a strange dream. We avoid each other in the halls, and I press closer to Zoe, until I can feel the wisps of her hair against my shoulder.

That fall Zoe and I discover drugs and careless make-out sessions with the boys who supply them. We lean back into the seats of the old red Saab my parents have bought me, and we blow cigarette smoke up through the sun-roof while we skip Ms. Cusak's class.

My relationship with my mother becomes both closer and more distant. Some nights I wake her in the middle of the night, sitting down softly in the darkness on her side of the bed. She is sleepy and warm and her voice is husky when she asks me what is wrong. It is past two in the morning, but I haven't gone to sleep yet.

Nothing, I say. I wanted to read you a poem that I just finished.

She clicks on the light and pushes herself up in bed until her back is resting against the headboard.

Okay, she says, I'm ready.

When I am done reading, she tells me all her favorite parts. She pulls me close to her and then pushes herself back down beneath the covers.

Turn off the light, will you?

I click it off and sit there next to her in the dark until she is asleep again.

In the fall of my senior year her cancer comes back. For months she is in and out of the hospital. Operations and chemo, doctor's appointments and more bills scattered across the dining room table.

In the morning, as I get ready for school, I can hear her throwing up in the bathroom. She is pale and gaunt and more careful with her movements. Her hair falls out little by little.

We have passed through whatever destructive phase of our relationship we went through. The anger and resentment have softened.

I have softened.

Henry and I still avoid each other at school, and my friendship with Zoe won't last through junior year, both of us finding circles of friends who aren't as complicated. Sometimes I want to call her and tell her about my mother, but I never do.

The day my college acceptance letter comes I open it quietly in the kitchen. Tears fill my eyes as I read the words written across the page.

I have only applied to one school. A tiny liberal arts college on a mountain in Vermont, far away from my mother and my father, far away from Atlanta and everything it ever meant to me.

I find my mother in her bedroom and hand her the letter. The late afternoon sun skates over the hardwood floors, and we stand near her dresser. She has a pair of earrings in her hand but takes the letter anyway. I watch her read the words, and then she looks up at me, tears brimming in both of our eyes.

This is the beginning of the end.

Part Three

◆

Bargaining

We will do anything not to feel the pain of this loss. We remain in the past, trying to negotiate our way out of the hurt.

—*Elisabeth Kübler-Ross*

Chapter Seven

2003, I AM TWENTY-FIVE YEARS OLD.

A TAXI IDLES, waiting for me in the circular driveway of a hotel in the Philippines. I take one last look at my companions, a motley crew of seasoned travel writers with whom I've spent the last seven days, and hand my pack to the driver, who tosses it lightly into the backseat.

I'm on assignment for *Student Traveler* magazine in Los Angeles, and I've been part of this group of journalists, all of us guests of the Filipino tourism board. But after seven days of touring Manila and the island of Cebu, I have yet to really generate anything worthy of a story for my publication.

While the rest of the writers are getting comfortable in their business-class seats, heading home to LA, I'll be making my way to an island I've only read briefly about in my guidebook: Malapascua.

The Philippines is a large and notoriously dangerous country composed of more than seven thousand islands flung carelessly across a corner of the Pacific Ocean. Before I left on this trip my friends and family expressed concern.

You could get kidnapped, my aunt said.

You could get, like, typhoid or something, my friend Lucy said.

You could get kidnapped, Liz said.

I've already learned a lot about the Philippines, and while those things are indeed true, they are unlikely. That said: it's been an intense experience. I've never been to Asia, or the third world, and the Philippines is definitely both.

There are very few Western travelers in this country, and for days I have been privy to the kind of treatment usually reserved for Hollywood celebrities. At every temple, every open-air market or on every bustling city street I have walked down, local Filipinos have grabbed one another, gesturing wildly at me: the tall white girl in their midst.

The cab driver peers at me, with interest, in the rearview mirror.

The bus station, please, I say firmly.

He puts the car in gear, and we leave the four-star hotel behind.

Where are you going?

Malapascua.

Malapascua?

I watch his eyebrows go up in the mirror.

According to my guidebook, the island of Malapascua is located in the Visayan Sea, just across a shallow strait from the northernmost tip of Cebu. Traveling there requires an eight-hour bus ride through the jungle, then a boat ride to the island.

There are no airports on Malapascua. In fact there are not even any cars. There is hardly much of anything, really. The island is about one mile wide by two miles long. The electricity shuts off at 10:00 p.m., and there is running water for an hour only twice a day.

There is really only one reason to go to Malapascua, and that is because it is one of a couple places in the world where you can dive with thresher sharks. I learned this two days ago, while paging through my guidebook, looking for something to do that would be worth writing about.

The common thresher shark ranges in size from ten to twenty-five feet and has a tail shaped like a scythe, which it uses to stun its prey. A pelagic species, thresher sharks generally reside at depths too dangerous for divers to reach.

Perfect, I thought when I read this. No matter that I haven't been diving in years. No matter that the idea makes my chest tight, my breath short.

According to my guidebook, Monad Shoal, off the coast of Malapascua, is one of the only places in the world where there are daily sightings of thresher sharks. The sharks convene there every morning because of their symbiotic relationship with a species of wrasse that lives in the shoal. The small fish rid them of bacteria by eating the dead skin from their bodies and the insides of their mouths.

Diving with sharks, a creature I am deathly afraid of, seems like the perfect antidote to the raging desperation I feel inside.

My father has been dead for exactly two months.

◆

YES, MALAPASCUA, I say to the cab driver, meeting his eyes in the rearview mirror.

Why are you going there?

I hear there's good diving.

The driver nods, his face serious as he contemplates my answer. A beat passes.

Who is going with you?

Oh, just me, I answer truthfully.

You're going alone?

Yup.

No husband?

Nope.

No friends?

Nope, just me.

I say this last sentence cheerfully, hoping to assuage any concerns the driver might have for my well-being. It doesn't work.

Do you know anyone on Malapascua?

Nope.

You're just going alone?

Yes.

This is getting tiresome. And it's also making me nervous.

When we get to the bus station, I will help you, the driver says then.

Um, I say hesitantly, that's very nice, but unnecessary.

I want to make sure that you find the right bus.

I relent, nodding at him in the mirror. I can tell that I'm not going to win this battle.

True to his word, he parks at the bus station and accompanies me inside. The station is hot and humid and crowded with people, all of them Filipino. As we walk through the open-air terminal people turn to stare and even point at me.

The driver leads me to a ticket window and leans forward, speaking rapid Tagalog with the clerk. The only word I can discern is "Malapascua." I watch the clerk make a surprised face and gesture questioningly at me. The taxi driver shrugs and repeats something.

Back outside, clutching my ticket in one hand, my backpack in the other, I follow the taxi driver down a long line of brightly colored school buses. I have a nervous feeling in my stomach. I've traveled a lot in my life, but never like this. Never alone. Never so far from home.

Each of the buses has been painted in wild streams of colors, and all of them are decorated with fringe and beads, random ornaments, and stuffed animals. We stop in front of one with the name Nikki emblazoned across the front in graffiti-style letters.

I try to act casual as the majority of passengers on the bus stop what they are doing and watch me make my way down the row of seats. I take the first open seat I see and scrunch down a bit, hoping to look less conspicuous.

The taxi driver stops to speak with the bus driver and then makes his way down the aisle to me.

Okay, he says, the ride will take about eight hours. You have to travel all the way to the top of Cebu. Yours will be the last stop. Once you get there you must find a boat willing to take you to Malapascua.

I nod. I am almost too stunned to thank him, but I finally manage to eke out a word of gratitude.

After he is gone I settle into my seat. Even though I haven't been in a school bus in a long time, the sticky seats and little rectangular windows are achingly familiar.

Hardly a minute goes by before the bus rumbles to life and we maneuver slowly out of the terminal. Just before we pass through the gates of the bus station two young Filipino boys in threadbare clothes hop aboard. And then I watch, through the big rearview mirror, as the driver slips on a pair of fluorescent Ray-Bans and pops an eight-track cassette into a player positioned just above the windshield.

Suddenly ABBA blares from tiny little speakers strategically placed all over the bus.

You can dance, you can jive, having the time of your life. See that girl, watch that scene, diggin' the dancing queen.

The music is so loud I can barely think, and my back is pulled flush against the seat as the bus lurches forward, gaining momentum with a fierce grinding of the gears. A warm breeze whips down through the top half of my open window and sunlight glances off the pleather seats around me. I close my eyes and lean my head back.

I have no idea what it is I'm trying to prove to myself with this trip, but I'm about to find out.

◆

THE HOURS ON THE BUS pass slowly. The jungle rushes by in a blur of humid greenery, and we fly up and down hills, twisting around curves and across long stretches of unpaved road.

The two boys who hopped on the bus as we left the station turn out to be ticket takers, and they fling themselves up and down the aisle as we hurtle along the road, collecting fare and chatting with passengers. Every once in a while I catch them looking at me, and I do my best to offer them a smile before they look away shyly.

Most of the time I stare at the passing scenery, smoke cigarettes, and think about the last two months.

My father died on a Tuesday night, just after seven o'clock in the evening. I was holding his hand when he took his last breath. Afterward I walked outside to the patio. The night air was warm, and I could hear kids splashing in the pool of the condominium complex.

My father was dead.

The whole world felt still and empty. Just like it did when my mother died. Except now I was really alone.

I had finally broken up with Colin a week before my father died, moving all my possessions into my dad's garage. I was now, in fact, the owner of his condo. My father left me in charge of everything, and I spent the weeks following his death making calls to Social Security and the VA, alerting them of his demise.

I kept waiting for someone more grown up than me to appear and take over, but no one ever did, and I was left to meet with the estate lawyers and plan the memorial service by myself. Those were lonely days. I smoked a lot of cigarettes on the patio. I drove my dad's car—a big, dumb Oldsmobile—to the beach, where I sat for long, quiet hours looking out at the water.

I felt an emptiness spread in me from the inside out. It was as though I was an astronaut, disconnected from my ship, floating in cold blackness, my breath coming in plumes, and static the only sound.

If grief was once like a whale, or like a knife, it became a vast nothing expanding outward from the very core of who I am.

Since there were no adults to tell me how to do things, I did them my way.

I blasted the Violent Femmes in the car the day I drove to pick up my father's ashes from the funeral home.

I hope you know that this will go down on your permanent record.

I wore my Seven jeans and aviator sunglasses the day I met with the estate lawyers.

I stayed up late, slept until noon, drank too much. Smoked cigarettes in the house.

The memorial service was on a Saturday. I wore a pale blue linen dress and stood at the podium in the little room and read aloud my eulogy with a shaky voice. There were fewer than twenty people there, most of them my friends.

After that I rented an apartment in Venice Beach. I couldn't stay in my father's condo anymore.

Venice was perfect, and my apartment was in an eclectic little neighborhood filled with canals that had been built in the 1920s. They were meant to replicate Venice, Italy, and for the most part they did. Ducks quacked softly at night, and on my walks to the video store I crossed over little white bridges covered in honeysuckle and bougainvillea.

But in the past two months a heaviness has settled over me. I'd been spending my days on the couch, with the blinds pulled tight against the harsh noon sun, unable to find a reason to leave the house.

Unable to find a reason to exist, really.

This last week in the Philippines has startled me out of my cloud of depression though, pulling me reverently back into the world. Several days ago I stood outside an open-air market in Manila, my eyes cast up to the blue sky as REM's "Losing My Religion" blasted through outdoor speakers.

For the first time in a long time I found myself grateful to be alive.

◆

Outside the windows of the bus the landscape is starting to change. We are nearing the coast again. When I finally look up, I realize that I am the only passenger left on the bus.

I catch the eye of one of the ticket takers, and he takes a seat across from me.

Where are you going?

He asks this timidly. And then we commence a repeat of the conversation I had with the cab driver.

Malapascua.

Why are you going there?

Oh, just to go.

Who is going with you?

Nobody, just me.

It suddenly occurs to me that this could all be some elaborate kidnapping plot. But if it is, it's already too late. I'm done for. In which case there's no harm in answering truthfully.

You are going alone?

Yup.

No husband?

Nope.

No friends?

Nope, just me.

Do you know anyone on Malapascua?

I shake my head.

You're just going alone?

Yes, I really am. I smile now, hoping that he'll finally get the picture.

But he continues. Where are you from?

Again, I briefly consider lying, but I'm a terrible liar.

America, I finally say hesitantly.

Where in America?

California.

LA?

Yup, LA.

He nods then. I will help find a boat to take you to Malapascua.

Thanks, I say.

I'm not sure whether I feel relieved or terrified.

Suddenly the bus rumbles off the main road and we're flanked on both sides by dense tropical forest. Oh God, I think. Here we go. I'm definitely being kidnapped. But before I can really panic, the trees clear and the huge, gleaming ocean opens up in front of us.

The bus chokes to a stop beneath a tree, and the driver hops off and immediately lights a cigarette. I follow the young boy across the road to a ramshackle dock surrounded by a cluster of wooden pilings. A few rickety catamarans sit in the water, and a surly looking group of men sit around a card table in the shade.

Hey, shouts the boy, this girl wants to go to Malapascua.

The men look up, not one of them making a move.

Hey, he shouts again, can one of you guys take her to Malapascua?

Finally one of the men folds his cards and pushes back his chair. He walks slowly toward us. His skin is topaz colored, and even though he's young deep sun wrinkles are etched in his face. He looks me up and down.

You want to go to Malapascua?

I nod at him, tighten my grip on my backpack.

Right now?

That would be great, I say, trying hard to sound friendly.

Give me ten minutes, he says.

I nod again.

Okay, says the ticket boy with a serious nod. Then he grins widely and trots off in the direction of the psychedelic school bus.

I lean against a little boathouse as I wait for the next portion of my journey to begin. On the map Malapascua didn't look too far from Cebu, but from where I stand all I can see is wide-open ocean.

True to his word, after ten minutes the boat driver emerges from out of nowhere with another guy. I watch as they climb aboard a little catamaran that looks as though it is made of matchsticks and Kleenex.

The boat captain flings some ropes around and pulls the sails tight. Then he motions for me to climb aboard. I pause for a moment. This is it, I think. I can either go forward or step back.

I take his rough, weathered hand and step precariously onto the boat. The only place for me to sit is cross-legged on a small square of canvas that is stretched taut between the two hulls. With a snap of his wrist the boat driver unmoors us from the dock and in no time at all we're skimming across the water.

What am I doing?

I have never been this far out in the world. My father's condominium, his death, those sad and lonely days on the couch, all of it seems impossibly far away.

Mom, can you see me?

There is no answer, only the warm wind whipping down over the hull.

After a while the captain squats down next to me.

Hello, he says.

Hi, I say and then we both stare out at the ocean for a beat.

What's your name?

Claire. What's yours?

Rafael.

Then: Do you know someone on Malapascua?

I groan inwardly. Not this again. I answer robotically, Nope.

Why are you going there?

Oh, just to go. It sounds like a really beautiful place.

Where is your husband?

I don't have one.

You have a boyfriend?

Nope.

But you have friends with you?

Uh-uh.

You're just going alone?

I'm just going alone.

The captain is quiet for a while, seeming to mull over my situation.

My aunt has some huts on the beach that she rents. I will take you there.

I realize that I haven't even given a thought to where I might stay when I get to Malapascua. Thanks, I say genuinely.

After what feels like hours, but is probably only forty minutes, a small mass of land finally comes into view: Malapascua. It looks bigger than I imagined, but I know from my book that you can walk from one end to the other in under an hour.

We glide right up to the sand, the shallow water a shade of pale turquoise that most people only ever see on vacation billboards. The captain offers me his hand again and helps me step down off the boat. I hold my sandals and wade through the warm waves. He points up the beach a ways to a series of thatched huts.

My aunt's, he says gesturing to them.

I follow him, my backpack hooked over one shoulder and my flip-flops in my hand. The sand is warm between my toes and the only sound comes from the waves breaking on the shore.

I've done it, I think. I've unmoored myself.

I GET SITUATED in my new abode, a small, pleasantly decorated hut just steps from the water. And then I head over to the island's only diving shop, Bubble 07. It's late afternoon, but the sun still seems high in the sky.

The divemaster is an affable British guy named Duncan, and I explain to him that although I haven't been diving in years I'd like to arrange to see the thresher sharks. He raises an eyebrow and leans back in his seat.

I give him the same look I gave the estate lawyer when he glanced up from his documents to ask why I had been chosen as executor over my three much-older half siblings.

Duncan sits forward again, pulling a form from a drawer.

Here you are, then, he says with a wink. Sign your life away right here.

We'll dive first thing tomorrow morning, he says. We'll leave at dawn. The dive is eighty feet, and we'll just descend and kneel on the sand and just watch the sharks go about their morning cleaning session. You'll probably see about fifty to sixty of them.

I swallow thickly.

Duncan looks at me expectantly, and I nod in return.

I'm in.

As I get fitted for the next day's dive I glance around at the photos papering the shop. Thresher sharks and giant manta rays, their enormous bodies gleaming in the deep-azure eighty-foot depths.

I haven't been diving in almost a decade.

For the first fifteen years of my life, we spent every Christmas on Grand Cayman Island. It had become such a ritual for my small family that even after my father lost his business and we moved to Florida, we still managed to go for a few more years.

My parents rented the same condo every year, and along with several other families who returned each December, we celebrated our Christmas on warm sand beaches, beneath rows of whispering palm trees.

Each morning my mother woke me at dawn so we could wade out into the shallow ocean, the water so clear that you could see your toes kicking up the sand below. She would bring with her a little bag of bread, and we would hold out bits of it to the gently orbiting sea turtles.

My mom was an avid diver, and each morning after feeding the turtles she tossed her gear onto a dive boat and would be gone until lunchtime.

When I was fourteen, I got certified too, and I became my mom's dive buddy on those early mornings. We held hands as we floated by the reefs, thirty, forty, fifty feet under the water. She pointed out all kinds of things only an experienced diver would notice: little anemones shaped like pine trees; fish that blended in to look like coral; long, silky eels lurking in dark crevices, their jaws opening and closing patiently.

It was some of my most favorite time ever spent with my mother, both of our eyes wide in our masks as we grinned at each other awkwardly around the regulators in our mouths, the bubbles rising to the surface like sparkling jewels.

But that was ten years ago. That was before I'd developed panic attacks, before I'd made friends with anxiety and depression, before the heart palpitations and the crippling fear of my body.

I scribble my signature on Duncan's form anyway.

◆

I LEAVE BUBBLE 07 and set out on a walk across the island. There is only one dirt road and it leads straight through the center of town. According to Duncan there aren't more than a few hundred people living on Malapascua.

The road is lined with shacks and huts, smoke rising from some, naked children playing in front of others, roosters strutting everywhere. I make my way carefully, wishing I could be less conspicuous but knowing that is impossible.

After a few minutes people start to emerge from their huts to stare at me. Little children run up and touch my leg or my bag, before darting off again.

Suddenly someone calls my name. A woman's voice, husky and inviting.

Claire! Claire!

Could I possibly know someone here? I spin around, trying to pinpoint the voice, and my eyes finally land on a robust woman with dark skin, her eyes dancing with light, a broken-toothed grin floating across her wide face. I've never seen her before in my life.

Claire! Claire! Welcome to Malapascua!

I smile at her and give a little wave, but before I can decide what to do next the kids start in on it too, calling my name and running circles around me.

Claire! Claire!

I will later find out that the boat driver and his aunt were the ones who spread the news, passing my name along on a whim, but this moment immediately becomes one of the most magical experiences of my life. I just give myself over to it, standing there on this little dirt road in a tiny village on an island in the Philippines.

Claire! Claire!

The name my mother gave me the day she first held my warm, slick body to hers.

◆

THE NEXT MORNING, true to Duncan's word, I am awakened at five thirty by a cacophony of roosters outside my window.

When I step outside, it is still dark, but I can see a light on in Bubble 07. I put on my bathing suit, underneath some shorts and a tank top, and make my way groggily over to the dive shop.

Duncan and a young Filipino boy are busy loading the dive boat with our gear. I stand for a minute, looking out at the dark ocean and trying to determine how I feel.

I have been thinking of my mother all morning. Although she has been gone for seven years I realize that I am waiting for her to show up. Waiting for her to stop me before I go any further.

Mom, can you see me?

The only answer is a soft breeze that blows across the beach.

Before I know it, I am seated in the front of Duncan's little boat, and we are streaming across the dark, choppy ocean.

I am filled with cold fear. Mom, Mom, Mom, I chant in my head. Where are you?

There is no answer. The boat just keeps plowing forward.

Duncan and the boy are behind me somewhere, piloting us into the deep, unknowable sea. When I can no longer see land in any direction, Duncan finally slows the boat. We moor at a little buoy that I am amazed he found at all, and I shakily begin to pull on my wetsuit.

Mom, please.

It is still fairly dark out and the water looks ominous.

Duncan repeats his instructions from yesterday. We'll simply descend to eighty feet and then kneel on the sand to watch the sharks. Fifty to sixty of them.

My heart is racing and I am silent as Duncan straps the heavy oxygen tank to my back. I sit on the edge of the boat, like I have done so many times in the past, my mother beside me, and I fall backward into the black, roiling water.

I tread quickly, swiveling my head in every direction.

Mom, where are you?

Duncan falls in beside me, and we make our way to the buoy line. My heart is beating so fast. I don't know how to slow it down.

You okay?

I nod at Duncan, even though I'm not okay.

I think about one of the major rules of diving. How you can descend at any speed but must ascend only as quickly as your tiniest bubbles, a rate as slow as fifteen to twenty feet per minute.

I think about how long it would take to get the surface from eighty feet.

I think about what it would be like if something happened to me in the middle of the ocean in the Philippines.

How long would it take for word to reach the States?

Who would be the first to find out?

Who is left to really care?

I take one last look across the choppy surface of the water, and then we begin to descend, both of us gripping the buoy rope. The regulator is awkward in my mouth, and my breath comes in giant gasps, the tanked oxygen cool in my throat.

The ocean current is strong, and I peer below me, trying to make out the sandy bottom, but I see nothing but darkness. I picture the massive school of thresher sharks waiting below.

Wait.

Wait.

Wait!

I thought she would be here by now. I came this far.

Here I am, Mom. Can't you see me? Can't you reach me?

And then I look at Duncan's face in front of mine and I realize that she is never coming.

I cut my finger across my neck, signaling to Duncan that I'm calling it off.

On the ride back to Malapascua I sit at the helm of the boat again, sipping warm coffee from a thermos that Duncan brought with him. I am wrapped in a towel, but still cold, and am thankful that there is no one to see the tears dripping down my cheeks.

Duncan was kind about it, had probably even expected it, but I still feel guilty. There was no need to inflict my stupid grief process on an innocent stranger.

I will tell the story of this trip many times in my life, and it will never cease to be anticlimactic. Except that for me, this *is* the climax. This is the very place—with my tear-soaked face, at the front of this little boat in the middle of the great Pacific Ocean—where I find a truth that I will test over and over in my life.

Nothing is ever going to bring either of them back.

Chapter Eight

1998, I AM NINETEEN YEARS OLD.

IN THE BATHROOM I pee on the little plastic stick and then place it carefully on the back of the toilet. I button my jeans and walk back into my bedroom, where I pick up the phone.

Colin is on the other end of the line.

Did you take it?

Yeah.

Well?

You have to wait, like, five minutes, I say.

Oh.

It is January, late at night, and the deep banks of snow outside the windows glow in the dark. Colin is in Atlanta and I am in Vermont. My mother has been dead for exactly one year.

I am back at Marlboro, picking up after a one-year hiatus following my mother's death. I'm living off campus, in a subsidized two-story condo in town, with a classmate named Tricia.

Like me, she is a poetry major.

We're like Anne Sexton and Sylvia Plath, she declares that first weekend. You're Anne because you're more glamorous, and I'm Sylvia because I'm more depressed.

As the ensuing months wear on we'll actually compete for the role of most depressed, both of us spending the same amount of time behind the closed doors of our bedrooms, both of us crying late at night in the other's doorway.

I have been back at Marlboro less than a week when I realize that my period is late. I count the dates backward and then forward again, give it a few more days, and finally buy a test kit at Walmart.

I call Colin that night. We had been seeing each other for less than six months when I left Atlanta to return to school. I had taken a year off from school after my mother's death, but my father and I both decided that it was time for me to get back in the swing of things.

I think that's the actual phrase he used. The swing of things.

It was around New Year's Eve when Colin and I realized that we were in love. The confessions came drunkenly, both of us left unsure the next day, not of how we felt, but of whether we had really said the words aloud.

Nothing could change the fact that I was moving back to Vermont though.

The plan was, and is, to see what happens. Colin is moving to New York City in a few months, to pursue his dream of becoming an actor. I've calculated that it's only three and a half hours from New York to Marlboro.

We'd talked for a while before I mentioned it offhandedly.

I bought a pregnancy test today.

What?

A pregnancy test.

I heard you. Why?

My period is late.

Do you really think you're pregnant?

No.

Did you take the test yet?

Not yet.

Well, maybe you should take it now.

While we're on the phone?

Sure.

Fine. Hold on.

And that's when I went in the bathroom to take the test.

Don't worry, I tell him, when I get back on the phone. I'm sure it's fine. I took a few of these in high school and they always turned out negative.

During my senior year of high school it seemed like every week one of us was taking a pregnancy test. We usually went to Lucy's house to do it. Her parents were divorced and her mom worked late. We had the house to ourselves for several hours after school let out.

Me, Lucy, Laura, Holly, and Sabrina.

I don't remember which of us was the first to lose her virginity, maybe Sabrina, but by senior year we were all sexually active. Some of our parents knew; others didn't. It's not even that we were particularly promiscuous. In fact we all had some form of serious boyfriend.

We were young though, and by proxy stupid.

Whenever one of us thought we might be pregnant, we would convene at Lucy's house after school. The rest of us would wait, whispering in hushed, respectful tones on Lucy's bed as the panic-stricken girl entered the bathroom alone.

Lucy had painted her room a deep, dark purple and posters of Robert Smith covered the walls. She dyed her long hair raven black on a regular basis and carefully maintained a ghostly pale complexion. Years later, when she is a bright and cheerful yoga instructor, I'll sometimes have trouble reconciling the Lucy I knew in high school with the radiant woman she has become.

None of us ever emerged from Lucy's bathroom with a positive test.

I tell Colin all of this and then I set down the phone and walk into the bathroom alone. The little plastic stick is exactly where I left it five minutes ago, and I peer into the plastic display window at the plus sign that's waiting there for me.

I am pregnant.

❖

MY EXPERIENCE BEING back at Marlboro is completely different from my first go-round. Even though it has only been a year since I was that freshman girl angrily stomping the recycling cans with my boots, pining after Michel and Christopher, and mourning the pending loss of my mother, it feels as though decades have passed.

I feel worldly and abused, fragile and desperate.

I've been avoiding the dining hall, the parties in Howland, even my old roommate Christine. I hurry to my classes and then back home again, where I curl into a corner of the bed, pulling the quilt tight around me.

Michel graduated last year. Christopher is in San Francisco.

I have insomnia and I've begun having regular panic attacks.

I stay up each night until three or four in the morning, smoking cigarettes and frantically feeling for my pulse, my heart pounding down from another palpitation.

Skip, skip, beat.

Skip, skip, beat.

A fleeting burst of sharp pain in my forehead leaves me breathless and frozen with fear. I sit, rigid like a hunting dog, for over an hour, certain that any movement might bring on an aneurysm.

My breath comes in shallow gasps. I think my throat is closing.

Each new symptom signifies my inevitable demise. It is exhausting.

Just months before, I ended up in an emergency room, certain that I was having a heart attack. Hooked up to monitors and an EKG for hours, the doctors found nothing wrong with me.

But it's not that there isn't anything wrong with me. It's that what is wrong is invisible.

Being pregnant suddenly gives me something real to focus on.

I determine that I'm not more than six weeks along. I go to the Laundromat the day after I take the test, and I pull a chair into a warm patch of sunlight and watch my clothes tumble dry behind the little circular glass window of the dryer.

I am pregnant.

I try to make sense of this fact but nothing comes. I have no context for this event. I think about my mother, and the time in high school when I thought I was pregnant. I think about how kind she was then. I wrap my arms tight around my abdomen and watch the clothes in the dryer tumble around and around and around.

I already know that I am going to have an abortion.

In fact I will never once consider keeping it. Not one time.

◆

I CAN'T REMEMBER if it was during my high school pregnancy scare or at another, later, time that my mother told me she had had an abortion.

She was thirty and living in New York. She'd just ended a brief relationship with some slick Wall Street guy, when she realized that he had left her pregnant. Calls to his home went unanswered and messages left at his office were not returned.

Finally, with a fury and impatience typical of my mother, she left a message for his secretary, requesting a check for the abortion she was about to have.

He shelled out immediately, and she went through with it. I don't remember any other details though. If she'd felt conflicted over the decision or if the experience was a traumatic one, I'll never know. Either she didn't tell me or the details left no impression.

I think about all of this as I watch the laundry tumble around and around.

Is it wrong that the idea of having an abortion makes me feel closer to my mother?

I write her a letter on the one-year anniversary of her death.

Dear Mom,
I don't know how to be without you. Please come back.

Colin doesn't protest when I tell him my plan. In fact I'll later wonder if he would have been so passive had it been the other way around. He tells me he'll fly up and be there for it.

The next call I place is to my father.

The same week that I moved back to Vermont my father moved to California. He sighs into the phone, three thousand miles away, when I tell him.

Just as the only time he will ever walk me down an aisle in a church was at my mother's funeral, the only time I'll ever tell my father that I am pregnant is this one.

Well, kiddo.

He sighs again.

I'm standing in the kitchen of the apartment in Vermont, twirling the phone cord around my wrist, as though I am in high school and talking to a boy I have a crush on instead of telling my elderly father about the abortion I am about to have.

Two days later I drive in my old red Saab to the Planned Parenthood clinic. It is deep, deep cold outside. The sky is a hard blue and slick; black ice coats the road. I smoke cigarettes as I drive, listen to Portishead.

How can it feel this wrong? From this moment? How can it feel so wrong?

The clinic is housed in a quaint, wooden A-frame house. The waiting room is really an old living room, with a comfortable couch covered in a knit blanket. A plain-faced receptionist insists that I make myself comfortable. I sit on the edge of the couch, my arms folded tightly across my flat abdomen.

After a while I am led upstairs, where a kindhearted and very butch old nurse examines me, confirming what I and the nurse-practitioner at school have already determined to be true.

I am pregnant.

Afterward we sit in the nurse's office. Instead of there being a desk between us, we sit in chairs pulled close so we can face each other. Although I've never been, this is what I imagine therapy would be like.

So, what do you want to do?

I want to have an abortion.

Have you considered any other options?

No. I want to have an abortion.

An alternative might be adoption. Also, there are more resources than you might think if you decide to keep it.

I want to have an abortion.

Okay, she says. Her eyes crinkle into a look of sympathy, and I suddenly envy her. I wish I *was* her. Wise, buoyant, practical. Sitting opposite some girl like me. Not me.

You're sure, she says, with one more look into my eyes.

Yes.

I don't know why I'm so firm about the abortion. In some ways it seems like the next logical step in the narrative of my life.

Mother dies at eighteen.

Abortion at nineteen.

It's as though I don't have a choice.

But we always have choices.

It won't be until over a decade later, when I am well into the actual world of parenthood, frazzled and overwhelmed with love and impatience for the tiny creature I have created, that I will realize that if I had actually had a baby at age nineteen it might have been the very thing that would have kept me from the years and years of misery and destruction ahead of me.

It won't be until I am finally a mother myself, and not until my cheek rests against my child's soft downy head, that I will realize the bleakness of what I did all those years before.

◆

I CALL THE NUMBER for the abortion clinic from the kitchen phone in my Vermont apartment.

A woman answers.

Clinic, she says plainly.

Hi, um, I'm calling because I'm pregnant. I want to have an abortion.

How far along are you?

Six weeks.

Not too far. She says this as though she is making a note out loud.

We settle on a date, and she begins to run through the details of the procedure.

Someone will need to come with you, she says. You won't be able to drive yourself home.

I nod into the receiver. Okay, I say.

The procedure itself probably won't last more than fifteen minutes, but you can expect the entire appointment to take one to two hours.

I nod silently.

Dress in comfortable clothing.

Nod.

Please don't eat anything the morning of the procedure. It's fine to have water.

Okay.

It isn't until the end of the call that she asks if I would like to be sedated for the procedure.

We offer a mild sedation, she says. You'll be awake but out of it. You won't feel anything. You may not remember the experience at all.

I pause before I respond, hanging on that last part: You may not remember the experience at all.

No, I say, no sedation.

If this is to be part of my narrative, I want to remember it.

◆

COLIN FLIES UP, as promised, and I am glad to see him.

We stand in the cold parking lot of the airport, our arms around each other. Even though it has been less than a month since we've seen each other, we are different people.

We have created something together.

Colin will move to New York in a matter of months and in the summer I will join him there. Everything about us will deteriorate from that moment on, but now, right now, we are the only two people in the world who make sense.

Or three people. Right now we are three people.

We spend the weekend huddled beneath the quilt in my bedroom, not talking about the baby growing inside me. We drink because it doesn't matter. Or maybe because it does.

Monday comes, a cold and overcast day.

We drive an hour north on Interstate 91, along the river that divides Vermont from New Hampshire. I lean my forehead against the window, the cold, crisp glass feels like the washcloths my mother used to lay over my forehead when I had a fever.

The clinic is a nondescript building. There is a lone car in the parking lot. No protesters to be seen.

Inside the waiting room, Colin wanders, his silhouette stark against the wood-paneled walls and library-neat bookshelves, while I fill out a large packet of forms.

Skip, skip, beat. I try to ignore the palpitations inside my chest.

I check off the little boxes on each form, indicating my medical history. There is nothing to report. Nothing has ever happened.

I cannot yet imagine the forms I will fill out for the rest of my gynecological history:

Number of pregnancies: ___ Number of live births: ___

When I am finished, I hand over the clipboard to the receptionist, who is as curt in person as she had been on the telephone, and then I sit on the couch beside Colin.

I am scared, yes.

But more so, I am lonely.

I feel distinctly alone sitting in this quiet abortion clinic in Vermont, on a cold Monday in January, one year after my mother has died.

◆

IN THE PROCEDURE ROOM a nurse tells me to remove my pants and underwear; I can remain clothed from the waist up. I leave my socks on.

I lie back on an examining table, my feet up in stirrups, knees pressed together, a plastic sheet covering my lower half. I am still wearing a sweater and a shirt, a bra under that. Something about being half-dressed like this is humiliating.

The nurse looks down at me. This shouldn't take very long, she says.

They are all expressionless—the nurse, the doctor, the receptionist—they have to be I realize.

I nod at her.

Colin is allowed to be in the room, and he stands next to me looking pale and younger than ever before.

The nurse runs through the details of the procedure.

The doctor is going to insert a speculum, and then a long, thin tube that he will use to scrape the walls of your uterus and suction out the contents.

I nod and think about the word "contents."

The cramping afterward may be severe. Are you sure you don't want a sedative?

I nod at her again. I'm sure.

The doctor enters the room, and I crane my neck to get a look at him. He is older, white haired, has a tired look in his eyes.

Years later, when I write this passage, I'll feel sorry that I did this to him.

◆

THE NURSE IS RIGHT. The procedure doesn't take very long. I grit my teeth and close my eyes as the doctor pushes and tugs about inside me with his instruments.

I cannot open my eyes. I squeeze them shut as hard as I can, trying to imagine that it is my mother's hand in mine, not Colin's.

And it's here, right here, on this exam table in an abortion clinic in Vermont, that I realize my mother is never coming back. Although I will have to realize this many times over the course of my life, nothing will ever be as strong a reminder as this.

Nothing is going to bring her back.

Some part of me, no matter how magical, believed right up until this very moment that she would make her way back to me before this happened. I realized that I had been ticking off the seconds all morning.

On the bright, cold drive up the highway.

In the warm, wood-paneled waiting room.

Mom, I'm here. Right here. Can you see me?

There's still time, Mom. Find me.

Please find me.

Don't let this happen.

But she is not here. She didn't make it in time. Or at all.

The doctor finishes and the cramps come. Thick and hard, they make me curl onto my side, the plastic sheet crinkling over me, perspiration dampening my sweater, tears running down the side of my face and soaking the exam-table paper beneath me.

I am nineteen and I have just had an abortion.

Chapter Nine

2008, I am thirty years old.

In the bathroom I pee on the little plastic stick and then place it carefully on the edge of the sink. I button my jeans and walk back into the living room, where I sit down on the couch. My husband, Greg, is sitting opposite me.

Did you take it?

Yeah.

Well?

You have to wait, like, five minutes, I say.

Oh.

It is September, early in the evening, and the first cool breeze of fall pushes through the screens of our Chicago apartment. My mother has been dead for almost twelve years.

You don't really think you're pregnant, do you?

I don't know. Like I told you, I feel really weird.

We'd had dinner that night at Greg's sister's house in Winnetka, an affluent suburb of Chicago. One of his brothers had been in town, from Cleveland, with his wife and baby, and everyone had convened at Sara's house.

The bottle of beer I consumed that night tasted funny. There was something metallic and repugnant about it, and I sipped gingerly, taking time to count and recount how many days past due my period was.

Just three.

Greg and I have only been married for two months, and although we have stopped trying to be careful, I am not exactly trying to get pregnant either. I have it in my head that getting pregnant will be no easy feat.

Thus I am surprised when I walk back into the bathroom and peer through the little indicator window at the plus sign that's waiting there for me.

I am pregnant.

◆

GREG AND I GOT MARRIED in the same church in Cape Cod where my parents were married thirty-three years earlier.

It was a hot July day and, although I hadn't expected it to be so, the happiest day of my life. I didn't feel sad about my parents at all. Not once, in fact.

I could only think about the man standing before me.

Gregory Thomas Boose from Ohio. Greg, with his thick brown curls and pale, pale blue eyes. Greg, with his steady hands and husky voice. Greg, who shares a birthday with my father. Greg, who has never been anything but kind and patient and grateful. Greg, who grew up on a farm, once worked as a banker, and is now a writer. Greg, whom I married only one year after meeting him.

Greg, who is the father of the child I am carrying.

He goes to the doctor with me on Monday and sits next to me in the waiting room as I fill out the paperwork and check the appropriate boxes.

Number of pregnancies: 1 Number of live births: 0

Greg doesn't look away. He knows.

He knows everything about me.

And he loves me for it.

The doctor dribbles my urine sample on another pregnancy test, shows us the little window, the plus sign waiting there.

She spins a few dials on a circular calendar.

You're due June 6.

Greg and I look at each other and smile.

Next summer seems at once impossibly far away and altogether too soon.

◆

I SPEND THE FALL in a dreamy haze, on the couch, coming home from work each day thickheaded and nauseated. I watch television blandly as afternoon slips into evening, until I hear the click of the door being unlocked, Greg's footsteps coming up the stairs.

I think about my mother every day.

But not the way I used to. After twelve years of absence she has become a kind of mythical figure in my life, a person I sometimes have trouble believing existed at all.

Being pregnant makes me think about her all the time again though. I wonder what this experience was like for her. If she felt sick. If she was scared like I am. If she wanted a girl, like I do. It's been a long time since I've allowed myself to miss her, and now I don't have a choice. With a sharp pang, I can't help but imagine what it might be like if she were still alive.

My mother miscarried once before I was born. My father told me that she didn't talk to him for two weeks after that, so devastated was she by the loss. She got pregnant relatively quickly again after that though, and I was born in late May. She'd been sure she was going to have a boy. I don't know if that's what she wanted though.

I wish I could ask her.

She kept up my baby book until the year she died, recording not just my birth weight and first words but the date I got my braces off, my first period, my first official date (Ben Holcombe, tenth grade). A baby book will end up being the only thing I buy for my baby too. And I choose a thick one with extra blank pages for me to record those extra firsts on.

I buy it in blue because I am sure that I am having a boy. If only because I want a girl so badly that it seems like it would be too good to actually get one. After all these years it seems impossible that I could actually have that mother-daughter relationship again, that I could, in a way, have *her* back.

I've been let down so many times now.

◆

DECEMBER COMES AND with it Chicago's long, stubborn winter. Snow piles up outside the windows of our apartment and ice cakes the summer screens.

Greg leaves work early to meet me for the first ultrasound. I am fifteen weeks along. We have told everyone we know. I have taken the first belly picture, posing in profile beside the dining room wall. I've been going to prenatal yoga, and we have begun a list of names.

Greg is wearing his work suit and he squeezes my hand in the waiting room. I lay my head on his shoulder and cannot believe that he is really my husband. It's a feeling I experience a lot, and not just because of how fast it's all happened. More because it seems too good to be true.

In the exam room I lie back on the table and lift my sweater. A nurse squeezes cold gel onto my lower belly, and Greg and I smile at each other as she begins to push the wand into my flesh.

We've already told her that we don't wish to know the sex. If it is indeed to be a boy, I know that it will be better for me to just meet him and love him than to spend six months in misery over a thing I know nothing about.

We all look up at the screen. A large darkness fills the space there. The nurse presses the wand deeper into my abdomen, circling the periphery of the screen.

Oh God, I think. My womb is empty.

Of course. Of course it is.

But then she pushes the wand upward and a little figure pops onto the screen, a fast-paced little heartbeat thrums out over the speakers.

There it is, she says, looking at us with a smile.

The figure waves it arms and legs dreamily.

We wave back.

Before the smile can fade from my face, before I am at all finished drinking in the inexplicable sight of my baby, the nurse zips the wand back down again and that same darkness fills the screen.

Did you pee before you came in?

Yes, I answer. Right before.

Hmm. Can you go pee again?

Um, sure. Is everything okay?

Probably, she says.

Probably?

I'm just trying to figure out what this is, she says, motioning to the darkness. It's possible that it's your bladder. Go pee and we'll take another look.

In the bathroom my hands shake as I unbutton my pants, sit down on the toilet. A dribble of urine comes out. Nothing more.

I already know that something is wrong.

I don't want to go back in there. I don't want to know what the darkness waiting there is.

I pause before I leave the bathroom, prolonging the moment between not knowing something and knowing it.

◆

I'VE BEEN LIVING in Chicago for two years. I moved here in September, when it was still warm. That first weekend Greg and I walked by the lake, the color an ancient kind of blue, as though it were competing with the sky.

I was living in Los Angeles when we met and, at the time, it made sense for me to be the one to move. But I didn't know anyone in Chicago, and that first fall was a lonely one. I rented a terrible, crumbling apartment on the north end of Lincoln Park, and it will forever go down as the worst place I've ever lived.

I'd signed the lease on impulse, with only a couple of days in which to find a place. The windowsills were peeling, there was only one closet—a dark, cavelike thing by the front door—and the living room received such little light that lamps were required even in the middle of the day.

Downstairs lived a band of college boys and above me a strange young couple prone to drunken late-night fights. The basement laundry room was accessible only through the college boys' apartment, and I had to creep through their living room in the morning, with all of them still asleep in various rooms, beer bottles and bongs left out on the coffee table and a video game paused on the big-screen television.

I worked hard that fall to make friends, and even though I met some wonderful people, I was still lonely. Greg and I never doubted what we were, never wavered on our commitment to making this thing work, but it was still hard. I missed Los Angeles, the sunshine, my friends there, my little apartment on the canals.

In December I came home one night to find my apartment broken into, my laptop and camera stolen, my bedroom riffled through. I stood in the center of my living room, a shattered Christmas tree ornament on the floor before me, and shakily dialed Greg's number.

He was there in minutes, with his best friend, Tarek, and they dutifully sat through the police investigation. Greg slept with a hammer on the bedside table that night, his arms tight around me.

I broke my lease after that, and two months later we moved in together. We found an apartment even farther north, on the edge of the Chicago River. From the dining room windows we could see ducks paddling down its brown waters, and every afternoon a rowing crew streamed upriver. We painted the bedroom walls pale yellow and lined up our books next to each other's on the built-in shelves on either side of the fireplace in the living room.

Greg asked me to marry him a couple of months after that. He took me to dinner at the Drake Hotel and got down on one knee, offering me the very engagement ring my father had given my mother. Greg had redesigned it to look a little different, but there it was: the diamond that had rested on my mother's finger as long as I'd known her. We went to Jamaica the next day, using money I'd won in a lawsuit against my old landlord, and as we floated in the warm turquoise water we reveled in how happy we were.

When we came home, I began to think about wedding plans, but every part of it overwhelmed me.

Greg is one of six kids, his family as large as mine is small. He grew up on a substantial produce farm in northeastern Ohio, about an hour from Cleveland, and while his friends spent the summer playing tennis and going to the lake Greg and his siblings picked strawberries and packed crates full of corn and zucchini until evening fell.

We couldn't have had more different upbringings, and during my first few years as part of the Boose family I continuously compared myself with his normal siblings.

If I have lived a life marred by tragedy and instability, the Boose kids have enjoyed the opposite. They are valedictorians and doctors and lawyers and teachers. Each one seemingly more perfect than the last. The oldest three are married, with healthy children and large homes and easily definable careers. The three youngest, Greg and his two younger brothers, are also wonderfully normal and remarkably unscathed by life.

Greg's mother is petite and sweet, prone to shopping and reading gossip magazines. She spins around the kitchen, churning out hearty buffets for her large family, and Greg's dad reads aloud tidbits from the newspaper as he reclines in the living room after a day of substitute teaching—a way to keep himself busy after selling the farm and retiring. They are like someone's idea of classic parents.

Something about planning a wedding in the midst of this giant new family struck right to the core of all the loss I'd experience. The absence of my parents was illuminated threefold, and I dissolved into daily torrents of insecurity and sadness.

I had no funny and charming mother to show off. No worldly and intelligent dad to put his arm around me as we all sat through some awkward meeting of the families. And I certainly had no one to pay for the wedding or to even walk me down the aisle. There was just me and my tenacity, an attribute that wasn't strong enough to see me through wedding planning.

After being engaged for only two months I gave up, and Greg and I eloped to Cape Cod where twenty-five family members and three friends witnessed our union in the same church where my parents were married. My oldest half brother walked me down the aisle, and my mother's sisters cried happy tears through the entire ceremony. Afterward we dined on lobsters in my aunt's backyard, and then we all donned swimsuits, skipping down Bank Street to float in the warm, green Atlantic Ocean.

It was more than perfect.

But six months later, as we sit in this exam room looking at the glowing darkness on the ultrasound screen, that day seems impossibly far away.

◆

WHEN I RETURN to the exam room, the nurse has been replaced by a doctor, a signal that there is officially something wrong with me.

Hmm, he says, pressing the wand into my abdomen. Do you have any pain when I do that?

I shake my head.

He moves the wand, and the baby comes back into view, a little figure smaller than the dark mass beneath it.

Well, it appears to be a very large cyst, the doctor finally says. Dermoid. Filled with fluid. It's likely benign.

Each sentence he says floats out of the room, echoing down the hallway, past all the rooms where other pregnant women smile up at their normal ultrasounds. I try to pay attention but I am disappearing into the blackness on the screen.

The doctor doesn't notice. No one does.

It looks like it's growing on your left ovary. We can assume that its unusual size can be attributed to the pregnancy hormones.

Greg is nodding, his hand tightening over mine like a wrench. I continue disappearing.

The doctor pushes the wand around the perimeter of the cyst as he talks, taking measurements, rattling them off to the nurse, who writes them down.

It's going to have to come out, he says finally.

◆

IN THE CAR my tears come in torrents. At home I throw myself into a corner of the bed, my coat still on, sobbing.

Everything I've done in the last few years, all the work I've done to find peace and stability and hope, is crashing to pieces around me. I'm shocked by how easily I am being demolished by this. I squeeze my eyes shut, rocking back and forth, calling, pleading in my head for my parents to come and get me.

Mom, Mom, Mom.

In the ultrasound room the doctor explained that these types of ovarian cysts are incredibly common but because mine is so large it will have to be surgically removed. The chances that it will rupture otherwise, an event that would probably cause me to lose the baby, are high.

The surgery will take place three weeks from now, when I am eighteen weeks pregnant. The doctor wants to wait until the baby is a little bigger and stronger, thus upping the chances of it surviving the procedure.

He explained that they would sedate me, possibly using general anesthesia, and then open up my abdomen with a deep incision in order to remove the cyst. I listened numbly as he went on to warn me that there would be a chance my ovary would have to be removed along with it.

If all goes well, I will be in the hospital for a few days and at home on bed rest after that.

It sounded so simple. The doctor even patted my leg reassuringly. Greg nodded at me hopefully.

But I had left the room already.

I fled through the blackness on the screen, and I ran and ran and ran until I was fourteen again. I ran all the way back to the time I learned that both my parents had cancer.

◆

I WAKE UP on the morning of the surgery surprisingly calm and rested. Sometimes I am most at home in the face of utter disaster.

Greg's mom has come from Ohio to be with us, and we all drive to the hospital that morning together. Greg kisses me sweetly, and I hand him my wedding ring to hold. It's the first time I've taken it off since the day he put it on.

And then I'm alone, in a hospital bed, being wheeled down an empty hallway. The sun cuts wide, warm swaths across the linoleum floor and I stare out the window at the snow and the parked cars. I am suddenly thinking about my mother and all the times she was in this exact place: in a gurney, in a gown, on her own.

Mom, I whisper, I'm so sorry.

Suddenly the orderly jerks me backward, swiveling and then pushing me forward into the operating room. It's lit up like a football stadium, and everywhere there are little tables covered with neatly arranged rows of gleaming, surgical tools.

It's like a nightmare.

I want to hop off the gurney, push my way past everyone, scattering scalpels and suctions everywhere, and just run away. But instead I do as the nurses tell me and sit on the edge of the surgical table so that the anesthesiologist can insert a giant needle into my spine.

Before I was even pregnant, I knew that I wanted to have a natural birth, to be as present to the experience as possible. But here I am, having an epidural before it's even time to give birth.

I am eased back onto the table at the same moment that the drugs flood into my lower half, turning my legs and hips to cement.

A nurse straps my arms down and out to my sides.

Another nurse fits an oxygen mask over my nose and mouth.

Someone fits a strap across my chest.

Someone else raises a curtain, separating my body into two parts.

Tears slip out of my eyes and fall to the table beneath my head.

Mom, Mom, Mom. Where are you?

◆

ON MY FIRST DATE with Greg I told him that I wasn't sure if I ever wanted to have children. Having corresponded for a long time before we actually met, I knew a lot about him, and one thing was certain: Greg wanted to be a father.

We were walking across a bridge in Millennium Park when I told him. It was late May and summer had officially descended upon Chicago. We were holding hands, and I felt like everyone we passed could tell that we were right in the middle of falling in love.

I'm not sure if I want to have kids, I said.

I can't remember what we'd been talking about before I said it. Maybe nothing. But there had been a shift, the kind where you suddenly know that there is an entire path opening up before you with this person, and I just had to tell him before we took another step down it.

He looked at me and smiled. Squeezed my hand.

I think he knew then that I would change my mind. In the beginning it seemed like he knew everything.

I'm scared, I would say sometimes about how fast we were moving.

You'll be fine, he always said back.

And I was.

He said it this morning too, just before we parted ways.

You'll be fine.

I think about this as the doctor begins her incision. The lower half of my body feels like dead weight, like something that isn't mine, but as she continues I begin to feel a fierce pushing and tugging. It's as though my abdomen is a suitcase and someone is angrily unpacking it.

I try to take deep breaths and I stare up at the ceiling. I want to wrap my arms around me, but they are strapped down. My vision goes in and out, blurring darkly at the edges. When I tell the anesthesiologist this, he spins a dial.

You need more fluids, he says.

The room comes back into focus.

I go in and out like this, and the surgery takes longer than I imagined it would. I'm having trouble concentrating on any one thing but I try to keep coming back to my breath.

Claire? Claire?

I can hear someone calling my name from far away. I finally realize that it is the doctor.

Yeah? My voice is garbled and slow.

We're calling in an oncology surgeon to help remove the cyst. It's a little larger than we expected.

More shoving and tugging.

It goes on forever.

I'm in a daze. Breathing. Breathing.

Breathing.

Claire?

The doctor's voice again. They are finished.

We're just sewing you up, she calls over the divider.

A nurse comes around and holds up a pink kidney dish for me to see. Resting inside is my cyst. It is the size of a grapefruit, smooth and pink.

Is the baby okay? My voice doesn't sound like mine. It sounds like my mother's did the first time I came to see her in the hospital: rough and disoriented.

The baby is just fine. Can't you hear the heartbeat over the monitor?

I listen, tuning out the other sounds in the room.

Flump, flump, flump.

THE RECOVERY IS much more painful than I anticipated. I was so focused on the procedure that I hadn't imagined what it would be like if I actually got through it.

I spend five days in the hospital while a winter storm rages outside the windows, whiting out the city. My stomach is too bloated to feel the baby kicking, but a kind nurse obliges me by letting me listen to the heartbeat once a day.

I drink in the sound. *Flump, flump, flump.*

Because I am pregnant I can't take anything stronger than Tylenol and I spend those first few days curled on my side, trying not to move so that I can't feel the pain of the incision.

Late at night, after Greg has gone home and I am alone in my hospital room, the fluorescent bathroom light casting a beam across the floor, I think about my mother. I imagine all the nights she spent, just like this one.

In the last year of her life I was convinced that she wasn't trying hard enough. I thought that some part of her enjoyed being sick. That somehow being a cancer patient was easier than being herself.

Lying here in my hospital bed on this snowy January night, the pain in my abdomen like hot knives, I weep for my ignorance, and for the girl who so flippantly judged her mother.

A year or so before she died I walked into the living room one night to find her writing in a notebook. When I asked her what she was doing, she admitted that she was writing a journal for me.

We never spoke of it again, but one night, a few weeks after she died, I turned the house inside out searching for it. My father watched helplessly from the couch as I dug through drawers and tore through closets. I was about to give up when my fingers closed around something at the bottom of my mother's knitting basket.

A simple spiral-bound notebook with a flimsy yellow cover. There were exactly seventeen pages filled with my mother's looping script.

I took it downstairs and read it on my bed, barely breathing until I got to the last page.

December 19, 1995

I got unplugged from chemo yesterday! A whole week without a leash. It was beginning to slow me down, me who doesn't know the term! It's okay though, given me some time to figure out some things in my head, which I don't often do. Maybe my life would have been different if I had. I always either reacted to things or just rushed in on impulse.

Have a plan, Claire, have goals, and I don't just mean material but spiritual as well. Get to know yourself deep, deep down, where no one knows you. Listen to that well, because that's who you are.

I think it took cancer, me saying I want some attention, the real me, not the one I've presented to the world, to make this happen. My body and mind are one and they were in trouble. Now that I'm dropping baggage all over, it will be interesting to see who emerges. I have to be quiet now and listen. Don't ever have to get a cancer of some sort as a wake up call, honey. Be as true to your inner self as you can. Listen to your real voice inside, because if you deny it, you will have to answer to it some day. I'm beginning to think that's the basis of most illness now—the denial of that voice within.

She ends the entire journal with this paragraph:

I'd say I was probably two or three when I knew it was sink-or-swim time. I was alone and desperate. I couldn't give in to my feelings because there was no one there to hold me and hear me and say it's okay. So I killed my feelings and got cancer. I remember blurting out to Dr. Benigno when he hypothetically asked, I wonder why this nice lady got cancer: I wanted attention.

❖

I TURN THIRTY-ONE at the end of May, just a couple of weeks before my due date. I'm enormous, only further fueling the speculation that I'm having a boy.

June 6 comes and goes. Greg and I go on long walks through the neighborhood. Summer has yet to bestow itself upon the city, and I wear long-sleeved shirts and shiver beneath the duvet at night.

Labor starts just before I go to bed, four days later. The contractions are strong and regular and I sit on the couch, rocking back and forth. In some way they feel good. There is something deep and strangely familiar about them.

Greg will later say that our drive to the hospital was like a scene in a movie. I sit in the backseat with our doula while Greg navigates the stop-and-go Chicago traffic. I am eight centimeters dilated by the time I am checked out in triage, but everything looks good and we are given the green light to use one of the suites in the natural birthing center.

I ride the contractions like waves for what seems like an endless span of time but is really only a few hours. I am amazed by the intelligent design of them, the peak, the drop-off, how still and peaceful I feel in between them. I never once consider having an epidural.

If this is to be part of my narrative, I want to feel every minute of it.

◆

Finally, just before midnight on June 10 the time comes to push.

It is the hardest thing I have ever done. During one of the early thrusts I feel the bones in my hips widen.

I am tearing in half.

I am ripping open.

I am bearing a child.

Greg is on my left. The doula on my right. The midwife poised before me on the queen-size bed, everyone waiting, everyone urging. And then in one final push it happens.

I become a mother.

Greg is there, his hands lifting our baby to me.

It's a girl, he cries. And then she cries too.

Part Four

◆

Depression

Invite your depression to pull up a chair with you in front of the fire, and sit with it, without looking for a way to escape . . . When you allow yourself to experience depression, it will leave as soon as it has served its purpose in your loss.

—Elisabeth Kübler-Ross

Chapter Ten

1997, I'M EIGHTEEN YEARS OLD.

I AM SITTING IN a dingy bar in Atlanta with two of my coworkers, Riley and Nathan. We have just closed up across the street at the café where we wait tables. Riley is a waifish girl who smokes more than she eats, and her roommate, Nathan, is a flamboyantly gay black guy with a ready laugh.

We are all underage, but we hold cocktails in our hands all the same.

Before now I've never really spent much time in bars. In the next year they'll become darkly familiar places to me. I'll know exactly which bartenders will avert their eyes when I order, not caring how old I am. I'll learn exactly what I like to drink and how many drinks I can handle or not handle. I'll learn how to swirl my cocktail just so, how to close out my tab at the end of the night. But right now all of this is new. I order gin and tonic because I've heard of it, and I lean my lithe, young body up against the edge of the bar, muddling the lime in the bottom of my glass with a little red straw.

Riley and Nathan have a funny relationship, bantering back and forth for hours about nothing—bands, movies, common friends. They tell story after story about getting drunk, about the trouble they get into. I nod and pretend like I know about those kinds of things.

The truth is that their world frightens me. I can't share in their stories yet, and I am afraid to talk about the things I do know: my dead mother, how

I've temporarily dropped out of college, or my elderly father who is at home by himself in front of the television.

I glance around the bar to see what the rest of my coworkers are doing. Although I've only worked across the street for a couple of weeks, coming to this bar has already become a nightly occurrence.

Another coworker, Lila, is over by the piano, flirting shamelessly with the balding piano player. She leans on one foot, laughing at whatever he's saying. In another corner, beyond her, I see my manager, a guy not much older than any of us, drinking whiskey with another waiter. One of them spills his drink across the table, laughs.

I keep scanning the room though. Looking for Colin.

Finally I find him sitting by himself on the other side of the bar. Both of his hands are wrapped around his drink and he's staring into space. I watch him for a moment and then push up from my seat. My body is humming from the gin and I glide across the room.

I ease myself onto an empty barstool next to him. He looks at me for a moment, then back at his drink.

We have something in common, I say. My voice feels like honey. The gin has made everything easy.

Oh yeah? Colin doesn't look at me, just takes a sip of his drink and waits for me to continue.

◆

EARLIER TONIGHT A COUPLE of my high school friends had come up to the café. They recognized Colin from his picture in the paper and told me about his sister's murder. I had been captivated by the story, watching Colin as they talked, and feeling as though I was looking at someone who lives in the same solitary world I inhabit.

So what is it that we have in common? Colin finally asks.

I look down at my drink. Little bubbles from the tonic fizz upward in streams.

My mother died in January, I say.

Colin doesn't reply.

I heard about your sister, I say then.

He looks up at me, holding my gaze until I blush, look away.

Just then the bartender appears. What are you drinking? Colin asks me.

Gin and tonic.

He orders one and a vodka for himself.

When the bartender is gone and we're both sipping our drinks again, Colin looks back at me.

I like your teeth, he says.

I twist nervously in my seat, suddenly aware of how little space there is between us.

Um, thanks, I say.

He asks about my mom after that, and I tell him bits and pieces. I'm afraid to bring up his sister again. We sip our drinks and stare straight ahead as we talk.

Colin grew up in Texas but moved to Atlanta with his family a few years ago. He's three years older than me, which means he's actually legal drinking age. He was attending a local college and living at home with his parents but has dropped out of school and been sleeping on a friend's couch for the past six weeks. I take this to mean that he's been sleeping there since his sister died but, again, I'm afraid to ask.

Colin and I don't have any friends in common. I sneak glances at him as he talks. His eyelashes are surprisingly long and his lips are full. He keeps his hands steady around his glass as he speaks, and he takes short, deliberate sips from it. Everything about Colin is deliberate.

The bar is closing and I am drunk. We all are: me, Riley, Nathan, Colin, my manager, and the waiter he's been laughing with. I watch Lila stumble away from the piano. We all fall in against one another, traipsing back across the street to the café parking lot.

I stand next to my car, waving stupidly at everyone as they climb behind the wheels of their vehicles. Colin is getting into an old Porsche, and Lila drives a station wagon, probably her mom's. I turn to open the door of my old Saab, my hands clumsy on the handle. I sink down into the seat, turn the key in the ignition. I've never driven this drunk before. I watch everyone pull away, their taillights fading into the bend in the road. Finally I put my car in gear and ease my foot onto the gas pedal.

It is four in the morning and Atlanta's streets are empty. It is only a ten-minute drive home and I take the turns easily. The traffic lights sway in the cobalt sky, all of them a steady green. I turn up the volume on the stereo, light a cigarette, and crack open the sunroof.

Driving feels powerful and calming. I think about Colin's eyes, about the way his hands gripped his glass.

At home I pull quickly up the driveway, parking beneath a fat clump of wisteria scenting the night air. Inside I walk mutely past my mother's desk. She's been gone for four months, but my father and I still haven't touched her things.

I glance at the purse still on her desk and I imagine the smell of its interior, one of waxy lipstick and cottony tissues. Mail still arrives for her, and we even get the occasional phone call from someone who doesn't know she is gone. A few weeks after she died I found a jewelry box in the bathroom. It was full of her hair that had fallen out during chemo.

In my room I fall across the bed, not bothering to undress. The room is spinning and it takes all my energy to sit up again, to click off the light.

I can't fall asleep so I lie there staring up at the ceiling. A smattering of old glow-in-the-dark stickers that I glued up there in tenth grade remains, and for a long time I just watch them come in and out of focus.

I think about how sometimes when my mother had too much to drink she'd want to come down here with me.

Let's look at the stars and talk, she'd say, her voice pleasantly slurred.

What do you want to talk about?

Oh, whatever. You. Boys. School.

I was slow to open up to her though.

Trust me, honey, she would say.

I would tell her little things. About my classes or my boyfriend. We talked about what it will be like when I go off to college. I told her that I was nervous.

Oh, honey, she said once, leaning up on one elbow. You're going to be fine. You're so much more together than I ever was. You're so smart. So self-aware.

I wanted to believe her. I wanted to trust her.

Smart and self-aware are the last things I feel right now.

This isn't what she would have wanted for me. The drinking and the café, the unmade bed and the thick heavy depression that has settled over both my father and me. She wouldn't have stood for any of it. Tears run down the sides of my face but I am too drunk to wipe them away.

By the time dawn seeps through the shutters I am unconscious.

◆

I WAKE PAST NOON, push back the covers, and make my way upstairs. My father has left the coffee pot on for me and he is sitting at the dining room table, bills and paperwork spread out around him.

Rough night?

I nod. Yeah, a little.

We are still figuring out how to be with each other. For eighteen years my mother was the epicenter of our family, my father and I orbiting her like distant planets, never quite lining up enough to actually be in each other's view.

Now that she is gone there is a gaping chasm between us. It's not just that he is seventy-five and I am eighteen. It's more that we have no experience of being me and him. Every move we make is new territory; we are still drawing the map of us.

Years from now, after he is gone, I'll watch an old home movie that takes place on Christmas morning when I am only four years old. In the movie

I throw myself frantically at my mother's feet as she ignores me, marveling over a gift she is opening. My father scoops me up, smoothing the hair back from my forehead and distracting me by singing to me in his funny, warbling voice.

I'll weep for how well he knew me, even though I thought the opposite for many years.

Most nights I linger on the couch with him after dinner, watching the news or flipping through movie channels. He drinks scotch from a tumbler, and I pour myself glasses of wine from a bottle in the fridge. We smoke cigarettes until there is a filmy haze hanging over our heads, until we are too sleepy or too bored to light another one.

I've been avoiding my high school friends, uncomfortable in their presence. Since my mother's death I have felt as though we were on separate planes of existence. No matter how hard my friends try to engage me I am no longer the girl they once knew. All the more reason why I find myself drawn to Colin.

On the nights I stay home my dad tells me about my mother, about when they first met. He also talks about World War II—long, drawn-out stories that make my attention wander. I fade in and out to the subject of fighter planes and prison camps.

My mother never had any patience for his stories about the war. Because of this I've always assumed his stories were boring, but the more I listen, the more I realize they are not.

They are, in fact, incredible. As is the way he tells them.

My father leans back in his chair, a glass in his hand, and really settles in for it, unwinding each tale as though it is a cord of rope. He begins with the day and the year, the weather, his age. He fills in as many details as possible until the image of him at age twenty-four, standing in a base camp in Italy before a giant, gleaming B-24 Liberator, is swimming in the room before us, like some great conjured-up hologram.

It must be like writing, I think. The way he tells these stories, the way he seems to unearth them from his being. I feel the same when I write out a new poem or begin the first gray sentences of a story.

Some nights I can't sleep, and after lying awake on the mattress in my room, listening to the ticks of the darkness around me, I go upstairs to my father's room and push the door open softly. He is asleep on his back, the covers pulled up neatly across his chest. He sleeps in the guest room now.

Dad, I say into the darkness. He is snoring softly.

Dad?

Huh? He wakes with a start.

Dad, it's me.

What's wrong, honey?

I can't sleep, Dad.

He pats the bed beside him. Come sit down.

I'm crying before I even cross the threshold. I sink down next to him, and he pushes himself back, props himself up, until he's sitting. He rubs my back as I cry.

It's okay, sweetie, he says. And we sit like that for a long time. Until the darkness has become an old, familiar thing again.

After a while, when I can speak, I say the things I've been most afraid to say. Here in my father's room at two in the morning, it feels like he is the only person who will ever hear them.

I wish I could have been a better daughter.

My dad shakes his head, starts to speak, but I cut him off.

I wish I could have been more loving. I wish I had told her how much I loved her.

The words take flight, like tiny birds escaping from the room.

My dad shakes his head again.

Do you remember when she came up to Marlboro for parents' weekend?

I nod feebly at him.

She came back and she was so damned happy and proud of you and what you're doing. I'll never forget her coming off that plane and saying, "Gerry, I got in that car, left the college, started driving through Massachusetts, and it was a beautiful fall day and the leaves were turning colors. It was a sunny Sunday afternoon. There was a Russian opera on the radio, one of my favorites." She said, "I was so happy with Claire being in that school and having friends like that. I was conducting the orchestra with one hand and driving with the other."

It was a very important day for her. And it meant a lot to her, and it meant a lot to me, because I knew it was just going to be rougher than hell following that.

I listen as he talks, but I'm crying again.

I didn't know, I say. I didn't really think she was going to die. I would have been a better daughter.

The words burble forth.

My father sighs. She didn't want me to tell.

I would've been more loving. I didn't understand.

I know. But she didn't want you to have that burden. She wanted you to leave the nest and go to college.

But I didn't anyway.

Didn't what?

I didn't leave. I came home after she died.

I know, but she didn't want you to go off to college worrying about her or not go to college at all because of her, and I think maybe she also knew that she was going to be a mess, and she didn't want you to feel that you were any part of it, responsible for it in any way. You had nothing to do with that. You didn't do anything—

I wasn't even there when she died.

I know you weren't, but you know what? She was so damned proud of you. It meant so much to her and her life to have had you. I mean you were the biggest thing that ever happened to her.

Just think if she'd never had you, if we hadn't met and married, if she'd never had a child and had this cancer and died . . . She'd have had no one. Instead she had loving you and all the years I gave her, which were a hell of a lot better than had she stayed there, in New York, dating all those guys and living in that damned apartment building by herself. And she would've done that.

You're better off to have the eighteen years so far and what you've got to go, you know? Love what you've got. Love what you've had. Think back and enjoy the past as you go ahead today, tomorrow. That's what the world is here for, why we're all here.

He presses a little blue pill into my hand after that. Here, take this, he says.

I don't know what it is. Xanax maybe. I swallow it with water from the glass on his nightstand and go back downstairs to my room, to sleep.

◆

MY RELATIONSHIP WITH ALCOHOL deepens by the day. That cool, clear fluid in my veins loosens and numbs me. It opens me up, let's me feel what I spend most days pushing away.

I move from gin to vodka. From tonic to club soda. Tonic masks the taste of the alcohol too much; soda makes it just tolerable enough to swallow. I'm one of the regulars now in the group that heads across the street each night after we close.

Lila and Riley and Nathan. Another couple of waiters, the manager. And Colin, always Colin. Colin with his dark eyes and steady hands. Colin who killed his sister. Colin who drives me back to my car one night after we've all ventured out to another bar, farther away. I am supposed to meet some friends, they are waiting for me back in my neighborhood, but Colin and I sit in his car, the engine off, talking.

The windows are down to let in the night air, and crickets chirp as a breeze rustles the trees. Colin leans over and kisses me. It's something we've both been waiting for. For weeks, ever since that night I first approached him, we've circled each other. In the café, at the bar, a careful dance, each of us afraid to get too close too fast.

His kiss feels like a drink—immediate warmth flowing through my whole body. I can feel myself opening.

We stay there in the car for a long time, leaning into each other quietly. My friends who are waiting for me back at home give up. Later I will find a note on my bedroom window, an empty bottle of whiskey in the grass. Nothing really missed. Not compared to the feel of Colin's lips on mine.

The summer goes on like this. Kissing in darkened cars at the end of drunken nights. There are no real dates, no formal meeting of each other's parents. The rules of this relationship are that there are none, that it isn't a relationship.

The last thing either of us wants is something more to lose.

We keep it a secret from the other kids at the café, avoiding each other for the most part but making sure we're always the last to leave, pushing against each other as we walk through the darkened parking lot.

Some nights I leave with the rest of them, angry at Colin, angry at myself, too drunk to know what I'm really angry about. My mother's death drags behind me, heavy and unidentifiable in the dark.

We sleep together a few times, and it's more than I want it to be. Colin inside of me is too much. It's too real. We push off each other, afraid of what we're starting.

I'm frightened by Colin. Not just by his anger and his intensity, but by the way he seems to know me. He sees straight through everything I've ever tried to cultivate about myself, sees past the girl with the dyed crimson hair and the nose ring, past the authors I've read, the music I listen to, the way I hold my cigarette. All these things I've worked so hard to become are immediately discarded in his eyes. He sees a much simpler version of me, a version I'd long forgotten about.

A month goes by and Colin and I stop seeing each other. I can't figure out what happened, but all of a sudden we're avoiding each other in the café. On the nights that I go out after work he's not there, and on the nights that he goes I find something else to do.

Part of me is glad for this end to things. No good would have come of it, I am sure. I force myself to go on dates with the kind of boys I think I should see. One night I let a tall, sweet customer named Chad take me to dinner. We sit across from each other in a restaurant downtown, and he stammers as he tells me how pretty I am. Later I let him kiss me in the bucket seat of his convertible, his lips dry and quivering against mine. I can't help but think about Colin, about the deliberateness of his kisses.

I start hanging out with some of my high school friends again too, going to their parties, leaning against balconies in depressing apartment complexes as I listen to some boy describe some band he plays in. I exhale my cigarette in long, thin streams and wish I were somewhere else.

One night when I show up to work at the café everyone is jittery with conversation. Riley pulls me aside excitedly.

Did you hear what happened last night?

I didn't.

Colin and Lila got arrested for beating up some cop.

What?

I won't see Colin for another day, and when I do the black eye he has will have deepened into a flushed eggplant, fading down one cheekbone. The skin will look tender and fragile, and I'll want to place my finger there. I'll turn my back instead, cry in the car on my way home.

They'd been drinking at a friend's apartment when some off-duty cop with anger issues got aggressive, asking them to turn down the music. Colin told him to go fuck himself, and the cop pulled a gun on him. Colin went ballistic. Lila, drunk and fierce, jumped on the cop. It's a wonder that none of them were shot. It all ended in handcuffs, black eyes, fuming anger, café gossip.

When I see his black eye, the skin there soft like a bruised fruit, I realize that I miss him.

It's obvious that something is going on with him and Lila though. I feel foolish for thinking it was me who was taking a break this last month. I avoid them both, leave each night as soon as I'm finished counting my tips.

One night Colin grabs my arm before I can walk out the door.

Can we talk?

I have to meet friends, I say.

Just have one drink with me.

I know he's going to tell me that he's moved on, that he's seeing Lila now. I feel like glass, transparent and breakable.

Just one drink, he says. I wait while he finishes counting out his drawer.

We drive in my car to a bar nearby. Once we're settled at a table he looks at me with a mischievous glint in his eye. I am annoyed.

Why did you bring me here?

I wanted to have a drink with you, he says, grinning.

Colin is arrogant. He's overly confident. In years to come we'll argue with each other wildly, debating for long hours absurd subjects like the idea of immortality and the malleability of one's core values. He never budges, never backs down. It's always me who gives in, gives up.

This is stupid, I say. I'm leaving.

No, wait. He touches my hand lightly and in that moment I know.

I sink back into my seat.

I miss you, he says. I made a mistake. I was afraid.

My insides are tightening. His hand on my wrist is like electricity, reaching into me.

After the bar closes we sit in my car in the parking lot. We are smoking cigarettes, listening to the Allman Brothers.

Let's go somewhere, I say.

Sure. Where?

New Orleans?

Okay.

Really?

He shrugs, and I start the engine.

Can I stop at my house first? I need a couple of things.

He shrugs again, and I press my foot against the accelerator.

Colin waits in the car while I tiptoe inside. My father is asleep. Downstairs in my room I throw things into a backpack. Underwear, a couple of shirts. Upstairs I look around the living room. Summer is almost over, and my father and I have begun to pack up the house. We are moving out soon, into a condo.

All week we have been on our hands and knees, sorting through the bookshelves, the trunks and closets. We are having an estate sale, and a woman comes each morning to help us. She has little stickers for everything. A pile of my mother's purses sits in one corner, her collection of Yves Saint Laurent dresses, her stacks of archived *Gourmet* magazines.

It's no coincidence that I want to run away.

In the kitchen I grab a bottle of red wine from the counter and a bottle of those little blue pills my father gives me when I can't sleep. I hurry. I am afraid that Colin will change his mind.

Or that I will.

He is still in the car when I return, leaning back against the headrest, his eyes closed. We drive all through the rest of the night, taking turns at the wheel. It is dawn when we reach New Orleans, that rare time in the city when the streets are empty. Dew glistens on the French balconies, strings of beads lie in the gutters.

Colin drives us to a hotel in the French Quarter, and I wait, bleary-eyed, as he parks the car, checks us in. Our room has a balcony overlooking Bourbon Street. I grab the bottle of wine from my backpack, open the doors to the morning air. Colin takes the two tumblers from beside the coffee maker and joins me at the wrought-iron table outside. He opens the bottle carefully, pours two glasses.

Light is breaking across the rooftops, and for the rest of my life I will never forget the way that glass of red wine tasted. I take gentle sips, breathing in the warm glow of the sun glancing off the buildings around us. I am afraid to look at Colin. I cannot believe what we have done.

It's not that we've run away to New Orleans in the middle of the night. It's that we've fallen in love.

Chapter Eleven

1999, I'M TWENTY-ONE YEARS OLD.

I AM SITTING IN the mayor's office in the small town of Troubky, in the Czech Republic. My father is on my left, and Michael, our translator and guide, sits to my right. Five minutes ago we were shown into the room by a secretary, and now we are waiting anxiously for the mayor to appear.

We arrived in Prague almost a week ago—I flew in from New York and my father from Southern California. This trip came together only a few weeks ago, my father calling me late one night with the idea.

Want to take a little trip with me?

Sure, where?

I half paid attention as I listened to him. I had just gotten home from my bartending job and was distractedly taking off my coat, unwinding my scarf and emptying the contents of the school bag that I'd been carrying around all day.

The Czech Republic.

I stopped what I was doing, allowing myself to fully tune in to what my dad was saying.

The Czech Republic?

Sure. Why not?

Why not was mostly because my father would turn eighty in a few months and his health has been deteriorating by the day. This would, in fact, be his last trip anywhere, something I think we both already knew.

I didn't have to ask why he wanted to go. For the last few years, ever since the availability of the Internet, my father has been obsessively researching his World War II past. He has uncovered information about his missing crew members and even been in communication with European war historians, trading back and forth obscure puzzle pieces making up the air wars that took place in December 1944.

One such historian, a man named Michael, in Prague, has been a major player in my father's quest to unearth just such information. They have been exchanging e-mail for months.

Michael thinks I should visit, my dad said. He's come up with some eyewitnesses and other people for me to meet with.

It sounds like an adventure, I said.

I've usually listened to my father's reports of his World War II findings with halfhearted interest. It's not that I don't care—it's more that I've never really been able to really connect with World War II.

Even the name World War II immediately dredges forth an image of dusty history textbooks and painfully boring descriptions of military operations. I've listened to my father's stories for my whole life, and they've always seemed like just that: stories. Compared with my bright, shiny New York City life, something like World War II never even seemed real.

Until now.

Sitting here, in the mayor's office of this small town, all of that has changed. My father's past has been brought to life, and it's more interesting than I could have ever imagined.

◆

MY FATHER WAS twenty years old when Pearl Harbor was attacked. He was a sophomore at Michigan State, studying engineering and going on double dates with his best friend, Bernie. When the reports of what happened in

Pearl Harbor blasted out through the speakers of the radio, my father dropped everything and enlisted in the war that very afternoon.

My father wasn't necessarily handsome, but he was deeply intelligent, with an inherent sense of mischief—both attractive qualities. He was brave too, even though he had no reason to be. I think it was those very traits that got him assigned to the Army Air Corps. He immediately began training to fly B-24 Liberators, huge, gleaming bomber planes. Although he'd never even been on an airplane, he instantly loved everything about flying.

By December 1944 he'd been stationed in Italy for several months carrying out one bombing mission after another. The name of my father's plane was *Arsenic and Lace*, and a scantily clad woman graced its nose. Like most B-24s, it was flown by a crew of ten men: Arthur Carlson, Vrooman Francisco, Milton Klarsfeld, Edwin Howard, David Brewer, Abraham Abramson, Clifton Stewart, Morris Goldman, John Modrovsky, and my father, Gerald Smith.

By that winter they were finally getting good at their jobs, these guys. Former kids from bland Midwestern towns, they had grown up a lot in the last months; they walked with a new sense of pride. They were flying airplanes, dropping bombs. They were saving the world.

On December 17, 1944, they were scheduled to conduct their biggest mission yet—the entire 765th Bomb Squadron, a flock of about thirty airplanes, was sent out from its base camp in Italy, to put an end to the Odertal oil refinery in Germany, in hopes of wiping out Hitler's most productive remaining fuel sources.

They weren't the only ones on a big mission that day. The Luftwaffe fighter command sent out a fierce squadron to stop them. Only one side would win that day, and it wouldn't be the Americans.

My father's squadron never even reached the refinery. In fact December 17 would go down as the day of one of the deadliest air battles in all World War II, with only one B-24 Liberator out of the whole group managing to survive the intense Luftwaffe attack and return to base.

The rest of the planes, my father's included, were shot to pieces in the air over the Czech countryside.

My father was forced to bail out of his bullet-ridden airplane when half of his crew was killed instantly. He stepped over the bodies of Art Carlson and Morris Goldman, and made a quick decision that the only way he was going to survive was if he jumped out through the burning doors of the bomb bay. My father dislocated his shoulder and hit his head during that jump, knocking himself unconscious. When he came to, he was falling through the sky. He pulled the rip cord on his parachute immediately and floated slowly to the snowy ground below.

He landed in a field outside the Czech town of Olomouc and was taken to an inn by a group of townspeople. Only hours later a group of German soldiers barreled through the town, whisking my father and all the other fallen airmen off to a prison camp on the icy lip of the Baltic Sea.

My father would remain in that prison camp for the next six months. He would discover four of his crewmen in its barracks. He would subsist on bread made of sawdust and, at one point, an old, dead horse that the German soldiers dragged into the prison yard.

In early May 1945, six months after my father was shot down, Hitler committed suicide and the war ended. The German soldiers fled as soon as they heard, and my father, along with several other men, riffled through the prison offices. He found his prisoner file and took it home as a souvenir. In the mug shot that is included with the file my father looks impossibly young, his mouth a hard, angry line.

My father returned to Michigan, to a wife he barely knew and a son who had been born while he was imprisoned. He would go on to live a long life, traveling the world, becoming a successful engineer, and marrying several times over. But for five decades he would carry with him many questions that would go unanswered until our trip to the Czech Republic.

Finding the answers to these kinds of questions is a feat that few veterans have ever been afforded, but my father had always been lucky.

◆

THE FIRST NIGHT in Prague we meet Michael in a loud bar downtown, and we spend the evening at a back table, huddled over maps and fresh pints of beer. My father acts boyish and excited, but I feel protective of him and a gnawing concern churns in my abdomen.

Michael is in his thirties. He is smart but nerdy, and when he met us at the airport he was wearing a leather bomber jacket covered in old air force patches, much to my father's delight. Michael is thrilled that we are here and he has brought along a historian friend of his who works at the newspaper. Michael pulls a sheaf of research papers from his bag, rattling in his warbling Czech accent about all the places he wants to go in the next two weeks, and the people he wants to talk to.

Michael does not realize my father's limitations. Rather, he sees a walking hero, a veritable history book come to life, and he can't wait to set out with him.

Michael does not see what I do: my incredibly fragile, overly exerted, only remaining parent.

I don't know how we are going to make it through these next two weeks. I haven't seen my father in four months, and he looks worse than ever. He has lost weight and takes long minutes to pause after simple things like getting out of a taxi or walking across the floor of a restaurant.

I keep quiet though. As feeble as he has become, I have also never seen him so excited. He runs his finger over a map of the Czech countryside, and Michael leans in close.

This has to be it, my father says. This has to be where I landed when the plane was shot down.

I take a sip of my beer and it dimly begins to dawn on me just what a big deal all of this is.

I've been doing some calculations, my father says, and he begins to break them down. I am in awe, reminded of just how smart he is. I am also reminded of all the times my dad ever tried to help me with math, and how much I hated it.

My father continues, moving his hand over the map.

Allowing for a descent rate of thirteen feet per second from an altitude of twenty-six thousand feet, the time of descent would be about two thousand seconds, or a little more than thirty minutes.

My father is talking quickly, Michael nodding along.

The stated wind at twenty-six thousand feet was fifty-two nautical miles per hour from 260 degrees, slightly south of due west. The wind at ground level, as I recall, was negligible. Using an average wind velocity of twenty-six statute miles per hour, I would have drifted to the east and a bit north in my chute for approximately thirteen statute miles.

Our formation had been on a northwesterly heading from a point about twenty miles east of Bratislava, en route to the next turning point near Uničov. That flight path passed about ten miles west of Olomouc. If I bailed out after passing Olomouc but before reaching Uničov, then my parachute landing should be north of Olomouc near Šternberk and Road No. 46.

Well, that's where we'll go, Michael says.

◆

After a morning spent sightseeing in Prague, we rent a little Fiat and set out for Olomouc.

The Czech countryside is peaceful, with verdant fields and old farmhouses. I tune out the conversation in the front seat, between my father and Michael; lean my head against the back window; and let my gaze wash over the unfamiliar landscape.

I think about my life back in New York. From this distance, it's so much easier to see it for what it is.

I've been in Manhattan for a year, living with Colin in the East Village, working at Republic, and going to the New School. Even with all of these things in place, it still feels like something is missing.

I am twenty years old, but I feel ancient.

Every day, on my way to school, I walk through a little park between a pair of apartment buildings on First Avenue. Several old women gather daily on the same benches, speaking in some undecipherable European language, their words clipped and polished like stones hitting water.

Every time I see them I make a silent wish to trade places with one of them. I want to skip past all the years of sadness I have ahead of me. I want to be at the end of it all, looking back. I wish I were done already.

I can't stop missing my mother. I can't stop worrying about how much time I have left with my father. Most of all I can't stop thinking that my life has been interrupted, that this is not the way it's supposed to be.

The only things that ever give a lift to my days are my writing class and the books I disappear into. The rest of my time is spent trudging from class to work to home again. Crying because I can't find a cab. Crying because I am drunk. Crying because I miss my mother. Crying because I feel trapped in my relationship with Colin.

My dad calls almost every night from California. He is lonely too. And sad. But here, on this trip, I realize how important this adventure is to him, how much meaning it gives his life.

Michael suddenly pulls over to the side of the road to consult the map, and I am shaken out of my reverie. We are almost to the city of Olomouc and they are buzzing with energy. Michael's friend has written a story in the newspaper about my father's visit and has put out a call for eyewitnesses from that time. Several have come forth, and we are on our way to meet them.

An hour later I am standing on a grassy hill overlooking a vast green field. In the distance is an old cemetery where the remnants of my father's plane crashed to the ground. We are looking at the answer to one of his long-held questions. My father scans the landscape, tears in his eyes, remembering that day fifty-five years ago.

Michael stands with an elderly man and woman, and I walk over to join them, wanting to give my father space to take this experience in. I smile at the woman. She is tiny but wearing so much clothing that it is difficult to tell her weight. She smiles up at me in return, and I try to imagine the ten-year-old girl she was five decades ago.

She was standing right here when she saw the pieces of the plane come down, Michael translates, pointing to the edge of the field.

She describes what it had been like to be a girl, what it had been like to see these planes fall from the sky. She describes how scared she was, how sad it made her to see all these young men dying. My father listens quietly, and I know that I will never fully understand what this moment is like for him.

The man, a doctor now, had also been about ten years old when he watched my father's plane crash from this hill. If there was any question as to these people having actually witnessed my father's plane crash, the doctor describes finding a heavy flashlight with the name Regan stenciled on the side.

Regan was the ground chief who worked on the plane between missions, my father tells him.

The doctor guides us down the street to a corner lot where, until recently, there had stood a neighborhood pub. He describes how the nose turret of *Arsenic and Lace* had come down right through the roof of the building, half-penetrating the ceiling. He had seen the turret hanging there over the beer taps. The body of David Brewer, one of my father's crewmen, came to rest not far from the bar.

Before we part ways the old woman presses a little gift into my hand: a miniature, hand-painted ceramic vase. It is wrapped in plastic and tied with a crumpled ribbon. I hug her good-bye and watch as she climbs onto a bus that will take her back to her home, over an hour from here.

After she is gone I open my palm to look down at the miniature vase, and something about this small gift becomes the singular thing to crack open the reality of the history book I am standing in.

◆

THAT NIGHT, AFTER DINNER with Michael, my father and I return to our hotel. It's the nicest hotel in Olomouc, but even so it only runs about forty dollars a night. Our rooms are lavish, with large four-poster beds, vanity tables, and luxuriously heavy curtains.

I stand at the window for a beat, watching cars circle a roundabout in the town center. I know I won't be able to fall asleep anytime soon, so I leave the room and walk carefully down the hallway and knock gently on my father's door.

Not tired, kiddo?

Not really, I say. You?

Not at all. I'm too damned excited.

I smile at him. I'll be right back.

I make my way down the hallway to a set of vending machines. One of them sells cans of beer and I feed a few heavy Czech coins into it.

Back in my Dad's room I pop the lids on the cans, and we each take a seat at a little table near the window. We light cigarettes at the same time, and my father leans back in his chair, a look of satisfaction on his face.

I'm glad you're here, monkey.

Me too, Dad.

I don't know if your mom would have had the patience for this sort of thing.

I laugh and shake my head. She would have been shopping in Prague right now, I say.

My father chuckles.

I miss her, I say.

Me too, kiddo.

We banter lightly like this. At some point I go down the hall for more beer. My father empties the ashtray. And after a while, for some reason, we start telling each other secrets.

Did you know that I used to sneak your car out when I was in high school?

The Lincoln?

Yeah. Zoe and I used to take it out after you guys had gone to bed.

Before or after you had your license?

Before.

My dad laughs, shakes his head.

One time I thought I should put gas in it but I'd never gotten gas before and I ended up hosing Zoe down. We had to wash all her clothes when we got home because she reeked of gasoline.

My dad cracks up here, snorting into his glass of beer.

It's his turn.

I went on a date the other week, he says.

I can't hide my surprise.

What? With who?

This older woman I met at Costco. She works on the weekends, handing out those samples at the end of the frozen food aisle.

Dad!

I'm horrified, yet also amused.

Where did you take her?

Oh, just to dinner. Went back to her place afterward.

And?

And we slept together.

Oh my God, I say.

I can't believe he's telling me this. But then I realize that there isn't anyone else for him to tell.

I take a sip of beer. And?

It was terrible, he says.

I start laughing so hard that I can't swallow my beer.

We stay up for hours that night, trading secrets, stories, memories. Later, when I am finally back in my room, finally drifting off to sleep I start back awake with a simple realization.

As much as I miss my mother, I am glad she died first. Otherwise I would have buried my father without ever having known him.

◆

THE NEXT MORNING we set out for Troubky. Michael has heard about a memorial there for a man named Tom West—a friend and fellow pilot in my father's squadron who died the day my father was shot down. We follow the map and park on a quiet tree-lined street in the middle of nowhere.

The memorial is in the center of a high-walled cemetery, and before we have even crossed the threshold we understand why we were told to come here. It's a small cemetery, the gravestones lined up in neat rows. The three of us pause in the entryway, taking it in.

In a few weeks, when he finds himself home again in California, my father will be unable to sleep for days and will stay up each night putting on paper the very things we are seeing right now.

He will write:

Upon entry, Michael asked if I could see the memorial. I looked around and against a distant wall was a very large edifice, the largest in the cemetery. It turned out to be what we had come to see. A huge vertical wall of granite about twelve feet tall and ten feet wide provided the backdrop. The granite itself was a beautiful gray color, polished to perfection.

On the face of the granite was mounted an extraordinary life-sized bronze casting of an airman wearing flight clothes and descending from the sky, the straps of his parachute stretching upward. His feet fall short of touching the ground by about eighteen inches and he gazes upward from whence he came, his left arm extended as if in farewell.

At the very front of the memorial were two identically sized and shaped blocks of matching granite, each with the same message inscribed. I knelt on the left to better read the English version, the other being in Czech. Tears came to my eyes as I read the message:

HERE REPOSE AMERICAN HEROES AFTER THEIR LAST START

WANDERER, READ AND ANNOUNCE TO ALL

WE GLADLY DIED FOR THAT YOU LIVE AND ARE FREE

DON'T FORGET US

Tears again mist my eyes as I type these words. I clearly remember looking up from my kneeling position, after reading the message several times. While viewing this heart-wrenching tribute in its entirety, I experienced a deep emotional experience. I was speechless.

For me, time had disappeared and I was back with these men over half a century ago. The images were, of course, as I had seen them last. I was brought back to the present by the knowledge that it could easily be Tom looking at a memorial of me.

Later we will all remark on the single most emotional moment of it all—the moment when we realized that there were fresh flowers placed on the memorial. A sweet bouquet of daisies, tied with a simple ribbon, had been placed at the foot of the airman. Clearly the war my father fought had not been forgotten.

My father slowly pushes his way to standing and turns to Michael.

I'd like to speak to someone about this, he says. But who?

Let's try the mayor's office, Michael suggests.

◆

WE FIND THE BUILDING in the center of Troubky and, after Michael explains why we are here, the mayor's secretary shows us into his office.

I fold my hands in my lap and take in the room, letting my eyes roam over the faded wallpaper and heavy draperies. After a few minutes the mayor enters. He is in his fifties, neatly dressed in a suit and tie. He shakes my father's hand and Michael's, gives me a little bow.

We all take our seats and Michael begins speaking in Czech, explaining who we are and why we are here. The mayor glances at my father while he listens. He is a serious man and his reaction to our presence is unreadable.

After a while the mayor begins to speak to Michael, who translates intermittently. He is telling us the story of the memorial.

It was actually built in 1945, the mayor explains, just a month after my father's plane was shot down. The townspeople were so saddened by the deaths of so many airmen, in particular the crew of Tom West's plane, which had crashed just outside the village.

Even though they knew the Germans wouldn't approve, and that they could possibly be severely punished for it, they pooled their money together to create the beautiful memorial that we saw today.

My father is taking slow, audible breaths, and I can tell that he is riveted.

Finally it is his turn to speak. He sits up straight in his seat, moving to the edge of it so that he can directly address the mayor.

He is choked up before he begins, but clears his throat and tries again.

On behalf of every American family, he says firmly, I want to thank you.

He continues. I can't tell you how much it means to me, to *us*, that you have honored our fallen men in this way. No one at home has any idea about this, he says. It will mean so much to the families of the men who died here to know . . .

He gets choked up again.

The mayor leans forward then, and Michael translates.

But sir, the mayor says, we are the ones who must thank you. You and your friends and family . . . You fought for us, for our country, for freedom.

The mayor is crying now too, and Michael looks back and forth between the two, working hard to translate.

I lean back in my chair and it is here, right here in this moment, that I finally realize exactly what it was my father did all those years ago in World War II.

◆

A WEEK LATER we are nearing the end of our trip. We have traveled across the countryside, sat in home after home, listened to stories from all kinds of people who were connected to that day in December 1944.

We have drunk cool, clear glasses of slivovitz on more occasions than I care to remember, and my father has fared better than I expected him to, making it in and out of the little Fiat and through each day without collapsing.

The day before we head back to Prague, Michael insists we stop one more time.

We wait outside a dilapidated apartment building for a long time before Michael beckons us to join him.

We make our way into the crumbling building, and then ever farther into a dark and sour-smelling apartment. An old man stands in a dimly lit and cluttered living room. He is clutching two weathered trash bags and he nods gruffly at my father.

This man has something he wants to give you, Michael says, and I watch as my father sits down on a grimy couch next to him.

The man fumbles around inside the trash bags, finally pulling out two wooden boards. He places one on his lap and the other on my father's lap. The boards are each the size of the laptop I will one day type this story out on, and they are painted an old but still-bright yellow.

On each board are glued bits and pieces from fallen B-24 Liberators. The pieces are tiny, none of them bigger than a fist, some of them just bolts or screws, little dials and bits that still turn in their casings. Each one has been carefully placed on the board, and there are words surrounding them.

Some of the words are in Czech, some in English. The phrase "I am alone" catches my eye. "We will never forget," says another.

He collected all of these pieces as a young boy, Michael explains, and has carried these boards with him ever since. My father marvels over the pieces, gently running his fingers across them.

He wants you to have them, Michael says, and my father looks up.

The man is looking expectantly at my father and I realize that he is crying.

No one understands what they mean anymore, Michael translates. The young people don't know what that time was like, what it all meant to us. I've carried these things with me my whole life.

I want you to have them.

He starts coughing then, and we all watch as his frail body collapses in on itself, each cough shuddering across his frame. My father places a hand on his shoulder, waits until he is done. He is crying again now too.

Thank you, my father says. Thank you for remembering us.

The old man nods. How could I ever forget?

THE NEXT DAY my dad and I part ways at the airport in Prague. I am anxious in the minutes before we do. I can't shake the feeling that this will be the last time I will ever see him.

We draw out our good-byes, neither of us really wanting to go home to our lonely life.

Over the next four years my father will write about our experiences in Prague many times. He will contact the families of Tom West and of his fallen crew, and he will do his best to share the information he discovered. He will even participate regularly in a program to visit elementary schools, talking to kids about World War II.

I'll go with him on one of those days, to a clean, modern elementary school in Southern California. My dad wears his bomber jacket and a hat emblazoned with the insignia of the 461st Bomb Group. By this time he carries an oxygen tank with him wherever he goes and the little container sits behind him hissing pleasantly.

The kids are fidgety and distracted as my dad talks, but he doesn't seem to notice. He has brought the yellow boards with him to show them, and they stand up one by one to walk over and touch the old B-24 parts glued to its surface.

I lean against a doorway, the warm California breeze filtering past me, and I watch the kids. I know they just see an old man going on about a war they don't understand, but I see so much more.

I see the man who swept my mother off her feet one warm June morning. The man who rubbed my back on the nights when I couldn't sleep after she was gone. I see a man who learned how to fly an airplane at age twenty, a man who dedicated himself to fighting for something bigger than himself. A man who survived when so many others died.

I see a man who made his life worthwhile.

Chapter Twelve

I GLANCE DOWN at the glass of red wine in front of me. It's one of those squat tumblers and the wine inside is a watery crimson. I see the waitress emerge from her station, heading toward our table, and I quickly knock back the contents in one smooth swallow. I smile up at her as she refills my glass.

I'm at C & O Trattoria on Washington Boulevard, with my friends Holly and Kevin, and a guy I'm seeing named Ryan. C & O is one of those cacophonous family-style Italian restaurants that caters to the tourists who flock to Venice Beach each day. We like it because it's cheap and the garlic knots are addictive.

I particularly like it because as soon as you sit down the waitress delivers a giant bottle of red wine to your table, encouraging you to pour freely throughout dinner. I fill my glass over and over again. By the time dinner arrives I've lost count of how many I've had. Five glasses? Six?

Kevin and Ryan are talking about books, and Holly and I lean conspiratorially into each other on our side of the table. I've known Holly since high school, and we always have more than enough to talk about.

How are you doing, dear? Holly's eyes are wide and probing as she asks this.

I nod at her, taking a sip from my glass of wine. I'm good, I say. This is an utter lie.

I smile brightly, hoping to appear convincing, but Holly knits her brow and leans in closer. I take another sip.

Are you?

I nod again. The fact that I've known Holly for ten years makes it hard to be deceptive.

No, really. I'm good.

I take one more sip of wine and then I continue.

I've been writing a lot. Every morning.

Really? That's great.

Again, this is a lie. A couple of months ago, right after my dad died, a large newspaper featured my blog in a list of the twenty best in the world. Ever since, I've had more readers than I know what to do with. An agent from New York even contacted me about writing a book, but facing the blinking cursor at the top of an empty Word document has been nearly impossible. I've written nothing.

Yeah. I'm working on getting everything settled with my dad's condo too. I slosh back more wine as I say this, and Holly nods at me encouragingly.

Lying suddenly seems kind of fun. It's interesting to hear what I would sound like if I actually had my shit together. The sad truth is that I've been waiting for someone to do exactly what Holly is doing, to step in and intervene before it's too late, but now that it's happening I can't help backpedaling.

A busboy clears our plates and Kevin asks for the bill. The waitress comes and marks off a line on the giant wine bottle, tallying up the total on her little pad.

I'm putting you down for fourteen glasses, she says.

Whoa, Ryan says. I didn't think we had that much.

Me neither, says Kevin.

I only had a couple of glasses, Holly says.

Me too, I mumble, even though I know the waitress is right and that most of the glasses belong to me. I'm just hoping none of them notice how much I'm slurring.

The waitress shrugs at us, dropping the bill in the center of the table.

Whatever, Holly says. I've always thought this whole bottle thing was kind of a scam anyway.

Ryan and I part ways with Kevin and Holly on the sidewalk. After they're gone I look in the direction of the beach. I can't tell if the streetlights look hazy because I've had too much to drink or if it's just from the ocean air.

I turn back to Ryan, and we begin walking along Washington Boulevard. We've only been dating for a couple of months, but after I moved to Venice we started spending most nights of the week together.

Ryan is a writer. He has just finished the first draft of a novel and works as a reality television producer. He's easily the smartest person I've ever met, almost to a fault.

Ryan has memorized every presidential team that ever existed. You can name a date—say 1883—and he will tell you who was serving in the White House, and often even more about that particular year in politics. It's the same with baseball. Strings of statistics and numbers spill out of his mouth like ticker tape at the merest prompting.

Ryan is the opposite of Colin. It wouldn't even occur to Ryan to put bars around me, to create rules about who I am supposed to be. After years of Colin doing just that, being with Ryan feels like freedom in the finest form.

Do you want to come over tonight?

Ryan shakes his head. I have to be at the office early tomorrow.

Okay.

I try to hide my disappointment, but Ryan doesn't seem to notice anyway. He's already talking about something that happened at work today. As I listen I try to keep my steps steady. I am drunker than I realized.

I don't want to go home. I just want to keep walking. I don't want tomorrow to come. Or the day after that. The thought of another perfect, sunny LA day spent not cleaning out my father's condo makes me want to vomit. Nonetheless Ryan walks me to the gate at the bottom of the steps that lead up to my apartment. He kisses me goodnight and walks away into the night, and I am suddenly alone again.

I'm crying before I even walk in the door. I stand in the middle of the dark living room, a tidal wave of fear and anger washing over me.

I don't want to be here.

I don't want to be alone.

I can't do this.

I can't do this.

The only response to my silent pleas is the sound of blood rushing in my ears.

I suck in deep, ragged breaths and look wildly around the room. I'm not sure what I'm looking for until I see the dark space underneath my desk.

I drop to my hands and knees and crawl there, tucking my head, and hunching my back under the frame. I pull the chair in against me, pinning myself to the wall. I close my eyes finally, breathing.

A few years from now I'll see a movie about Temple Grandin, an autistic woman who used to lock herself into cattle-holding stalls in an effort to feel secure and contained. I don't realize it now, but that's exactly what I'm doing.

Finding some way, however desperate, to hold on to myself.

◆

THE NEXT MORNING I park in the carport of my father's condominium complex and walk up to his front door. I pause for a moment, unable to bring myself to unlock it yet.

A breeze blows around a corner of the building, and I close my eyes for a moment. It's another balmy, Southern California day and the temperature hovers around seventy-four degrees.

My father has been dead for three months.

Finally I push the key into the lock and turn the doorknob, making my way inside. I take two steps into the living room and then I just stand there, breathing in the stale air.

The blinds are pulled on every window, and the living room is dark. Everything is exactly as it was when my father still lived here. The dishes sit quietly in the cupboard, the cable is still connected and my father's dentures sit in their little plastic case on the bathroom counter.

I begin to walk around the condo, turning on lights here and there but leaving the blinds closed. The air is old, the rooms quiet. I lean against the door to my father's room, letting the memories wash over me.

My father's hand in mine that last afternoon. His funny, bushy eyebrows. The creases around his mouth.

The way he was gone so quickly from his body.

After he took his last breath, I untangled my hand from his and let it drop to his lap. I backed away from the bed. All the blood drained quickly from his face and hands, leaving them a marble white color that I'd never seen before. His eyes were half-open, his mouth a wide, gaping place.

The hospice nurse drew her hand across his face like they do in the movies, and then his eyes were closed. I stood still a moment longer, taking in the sight of his dead body. It was the first I'd ever seen.

I turned then and walked outside to the little patio off the living room and lit a cigarette. I picked up the clunky cordless phone, punching in the numbers that would connect me to my half brother Mike.

He's gone, I said, sinking down into one of the plastic patio chairs.

Mike didn't say anything, but I could almost hear him nodding in response.

I went back to my father one more time before the funeral home workers arrived to take his body away. The room was unnaturally quiet without the hiss of the oxygen he'd used for the last several years. I stood over the bed and took in the sight of his body. I touched my fingertips to his eyebrows and then held each of his hands in mine. They were already growing cold.

My father was gone. His body, the familiar house of his self, his limbs that I'd clambered in and out of as a kid—they were just dead, heavy things.

I turn away from these memories and walk down the hall and into the kitchen. I open the refrigerator, surveying the contents: half-full bottles of mayonnaise and salad dressing, a slim jar of cocktail onions that my dad always put in his martinis, a dented box of baking soda, some congealed ketchup. I had told myself that I would clean out the fridge today.

I close the door instead and go into the living room, where I lie down on the couch and cry until I fall asleep.

When I wake up, an hour later, I push myself up and walk outside into the bright afternoon; then I drive the thirty miles north back to my apartment in Venice Beach.

◆

A FEW WEEKS after my father died I rented this little apartment. It was an immediate relief not to sleep alone in his condo anymore and for the first time in my entire life I began to make a home for just me.

Venice Beach is an eclectic beach community, completely different from the rest of Los Angeles. My apartment is two blocks from the ocean, nestled into a series of canals built in the 1920s to replicate the real ones in Italy.

At night ducks quack softly from their perches on the banks and fish slumber under little white bridges that crisscross the canals. Bougainvillea and honeysuckle drip down onto the sidewalks, and when the mist rolls in from the ocean the whole place takes on a dreamlike quality.

My apartment is a one bedroom above a set of garages, and from my deck I have a view of one of the bridges. I've never lived alone before, and while I love the freedom of it, I'm also lonely. I go out almost every night, meeting friends for drinks or dinner.

Colin and I broke up only a week before I became parentless. At the time I didn't know that my dad would be gone so soon, but the intensity of the situation helped propel me out of that relationship.

It's the oddest feeling, not to have anyone checking in on me. For the last six years, between my father and Colin, I was either being watched over or doing the watching. Now there is no one to tell me what to do or where to be, what time to get up or how to spend my days.

No one knows exactly how depressed I am, and there is no one who knows that I spend most of my days trying to sleep.

When I get home from another failed morning at my father's condo, I curl into a corner of the couch and try to sleep. I wrap my arms around me and close my eyes to the bright California day. I can hear palm fronds rustling in the breeze and seagulls cawing at one another as they circle overhead.

Sleep does not come.

I open my eyes and glance at the clock again: 2:11.

I look at the wine rack on my kitchen counter and try to determine if it's too early to have a glass.

I close my eyes again.

◆

ONE YEAR AFTER my father's death I fly to Europe. I spend a week in Sicily with a friend of my parents' and his three daughters, who are my age. After that I make my way to more family friends in Rome. While I'm there, I scatter some of my father's ashes.

After a week in Rome I'm headed to Switzerland, where I plan to stay with one last set of family friends before flying home to Los Angeles. Most of these friends are ones my parents made when I was growing up in Atlanta. They tell me stories about those years, about the late-night dinner parties when we were babies and how they all thought that time would last forever.

I'm on a train to Zurich when the accident happens. Or I guess it's not really an accident at all.

I'm sitting in the first train car. I have just put down my book; something I read made me look up and out the window. I am thinking about my life. Just before I left on this trip I had told Ryan that he could move in with me. I felt uneasy about the situation but I couldn't come up with an alternative.

We've been dating for close to a year and have been spending practically every night together. He wants to move forward and so do I, but I can't shake the feeling that I am not ready to live with someone again. I have only just been starting to feel comfortable about living alone for the very first time in my life.

We talked about it over Chinese food one afternoon, and Ryan was firm about what he wanted. I remember opening my fortune cookie hoping that it would give me the answer I sought but finding something frivolous there instead.

Okay, I'd finally agreed, and the timing had worked out so that he would move in while I was traveling. But the uneasy feeling had not abated.

This is what I'm thinking about while staring out the window. This is what I'm thinking about when the train suddenly decelerates. This is what I'm thinking about when the sound hits my ears.

It's a crunching sound, like rocks in a blender.

The train slides to a complete stop.

I sit forward in my seat, looking around the car. Everyone else is leaning forward too. We are in the countryside outside of Milan. There is nothing but trees outside the windows.

The crunching sound replays in my ears. The thought that it might have been a person pops into my head before I quickly dismiss it and scold myself for being morbid.

Suddenly the conductor rushes past. His face a blanched white. More officials rush back and forth.

Then suddenly the news branches out through all the cars, reaching each passenger as though we are playing a grown-up game of telephone.

It was a suicide.

◆

A MAN HAD THROWN HIMSELF in front of the train. The source of the crunching sound was exactly what I had imagined it to be.

We stay where we are for hours. I miss my connection. We are not permitted to disembark. The police arrive and we watch them walking alongside the tracks, their backs bent beneath the late afternoon sun as they scour the tracks for remains.

When we finally inch forward to Milan and are allowed to get off the train, I cannot help following the craned necks of the other passengers as they turn to glance back at the front of the train. Yet I deeply regret seeing the blood that is dried in streams along the nose.

In Milan I hop aboard a train to Zurich that is literally pulling away from the station even as I am stepping into the very last car. I sink down into my seat, tightening my arms around me and watching the station recede in the distance.

After a while I don't want to be alone so I venture into the next car to smoke a cigarette. The car is empty except for a tired-looking train official slumped in a seat and a young man reading a book. I sit opposite the train official and light my cigarette. He looks like I feel, and I watch him for a moment before I speak.

Were you on the last train? I ask. The one with the suicide?

He vaguely nods but does not look in my direction. I feel guilty for engaging him, but I already miss the company of passengers who have shared in that experience.

Suddenly the young man stands up.

What suicide?

I let him walk me back to my seat as I describe the accident.

Patric is uncommonly lovely, with an aristocratic nose, warm brown eyes, and messy blond hair. He is Swiss, on his way home to Zurich. He listens with interest, taking the seat opposite me.

For me, the suicide had been one of those moments that made me sit forward in my seat, startled not just by the incident itself but by the unexpected depth of life—the way one moment can fling your life in any of a hundred different directions.

I cannot help but wonder what it means that I was sitting on that train, on that day. That my connection was delayed, that I only just made this one, and that I am here right now, speeding toward Zurich, sitting across from a man I don't know. Some of the most pivotal points of my life seem to be made up of moments such as these.

It is a long train ride to Zurich, and Patric and I talk for hours. At one point we venture out to the dining car to buy little bottles of wine, packages of chocolate, and more cigarettes. He is recently out of school and has been traveling, trying to figure things out. It's easy for us to tell each other all our secrets. We will never see each other again.

He explains the recent confusion he's had over a girlfriend, and I reveal my uneasy feeling about Ryan. We blow long, thin streams of cigarette smoke up toward the ceiling and are lulled into even deeper subjects by the rocking of the train car.

Hours later Patric gets off in Zurich, but I stay on, having to travel a bit farther to reach the town where my parents' friends live. He stands silently on the platform, one hand raised in good-bye, and I touch my fingers lightly to the glass.

It's a simple thing, meeting a stranger and opening yourself up, but it's not something that happens often. As the train pulls out of the station I think about that night in Vermont with Michel, and then about the night in Spain.

I lean my forehead against the cool glass and I know something about life—about how even in the moments when you don't think you are moving forward, you really are.

◆

WHEN I GET HOME to Los Angeles Ryan has moved in. My dresser is half full of his clothing, his books have been crammed in with mine, and his jackets hang in my closet. I shake my head against the resistance I feel and try to move forward into life.

My father has been gone for over a year, but I still find myself driving down to his condo now and then. I ended up selling it a few months after he died, but I find a weird comfort in just sitting in my car near his old garage. I will in fact do this for years to come.

My half brother Mike had to fly out from Atlanta to help me clean out the condo. I realized one day that I was never going to be able to do it on my own. Together we finished it in a weekend, moving systematically through each room, Mike holding up object after object. "Toss, sell, or store?" he'd ask patiently.

I was incredibly grateful for his help, but I felt guilty all the same. Of his four children, my father had left me, the youngest and least capable, in charge of everything. My half siblings, two brothers and a sister, are all at least thirty years older than me.

Mike, the oldest, lives in Atlanta and works for Delta. He is gruff but kind, and over the next several years we will grow closer than we ever were when my father was alive. In fact years later it will be Mike who walks me down the aisle at my wedding, his face bursting with pride as though I were his own daughter.

Candy is a lawyer and lives in DC with her husband and son, Brian. It was in the driveway of her house that I last saw my mother.

Eric, the youngest, is actually the least capable of all of us, having lived a scattered and tragic life. He will die of a sudden heart attack two years from now, in Candy's basement in DC, surrounded by his beloved blues record collection, and I'm not sure that I will ever figure out how to feel peaceful about his swift passing.

Sitting there, outside the condo, I close my eyes and talk to my father silently in my head.

Dad, I don't know where to go from here.

◆

A COUPLE OF WEEKS later I find my answer.

A few years ago Holly and Kevin went to hear Dave Eggers read from his first book—a memoir called *A Heartbreaking Work of Staggering Genius*—and Holly later mailed the book to me in New York.

I scanned the book before I finished reading Holly's accompanying letter. I could tell from his picture that Eggers was just a couple of years older than me and that the book was about how he had lost both parents in his early twenties. I felt a hopeful twinge and went back to Holly's letter:

I thought you would enjoy this book. While he was signing it, I told him that my friend who he was inscribing this to had had a somewhat similar experience and was writing about it. He said that he thinks it's a bad idea to read a book like the one you're trying to write, but I don't buy that. I think you'll like it. I hope so.

I read it in only a few sittings, fascinated by Eggers's similar story. I'd never met anyone who had lost even one parent.

I often wonder who I would be had my parents not died. I watch my friends, envying the security they feel in their lives. They don't even realize they feel so safe, but I can see it in the way they try out different career paths and relationships. In the ways they move toward each mile marker with a seeming confidence that it will be there when they arrive.

I imagined that Eggers has watched his friends in a similar way.

A few months after Holly sent me his book, Eggers was reading at my college in New York. I went by myself, sitting in a center row in the large auditorium. I was surrounded by young women, all of them whispering about him. I felt a stomach-tightening sense of possession over the author and I bristled each time one of them wondered aloud if he was cute.

When he finally appeared on stage, he was indeed a little cute, but mostly he was funny and irreverent and the packed auditorium responded at the end with a standing ovation. My heart raced throughout the reading, wanting so much to connect with this man who surely understood my plight.

There's something incredibly lonely about grieving. It's like living in a country where no one speaks the same language as you. When you come across someone who does, you feel as though you could talk for hours.

It's been years since that reading at the New School, but when I see that Eggers will be reading at UCLA, I buy tickets and decide to take my friend Abby. I can't help the tingling feeling I have at the thought of seeing him in person again.

It's a good reading. They Might Be Giants play first and then Dave does the usual unexpected stuff involving random guest participation. The crowd is made up of the typical twenty- to thirty-five-year-old hipsters who fanatically follow Eggers's San Francisco–based magazine empire, McSweeney's.

At the end of the reading Dave leans into the microphone and announces that he is starting a Los Angeles branch of his literacy nonprofit 826 Valencia. He rattles off an e-mail address, and I memorize it so hard that I may as well have tattooed it on the inside of my wrist.

Twenty minutes later I'm standing in line to get another book signed, so nervous that I feel woozy. I look around at all the other audience members who have lined up to have their books signed. Girls and boys alike, we all want to marry Dave Eggers.

When it is finally my turn, I fumble with my book.

I'm sorry, I say. I'm nervous.

Don't be nervous, he says kindly. Here, do you want a pen? Some water?

I laugh. In my book he writes:

"Claire . . . and always they gave them light of their own creation. Dave Eggers"

I wait until I'm in the car to cry. Something about seeing someone who absolutely must know how I feel tugs at me relentlessly. I can't shake the feeling that he has answers to my questions. That he has salves for my wounds.

As soon as I get home I send an e-mail to the address, and a few weeks later I find myself walking down Venice Boulevard, carefully balancing a tray of homemade raspberry muffins. I'm on my way to a breakfast meeting for 826LA, and I'm determined to stand out in the sea of obsessive Eggers fans. The muffins will, in fact, earn me a mention the next day in a *Los Angeles Times* article about the impressive turnout.

It's funny to be in a regular house with a person I don't know but have spent so much time focusing on. Dave's wife, the writer Vendela Vida, is also in attendance though, and her presence is an adequate enough reality check. I take a seat on the floor with the other thirty or so people who have shown up.

Dave stands before us and speaks enthusiastically about his plans for 826LA. This is to be the third location, with centers already up and running in both San Francisco and New York. The main part of 826LA will function as a free tutoring center where local kids can drop in for homework help, but there will also be workshops and classes, partnerships with local schools, author readings, and bookmaking projects.

Each of the branches comes with a storefront—the San Francisco location hosts a pirate shop, Boston a bigfoot store, and LA's will feature time travel. It's a unique way to draw people in, Dave explains, in the hopes that they stick around long enough to see what's going on behind the scenes.

I've never heard of anything like it, but I'm in.

In a weird twist of fate, the location for 826LA is just blocks from my Venice apartment. Since I'm still unemployed I begin showing up every day. A handful of other volunteers do the same, and we spend the mornings painting the second floor walls of an old public building, working to make this the future home of a tutoring center.

I chat with the other volunteers and get busy acquainting myself with a paint roller.

Eggers is there that first weekend, and I keep tabs on him out of the corner of my eye. He is friendly with everyone and works hard building bookshelves and making runs to the hardware store. On the second day we end up painting a small office together. The color is a pale, creamy yellow and it's satisfying to lay it on the wall. The more we paint, the brighter the room becomes, until we are bathed in a warm, golden light.

I can't know that a few weeks from now, when I am asked to come on board as volunteer coordinator, this very room will be my office, but nonetheless I love the room for its light, for it being the place where I finally got to say my piece to Dave Eggers.

As we paint we banter, mostly about the space, about plans for the organization. I ask him questions about 826 Valencia, and he answers readily, obviously proud of the work they've done. As I listen to him talk I ponder the actions he's taken. We both lost our parents. We have both experienced incredible loss and sadness in our lives.

But Dave doesn't seem sad. In fact he seems the opposite: energized and passionate. It doesn't sound like he has ever spent all day on a couch feeling sorry for himself.

How did he get past all of it? I wonder to myself.

My parents died too, I say suddenly. We are working on separate walls, and in the brief silence that follows my sentence, I listen to the sticky sound of his paint roller.

That must have been hard for you, he says finally.

I swallow. It was.

I have this dreadful feeling, suddenly, that a million people have told him about their losses. My confession, my big connection, is nothing new. In fact I realize, with a pang of insecurity, that he's probably cringing right now.

I want to fix the moment somehow, take it back maybe, but I can't think of anything else to say.

I want to ask him how he got where he is now, but I'm too intimidated.

Before either of us can say anything else, someone comes into the room and asks Dave to inspect some tables they're putting together.

Excuse me, he says.

And just like that it's over.

◆

DAVE HAS GONE BACK to San Francisco, but I continue to walk down to the 826LA space every day. There's constantly something to help out with, curtains to hang, bookshelves to hammer together. The walls are all painted. A globe hangs in one corner and there are neat cups of freshly sharpened pencils all over the room.

As the launch date approaches, I spend hours there, and am often the last to leave. Walking home each night, staring down at the yellow paint on my sneakers, I have this new feeling fluttering around inside me.

Something like satisfaction.

Maybe something like happiness.

Shortly before the official opening the executive director asks me to come on board as the volunteer coordinator, and I accept in a heartbeat. Even though we've hardly begun, I want nothing more than to be officially part of this organization.

That first Monday a few of us stand nervously at the windows, watching kids pile out of a school bus. We've been working hard to get the word out to parents and schools, and a local teacher has arranged for her high school essay class to drop by for the afternoon. The students glance suspiciously around the room, not sure what to expect, but one of the volunteers jumps in before they can backpedal.

Hey, guys, how about you grab a seat right here?

Slowly the kids fill the room, scattering the contents of their backpacks across the brand-new tables, grabbing pencils from the little cups we've so carefully stocked.

I end up at a table with three boys: two eleventh graders, Freddy and Ismael, and a shy, sweet ninth grader named Robert. Their essays are supposed to focus on teamwork, and I begin by asking them each to go around and read what they have out loud. They are here today to get help on their final drafts.

Before they start I fight back a breath of nervousness. I'm worried about what they're going to read and how I'll respond. I wonder if they're annoyed with me for asking them to read out loud and if any of them are going to volunteer or if I'll have to pick on one of them.

Suddenly Freddy shrugs his shoulders, leans forward, and begins reading aloud from a crumpled piece of paper. I am immediately captivated by his vivid description of the feeling of handcuffs encircling his wrists when he was fourteen and being arrested for beaming lasers at passing helicopters. When he finishes reading what he has so far, he explains that he plans to incorporate teamwork into the essay by recounting how he and his friends, by *not* working as a team, had failed to escape the LAPD.

We move on to Ismael after that. He's written about his grandfather in Mexico, known to have had "less than fourteen but more than eight" children. Ismael isn't quite sure how to bring teamwork into the essay, but after a thorough discussion between the four of us he comes to the realization that his grandfather had been the leader of the team that is his family. Robert, only fourteen but already a gifted writer, has finished his entire piece already, a story about getting trapped on a boat with his family on Lake Mead one summer, as a dangerous storm threatened to capsize their vessel.

We are all impressed with Robert's essay, especially by the way he so easily describes the teamwork required to keep all the family members afloat. After an hour the boys are grinning at one another, energized by all the new ideas they have come up with for their essays. We make plans to meet up often in the next few weeks to continue working together.

When I walk out of the center an hour later, I'm buzzing with happiness. I realize that for the first time since my father died, an entire afternoon went by in which I didn't feel sorry for myself.

In fact I didn't even think about myself.

Months and months later I'm sitting in my office at 826LA. The sounds of the afternoon tutoring session echo in the hallway and I pause, looking up from my computer. I glance at the walls around me, at the walls I painted all that time ago with Dave Eggers, and I realize that he did have an answer for me after all.

Part Five

❖

Acceptance

In a strange way, as we move through grief, healing brings us closer to the person we loved. A new relationship begins. We learn to live with the loved one we lost.

—Elisabeth Kübler-Ross

Chapter Thirteen

2007, I'M TWENTY-EIGHT YEARS OLD.

I'M ON MY WAY to my 7:00 p.m. psychopharmacology class when the accident happens. I've been cruising down Sepulveda, my body still warm and relaxed from the yoga class I just left. I'm listening to Peter Bjorn and John, thinking about how I'm going to see them at the Roxy tomorrow night.

I glance down for just a moment, at my phone or at the little illuminated buttons on the stereo, maybe both, but when I look back up the car in front of me isn't moving anymore.

I'm going too fast to stop. Even as I slam on the brakes, my car makes impact.

My books and bags fly off the passenger seat. *Thwack, thwack, thwack.* The hood of my car crumples. My head snaps forward and then back.

Everything comes to a halt. I quickly turn off the stereo.

I give myself a once-over to make sure that I still have all my limbs, and then I ease my foot tentatively onto the accelerator, following the other car into the parking lot of a nearby gas station.

The other driver is a woman, and we get out of our cars at the same time. Her car looks relatively fine. It's mine that illustrates the intensity of the impact. The hood has crunched up toward the windshield and a tiny tendril of smoke sifts upward into the night sky. I try to smile as the woman approaches, but my breath is already quick and shallow. There is a lump at the back of my throat and I feel the prick of tears welling up.

Breathe, Claire. You can do this. Don't cry yet. Please don't cry yet. You can do this.

We begin to exchange information, and she takes a long time filling hers out, searching for her insurance card, huddling over in the car seat, scribbling down various numbers and information.

Leave, leave, please just leave so I can sob in peace. I chant this in my head over and over while she writes.

She finally hands me a piece of paper, and I give her one in return.

Will you be okay? Do you want me to stay? She looks concerned for me.

No, no, I'm fine, really. Thank you.

I sink back into my car, pull the door closed, and let out a sob. I hold my phone in my hand, my thumb ready to depress any button.

And it all comes crashing down. It swells up and crashes down like a tsunami.

What the fuck am I doing any of this for? What is the point of all of this?

All day I'd been a little sad, could feel the weight of things slightly pressing down, and all day I'd been fighting it. It's okay, Claire, I whispered in my head all day. It's okay. You can do this. You're already doing it. It's working. You're changing. You're getting better.

All day I told myself these things, held my head high, took calm, even breaths.

But suddenly, sitting here in the car, phone in my hand, it all comes crashing down. This thing that I'm fighting every day, all the time.

In this moment, twenty-eight years old on a cool Los Angeles night, my thumb is ready to press a button, the button that will connect me to that person, the person you call when something like this happens.

Except I don't have that person anymore. They're all gone.

I'm nobody's most important person, and I don't have a most important person. The tears are streaming down my cheeks now.

This is it. This is the thing of it.

The thing that leads me to those moments when every part of me is screaming.

I'm nobody's most important person.

Ryan and I have been broken up for months now, and it wasn't long after he moved out that I realized I'd lost a vital connection. I'd lost that unconditional attachment. The one person you call when something like this happens.

I fight this all day. It's okay, I tell myself. It's okay to feel alone, to feel unattached. It's okay to want to attach to someone. It's okay to want to be loved. It doesn't make me a bad person. It's okay.

Except, it's not okay.

I hate myself.

In these moments I hate myself so much. I can't think of one person I know who is no one's special person. I can't think of one friend of mine who isn't a daughter or a sister or a wife or a girlfriend. I can't think of one person who wouldn't have that most important person to call if they got in a car accident, or if they found out that they had cancer or that they won the lottery.

I feel like there's something wrong with me because I'm no one's special person.

Like I'm damaged.

Like I'm not worthy of being someone's most important person.

After a while my sobs subside and I call my friend Timbre. She arrives within fifteen minutes. A big hug. I don't even have to tell her why I'm so upset. She knows. And she is wonderful, so loving. She handles the tow-truck guy, makes decisions, even gives me her husband's car so I can make it to class to hand in a paper on time.

Anything, sweetie, she says. Anything you need.

I cry again on my way to school in her husband's car, feeling so grateful.

I know I'm going to get through this, that I won't always be alone, that I will one day be someone's most important person.

I know that the work I'm doing right now will make me all the more important.

◆

On my way home from school in Timbre's husband's car I try to tamp down the emotions swelling in me.

I don't want to go home. I want to keep driving. Anywhere. Up the coast. Harder, harder, harder—I want to press the accelerator as hard as I can. I can imagine the dark, winding curves of the Pacific Coast Highway. Mountains crashing upward out of the earth on one side of me. The roiling, churning sea on the other. Moonlight glinting in the cresting waves.

Instead I walk up the stairs to my apartment, pick up a package from Amazon that's on the deck, turn the key, calmly open the door, greet the cats, prop my yoga bag up against the door, put my purse on a stool under the kitchen counter, and open a piece of mail.

I walk into the kitchen then, clicking on the light as I enter. I look at a bottle of wine up on a shelf. I imagine removing the cork and just pouring the whole bottle down my throat, can picture the crimson stains, pretty and fading against my skin. Drinking, drinking, filling. I imagine biting down on the glass, consuming the whole bottle, literally eating, crunching, the glass.

I haven't had a drink in thirty-one days.

I lean against the counter, both hands down, cool against the tile. I am screaming inside. I want to drink, to die, to run away.

I can't do this.

I can't make it through this.

Breathe, breathe, breathe—yes you can.

My eyes roam the apartment. I need to find something to do before I cave and open that wine bottle. In the bathroom I turn on the shower, run it hot, hotter. I peel off my clothes and step into the steaming, scalding, water.

I'm fucked. I'm fucked. I'm fucked.

I can do this. I can do this. I can do this.

I turn the shower head off and the tub faucet on, and I let the water fill up and I crawl beneath it, twisting and turning as though the water is a blanket and I am trying to cover myself. I'm pushing hard against the walls of the tub, my arms taut and straight, and I am crying, except I'm not because there are no tears, only breathlessness and an inward wail.

I wrap my arms around myself. I can do this. I can do this. It doesn't matter if I'm fucked.

I'm fucked. I'm fucked. I'm fucked.

It doesn't matter. I'm okay. I can do this.

I'm fucked.

I can do this.

I'm fucked.

Breathe.

I can do this.

Breathe. Breathe. Breathe.

And then I'm standing, and dripping, and lightheaded, and I'm pulling the towel soft and tight around my steaming body.

I crawl into bed and fall asleep, with wet hair, listening to the gurgle of the drain.

◆

I WENT TO MY FIRST AA meeting on Christmas Eve. It was the first Christmas I'd ever spent alone, and that night I went to dinner with my Jewish friend Paul and his dad. We ate Oaxacan food and didn't talk about it being Christmas Eve.

After dinner Paul was going to drop me off so that he could make his regular AA meeting, but I shook my head and told him I'd go with him. He'd been asking me to go for months.

You don't have to do anything, he always said. You don't even have to quit drinking. Just come. Sit in the back.

Paul and I met last summer, in yoga class. He's lean and gentle, with full-arm tattoos and big liquid brown eyes. I was right in the middle of my breakup with Ryan, and, even though we'd never spoken, Paul seemed like the kindest person in the room. I wasn't necessarily attracted to him, but something about him pulled at me.

We'd only spoken a few times, in the hallway, when I asked him if he wanted to go on a yoga retreat with me. The studio had been promoting the retreat for a few weeks and the idea seemed appealing, but I didn't want to go alone.

Paul looked at me for a moment before answering.

Sure, he said finally.

We exchanged numbers, and two weeks later we were in his car, driving north to Ojai to spend an entire weekend doing yoga. We got to know each other during the drive.

I just broke up with my live-in boyfriend of three years, I said.

Ohhh, Paul replied. You're in it, huh?

Yeah, I guess so.

And you're dragging me along for the ride? He laughed when he said this, a twinkle in his eye.

Hey, you're the one who agreed.

We talked for the next two hours. It turned out I was right about him. Paul had been through his own hellish years, so much so, in fact, that there wasn't much left in him but kindness.

It was Paul's kindness that saw me through much of those first months after Ryan moved out. We went to yoga classes together several times a week and sometimes out for dinner at a vegan place.

But despite my friendship with Paul, and the rest of my friends, I was a mess. I'd never really been alone. My whole adult life up to this point had been spent in relationships. First with Colin, then with Ryan.

I combated my loneliness by alternating excessive yoga with excessive drinking. Not a good combination, but my drinking had reached an all-time high even before I left Ryan, and I was at a loss for how to control it.

After that first AA meeting I went home and drank half a bottle of wine. And then the next day, Christmas, I drank even more. The next week I bought a case of wine.

But something about that one meeting had gotten under my skin. The meeting took place in an old house in Santa Monica and, just as Paul suggested, I sat in the very last row and simply listened.

The stories were incredible. Some were far beyond my scope of addiction. But others were simple, like mine. The simple ones even seemed to have a formula. Something bad happened to someone and they started drinking. Just a little at first. They liked the way it dulled things, the way it loosened something inside. A few years would go by and suddenly they couldn't remember the last time they went a day without a drink. A few more years and they had a list of things they regretted saying, things they regretted doing.

My downward spiral was like that too.

I still remember that first summer after my mom died, leaning my young body up against the bar. The unusual taste of a gin and tonic. The slow warmth that spread through me. The way it dulled the grief and eased the fear.

At that first meeting one guy talked about his first thirty days, about what it felt like to reach that milestone.

Thirty days, I thought. I could do thirty days.

Right?

◆

Quitting drinking has definitely made my life a little easier. I'm working full time at a community mental-health clinic and I'm also in grad school, getting a master's degree in clinical psychology. I worked at 826LA for over a year, recruiting and training volunteers, falling in love with every kid who walked through the door, and making a whole slew of friends.

Over the course of that year the feeling I had the very first day grew and grew until finally I couldn't remember the last time I'd felt sad or lonely. I only knew that it was before I started working with those kids, before I started giving myself over to something more important than myself. It was an easy decision to go back to school to be a counselor.

My program requires that I be in therapy, and so a few months ago I began seeing a shrink. I like her. She's older and British and sharp, and I like her office. I like the chairs and the light and the slanted ceiling. I see her on Friday mornings.

The subject I spent the majority of our first few sessions talking about was my pending twenty-eighth birthday. I couldn't believe I was going to turn twenty-eight. It had seemingly come out of nowhere, and not in some apathetic, MTV kind of way, but rather I was genuinely shocked that I was about to turn twenty-eight. It seemed impossible, and the more I thought about it, the less I could understand why this seemed so impossible or why it made me cry every time I thought about those numbers.

Twenty-eight.

We spent quite a few sessions talking about it, my throat closing up as I tried to describe the feeling associated with those numbers.

It's confusing, my therapist remarked, because usually people become anxious before turning thirty. What is it about twenty-eight?

Finally I realized that twenty-eight marked ten years since my mother died.

I realized that when I was eighteen, it wasn't just my mother who died but a part of me as well. Something happened inside me. Something failed to continue. Some part of me just stopped. Stopped growing. Stopped imagining. Stopped becoming.

It was like, without my mother, I couldn't possibly go on. I couldn't grow up, become a woman, do things that she would never know about, go places she'd never been, think things I couldn't tell her.

So even right now, there is a part of me that refuses to believe that I am the woman I have become. Except, every so often I catch a glimpse. I see it in a passing glance in the mirror, hear it in an accidental laugh, stifled and throaty, find it in a footstep, an echo in a hallway. Suddenly there are these two parts of me, then and now, staring back at each other, wondering where the other came from.

I see myself this morning, my body twisted and warm beneath the sheets, the cat curled against my softly rising abdomen. The room is dark from the curtains and the alarm bleeps at 7:20. I watch myself roll over, one hand brushing the hair out of my face.

I take a deep breath, push the covers back in one heavy go, and get out of bed.

There I am, twenty-eight years old, walking into my living room, the warm Los Angeles sun already flooding the apartment. I'm opening the blinds, putting on music, making coffee in my little kitchen. It is Wednesday morning and I have to go to work.

I am in the shower, my head tilted forward, the water as hot as it will go, and then I am getting dressed, opening drawers, pulling on a pencil skirt, slipping on high heels, making the bed.

All the while there is a part of me that stands back aghast. How can she do these things? How can she just go about her life, putting on makeup, turning on her phone ringer, making lunch?

Then I am walking out the door, walking down the stairs, and I'm opening the garage and getting in the car. I'm driving to work, listening to NPR, sipping coffee.

Then I am parking in the garage and walking up the stairs into the clinic. I am unlocking the front door, heels clicking down the hallway, coffee in one hand, purse slung over my shoulder, binder pressed against my chest. Part of me wants to scream when I see this.

Stop. Stop walking. Just stop.

But I can't. I can't stop her.

She's unlocking the door to her office, flicking on the lights, the computer, sitting down, checking messages, hair pushed back over one shoulder, legs crossed under the desk.

And there's nothing I can do.

It's nine thirty and I'm joining my coworkers, my supervisor, for our weekly staff meeting. I'm still drinking coffee, eating a protein bar, balancing a clipboard on my knees, nodding in agreement about a client.

Then it's noon and I'm eating my boring turkey sandwich, responding to e-mail, listening to voice mail, chatting with a coworker, talking with my boss, printing a payroll adjustment form, reading about existential psychotherapy. Then it's three and I'm getting in the car again, spinning up Sepulveda.

I'm tired at this point. And I'm sad. I want more than anything to go home, to crawl between the sheets and close my eyes. I want to turn it all off: the phone, the computer, my awful screaming head.

But I don't.

I park and pull my yoga bag from the backseat, and I see myself standing there at the corner of Westwood Boulevard in my high heels and pencil skirt, yoga bag over one shoulder, hair in my eyes. I'm twenty-eight years old.

And then I'm off again, crossing Westwood, walking into the yoga studio, up the stairs, stopping to check in. "Claire Smith," I say, pulling off one high heel then the other. In the changing room my bare feet feel good on the tile. There is another woman in there with me at first, and as she leaves, the door swishing shut behind her, I look up at myself in the mirror.

And I see her.

Suddenly I see her.

This woman, this twenty-eight-year-old woman.

I am frozen. I know that if I move I'll lose her. She'll go back to being the girl I think I am, and I'll no longer be able to see this woman standing before me.

And so there I am, frozen in front of a mirror in a yoga studio on Westwood Boulevard in Los Angeles, and it is four in the afternoon on a Wednesday and I am twenty-eight years old and my life has in fact continued.

◆

THE FIRST YOGA CLASS I ever took was at Marlboro College when I was nineteen.

I hated it.

I felt self-conscious and awkward. My body didn't do the things the teacher was urging us to try. I had trouble concentrating on my breath. I couldn't stop the constant waves of thoughts coursing through my mind.

I didn't try again for nearly ten years.

When I went to my first class in Santa Monica, I still felt awkward and insecure. But I felt something else too. It was a few months before Ryan and I broke up, and I was desperately searching for something to quell the buzzing in my head.

Walking home along Main Street after the first yoga class, with my friend Elizabeth, I felt the tiniest sensation of relief. A hint of serenity. My mind was relaxed for the first time in weeks.

The feeling wasn't much different from the one I had after an afternoon spent tutoring kids. All the anger and frustration that I'm always carrying around inside of me, all that self-hatred and despair, it suddenly felt soothed.

It was an addictive feeling, and the very next morning I found myself back in another class. I went the day after that too. In fact I went to yoga almost every day that week. The feeling growing inside me was too good to let go of.

Yoga was hard though. I'd grown so used to filling up my life with distractions that it was startling to strip them all away. On the yoga retreat with Paul I sat out in a hammock on the first night and just cried.

All my usual distractions were absent. My evening glass of wine was missing, my phone didn't get any service, and there was nowhere for me to be.

I sat in the hammock, looking up at the bright stars above the canyon, and had no choice but to deal with everything inside of me.

My dead parents. All the years of hospitals and surgeries and bedpans and oxygen tanks. All the years of drinking. All the years of disappearing into relationships and jobs and parties.

After a while I found myself staring, not up into the night sky, but instead into myself. Looking right into all the things I'd been trying so hard not to see.

I'd been running for so long that I didn't even know what I was running from.

When I got home, I went right back to my old habits though. My hectic schedule, frantic social life, and frenzied drinking started up right where they had left off. The only difference was that I knew there was another choice.

That knowledge is what gave me the courage to finally leave Ryan. To quit drinking. But it's still not easy.

The night after the car accident I take another bath. This time I just sit in the scalding water.

The apartment is quiet. I pull my knees to my chest and look around the bathroom. The window is cracked and I can smell the ocean air wafting into the room. The shower curtain blows just a bit.

I look at the shampoo bottles and the towels hanging on the rack. I look at the soap sitting in its dish.

I feel a wave of disappointment. I have no idea who I am. My whole life seems like a series of reactions to my parents' deaths.

I wonder if I'll ever be able to get my shit together.

I don't yet realize that just by sitting here I'm beginning to do exactly that.

◆

I start taking baths every night. In the beginning I hate listening to the thoughts in my head. I constantly battle the urge to get up, to turn the TV on, to call someone, to go somewhere.

Sit here, Claire. Listen to yourself. You owe yourself at least that.

And so I listen.

At first what comes is nothing new. A report I have to finish at work tomorrow. A paper due at the end of the week for my personality theory class. A client I've been seeing who keeps cycling through the same damaging relationships.

Then older stuff.

Those last months with Ryan. The denial we were both in about the state our relationship. The look on his face that last morning before he moved out.

I squirm in the warm water, uncomfortable at having to relive these memories. I lean my head back against the cold tile and take slow, deep breaths.

More memories come.

The last few days with my father. What his hand felt like in mine after he was gone.

I cry, but I force myself to stay still, to keep my eyes closed.

My mother comes next. The color of her skin on the last day that I saw her. That awkward hug we shared. The distant sound of her voice.

I sit up now, lay my cheek on my knees.

I think about all the things she missed. My college graduation. My first time reviewing a restaurant. My father's death.

I dry-heave over the side of the tub. There is a lake of grief inside me, churning open. I can't believe how much this hurts.

Finally I allow myself to get up. I towel myself off, put myself to bed. But the next night I make myself do it again.

After a few weeks the baths actually become relaxing. The bad memories are replaced by softer ones.

One afternoon I clean out all the soap-scummed shampoo bottles and replace them with candles and sea sponges. I grow familiar with the way the shower curtain moves in the night breeze, begin to feel comfortable with the way my thoughts come and go.

I start to find new parts of myself, places that exist beneath the pain. I hadn't realized there was anything there at all.

Each night I put myself to bed, and each morning when I wake up something is a little looser.

◆

MY DAY-TO-DAY LIFE stays the same, but I can feel something breaking open inside me.

Something is changing.

On the ten-year anniversary of my mother's death I write her a letter, like I always do.

Dear Mom,

You have been dead for ten years.

This letter will be different from the others. Things aren't the same anymore. It has taken a decade for me to really care about myself. In my last letter to you I wrote that the upcoming year would be one of my biggest because I would spend it helping other people. I've actually spent it helping myself.

I never realized how much I hated myself. How afraid I was. This last year has been terribly hard and wonderfully healing. I'm alone now. All alone. No more men, no more alcohol, no more self-destructing, no more hiding.

I miss you so much. Ten years feels like a lifetime. I no longer know the girl I once was, the girl who had a mother.

But the thing is: I don't want to do this anymore. Obsess over your and Dad's deaths. I don't want my whole life to be about those experiences. I am grateful, so incredibly grateful, for who I have become because of these losses, but I don't want to live my life based on them anymore.

I don't want to be terrible to myself anymore. I don't want to hide. I don't want to feel desperate or lonely or hateful anymore. I want to stride forward. I want to shirk the heavy weight of all this loss. I want to throw it off like a coat worn on a summer day. I am tired of it all. I just want to be me.

I want to let you go.

I think that maybe, just maybe, in trying not to hold on to you, I can be at peace. I haven't been at peace, Mom. All these last ten years I've been in so much pain. It's been so hard. And I don't want to do it anymore. I need you to release me as well.

I'm so proud of myself now, Mom. I'm twenty-eight years old and I'm living alone in Los Angeles. I have a lovely little home filled with pets and plants and music. In the mornings I get up and make coffee, feed the cats, get ready for work. At night I tuck myself into bed, the curtains drawn, the door locked. I am almost finished with my master's degree. I help people every day. Doing so has taught me how to help myself.

I discovered yoga last year and it has helped me to discover my body again. I'm not afraid of it anymore. I kind of even love it. I hated it for so many years, was so frightened and ashamed of it. And now it's mine again and it's beautiful and strong and young.

Oh Mom. Ten years. I don't need you to be proud of me anymore. I'm proud of myself.

I'm letting you go this year.

Your only daughter,

Claire

◆

SPRING COMES AND with it a torrent of happiness. I feel free for the first time in my life.

I say yes to everything. I won't have a drink for another couple of months, but even when I do it will never again be like it was before. I go to parties and out with different people all the time. I even start going on dates. I'm slow and careful though, afraid of taking things too far with any one person.

Once I stay up all night talking with my neighbor's best friend. He's a young movie producer, and I like the way he uses his hands when he talks. I like the way he looks at me. I go on a blind date with a friend of Timbre's husband. It's not a match, but it's fun all the same. I exchange e-mail with a guy in Chicago who writes for the same literary website I do. The e-mails we write are lengthy and full of an unrelenting kind of honesty.

Everything feels strangely magical. Nothing feels serious.

My grandmother dies on my twenty-ninth birthday. In an odd way I find the date kind of beautiful. My mother's mother, she was my last remaining grandparent. She lived on Cape Cod with my aunt Pam and uncle David, and over the last ten years, since my mother died, I made a point of visiting her at least twice a year.

It took me a long time, after my mother's death, to feel comfortable going to Cape Cod without her. Aunt Pam's persistence in offering herself as a parental figure won out eventually, and after a while Cape Cod began to feel like the only place in the world that really resonated with tones of home.

My grandmother was a big part of that though.

I've been thinking of you, she'd say each time I saw her.

And I knew she really had been. Thinking of me. It felt good to know that someone was.

She was ninety-three, so I'm not sad that her life is over, only that I won't see her anymore. I sit on my deck that morning, the morning of my birthday, and lean my head back into the warm sunshine that's peeking over the roof.

I can't help but feel like I am part of something bigger. Like there really might be a purpose to it all. Like I'm not alone.

I get on a plane a few days later, to go to Cape Cod for my grandmother's memorial service. I haven't been away all spring and the feeling of the plane lifting into the air feels good. I peer out the tiny window at Los Angeles glimmering on the very edge of the continent.

I feel like I can see my whole life from up here. As the plane climbs higher and higher I see all the progress I've been making in the last year. All the yoga and the baths, the dimly lit back rows of the few AA meetings I went to. I see myself happy too, padding around my apartment in the mornings, making coffee, turning on music. Alone but happy.

A feeling of lightness spreads through me.

◆

THE FEELING ONLY GROWS when I arrive in Cape Cod. I'm so happy to see my family. My *family*. My aunts Pam and Penelope. My uncle David. My cousins. These old, weathered houses on the beach that I've been visiting since I was a kid.

At my grandmother's funeral I look around and I am so filled with gratitude. All these years I've been focusing on what I don't have and not appreciating what I do.

After the service we all go back to Aunt Pam's house, and I take up residence in a hammock in the yard. It's Memorial Day weekend, and beachgoers trickle by on their way to the water. My cousins are down at the beach. I'll join them soon. I just want a moment to be still.

I have no idea that just over a year from now I'll be getting married in this very backyard. That it will, in fact, be the happiest day of my life.

I can't possibly know that. Yet I do know something.

I know that everything about the last few months of my life has been magical.

I know that I've changed.

I know that I'm happy.

I know that I've finally learned how to listen to myself.

I smile as I think about all the things I've said yes to in the last six months, all the adventures I've had, all the people I've met.

And then I frown for a moment.

There's one person I haven't said yes to.

The guy I've been e-mailing in Chicago: Greg. He's been asking me to come visit him for weeks.

Each time I said no.

After we became friends in April it wasn't long before we were e-mailing almost every day. Greg is twenty-eight. He works at some boring job in Chicago that I can never retain the details of. He has curly brown hair, blue eyes. He's a writer.

I quickly came to depend on my morning e-mails from him, loved the funny notes he sent me when he got to work. Both of us single, living in big cities, trying to figure out who we are—there was never a lack of things to say.

Eventually we started talking on the phone. I liked the sound of his voice, husky but kind too. Before long we knew everything about each other. The farm he grew up on in Northeast Ohio. His five siblings and MFA. That he shares my father's birthday.

It wasn't long before he suggested we meet.

I'll come to LA for the weekend, he said. Or you could come here.

I shook my head into the phone.

No way. It would be awkward. We wouldn't live up to the ideas we have about each other. And then we couldn't talk on the phone anymore.

Greg laughed. Come on, he pleaded.

Nope.

So we broke up. Or whatever it's called when two people who only know each other online and the phone stop talking.

That was two weeks ago. I miss him though. I miss his e-mails and his voice. I miss his stories and his insights into my silly LA adventures.

Why didn't I want to meet him? I, a person who goes on yoga retreats with people I hardly know and gallivants around the Philippines in search of sharks?

I know it's because I've been afraid of losing this newfound ability to be on my own. I'm afraid of disappearing into another relationship. But I also know that I can't let that hold me back for the rest of my life.

At some point I'm going to have to test my new strength.

I look toward the beach. The breeze carries the scent of salt and suntan lotion up to me.

I pull out my phone and text Greg.

What if I stop in Chicago on my way home from Cape Cod tomorrow?

Hardly a minute goes by before my phone beeps with his response.

Yes. Please. Do it.

THE NEXT MORNING I find myself, not on a plane back to LA, but instead on one bound for Chicago.

I'm nervous and I stare out the window, watching Boston Harbor recede below us. I went out with my cousins last night. When I told them about my Chicago plans, my cousin Chris laughed.

Just like your mom, he said.

I realize he's right. I think about how my mom got on a plane with my father on the afternoon of their first date. I wonder if she felt like I do right now.

I have this feeling like I'm altering the course of something. I'm supposed to be on my way back to Los Angeles right now. I have a party to go to tonight. My friend Lucy is in town from Atlanta. I'm graduating in two weeks from my master's program.

What am I doing on this plane to Chicago?

At the very least, I think to myself, I'll see a city I've never visited before. And if Greg is a total weirdo, then I only have to put up with him for sixteen hours. My return flight to LA is scheduled for eight tomorrow morning.

As the plane rounds its way across the lake, I can see the city gleaming, curving around the lip of the water. We touch down before I can decide if any of this is a good idea. As the plane taxis to the gate I text Greg.

Just landed.

I'm in baggage claim, he writes back.

I'm nervous.

You'll be fine.

The seat-belt light clicks off and everyone stands up. I grab my only bag, a canvas one with my name embroidered on it—a bridesmaid's gift from Liz—and make my way off the plane.

I follow signs to baggage claim, my heart pounding. And then I'm riding the escalator down. In years to come I'll walk by this very escalator a hundred times, and each time I'll look at it in wonder, remembering the final moment before Greg and I really knew each other as it hovered on this moving, silver staircase.

And then he's walking toward me and all I can think is, It's you.

It's you.

The feeling is strange, if only because it is so simple.

We embrace, and the heat from his body tempers my air-conditioning cooled skin. After that we ride the same escalator three times, both of us too nervous and too distracted to figure out how to get out of the airport.

Once we finally make it to his car Greg drives us back to his apartment in Lakeview, where we stand in the kitchen and eat strawberries from a bowl. Greg cut them himself earlier that morning in preparation for my visit, and I can tell it is something he doesn't normally do. The windows are open to let in the summer air, and during our silent moments we listen to the happy sounds of laughter filtering up from the bar across the street.

We kiss for the first time, there in the kitchen, and I'll always remember it for many reasons. One of them is because, for the first time in a long time, nothing about the kiss serves to fill a void.

Again, it is much simpler than that.

He is a boy and I am a girl, and we are standing in a kitchen on a warm summer day, the taste of strawberries sweet in our mouths.

Sixteen hours later I get on an airplane back to Los Angeles. It will be another couple of weeks before I admit to having fallen in love, but as I stare out the window at the Chicago skyline growing distant beneath me, I remember something my mother wrote in a letter a few months before she died.

You'll meet so many men, will attract them like flies. You have that shy sweetness that men love. Don't marry anyone because of money, name, class, need of any kind. Be so much in touch with who you are and what you really want—and then it will happen. Your complement will appear.

Find yourself and you'll find your other self. Give each other space and respect. There can be no nagging doubt. The Italians have a name for it, which I adore, but which I've forgotten. It's likened to being struck by a lightning bolt.

Accept nothing else.

Chapter Fourteen

2003, I'M TWENTY-FIVE YEARS OLD.

IT'S A WARM California evening and I'm driving west on the 22 toward Garden Grove. My father is in the passenger seat beside me. I am taking him home from the hospital where he has been for six weeks, ever since his legs stopped working and we found out that the cancer had spread to his hips.

Must be nice to be outside again, hmm?

My dad doesn't answer and I glance over at him. He's staring out the window at the cars streaming by, at the brightly lit billboards on the side of the highway. He's looking at the world like he's never seen anything like it.

Something inside of me crumples. Then I feel a snag of fear.

My mother had the same look on her face in the weeks before she died.

I look back at the road, gripping the steering wheel with both hands. I am determined to get my father home. To nurse him back to health.

Inside his condo complex I pull the car up alongside the curb. It's about twenty-five feet to the front door. I shift into park and turn off the engine.

I'm going to run in and get the walker, I say. You okay?

Yup, my dad says.

It's early evening and there is still light in the sky. Inside the condo I flick on a few lights and grab my dad's walker.

Back outside I open the passenger side door.

Okay, you ready?

My dad nods but looks nervous.

I help him to swing his legs out the door, making sure they're planted firmly on the asphalt below. I position the walker in front of him, and he grips the handles on either side.

Okay, Dad. One. Two. Three . . .

I watch the muscles in his arms tense, see the tendons strain in his neck. But nothing happens. My father can't stand up.

I think I'm gonna need some help, kiddo.

I lean forward, placing a hand beneath each of his arms.

One. Two. Three . . . I pull upward but I'm not strong enough to lift him, and again nothing happens.

Fear finds its way into my throat. I swallow it down, gulping.

I can see that my dad is growing nervous too.

It's okay, Dad. I'll figure this out.

I run around and climb in through the driver's side. I perch on my knees, wedging my hands underneath my dad's butt. It's an awkward position, and I already know that at this angle it isn't going to be easy to utilize my strength.

One. Two. Three . . .

I try as hard as I can to push him upward. He rises out of the seat an inch or two. His arms are shaking. Mine are shaking. He drops back down.

Oh fuck, Claire. What are we going to do?

It'll be okay, Dad. I promise.

He exhales in a loud puff. *Pfft.*

Yesterday I sat in a roomful of doctors and promised them all that I could handle this. A social worker tapped her pen skeptically and one of the doctors sighed audibly.

I really think you should consider a skilled-care facility, he said.

Before I could object, the social worker spoke up.

I don't think you realize what a big undertaking this is. It's a lot for anyone, let alone a twenty-five-year-old on her own. Your father is very weak.

I cleared my throat, swallowed the bubble of fear lodged there.

I'm going to take him home, I said.

My father looked up hopefully.

I will not cry. I will not cry. I will not cry.

I gritted my teeth and cleared my throat again, just to buy time. If I thought I could have gotten through it without breaking down I would have told them about my mom. About all the years that we'd all been through. About how I wasn't there the night she died.

I can do this, is all I managed to say instead.

But now I'm not so sure. I haven't even gotten my father inside the house and I'm already failing.

Let me try again from the front, Dad.

As I crawl out from behind the wheel and make my way around to the passenger side I have this sudden flash of myself. It's like I'm watching all of this from another place, another time. I see myself at age twenty-five, on a warm June night in Southern California, trying to lift my dying eighty-three-year-old father from the passenger seat of his car.

Tears are running down my cheeks now, but I swipe them away, push down the panic rising up into my chest.

Okay, Dad. One. Two. Three.

I get a grip under each of his arms and pull as hard as I fucking can.

Nothing.

He's breathing heavily now. He is shaking his head.

It's going to be okay, Dad. It's going to be okay. It's going to be okay. We just need to get you inside and everything will be okay. It's going to be okay.

I'm verging on hysterical and I know it.

Wait here, I say.

I take off down the sidewalk, rounding the side of the complex.

Please, please, someone help me.

I knock on the door of a neighbor. Please let this guy be home. Please, please, please.

The unit belongs to a young couple, Mike and Melanie. They're only a few years older than me, married with two little kids. My dad has always been friendly with them, and Mike has helped us out with a couple of things before.

The door opens and it's Mike. He's a big guy and I immediately take in the muscles in his arms, the sturdiness of his shoulders.

Don't cry. Don't cry. Don't cry.

My throat is so tight that the words come in a whisper.

Mike, can you help me?

Back at the car my dad offers him a weak grin. Hey, Mike.

Hi, Mr. Smith.

In one fluid motion Mike has my dad on his feet.

My father sighs in relief and leans heavily onto the walker. I can see his legs wobble and he's still breathing in puffs.

Pfft. Pfft. Pfft.

I wheel an office chair out onto the sidewalk, and we quickly get my dad settled in it. As Mike and I push him toward the front door I reflexively glance behind me. I have this feeling like I'm being watched. Like someone is just waiting for me to fuck up.

Like I already have.

I SPEND THE NEXT WEEK trying to get my dad back on his feet. I'm still convinced that he'll get better now that he's home, surrounded by his books and plants, by all the photos of my mom on the walls. I cook dinner every night, rent all his favorite movies.

A physical therapist comes every day, and together we help him walk back and forth down the hallway. Watching him slowly place one foot in front of the other is excruciating. Time drips by. More than half the time, I realize, I'm holding my breath.

Although I technically still live in Hollywood with Colin, I haven't been home in days. My dad needs too much care to be left alone. Every night I run through a lengthy checklist of medications and comfort measures. I take a baby monitor to bed with me, awakening thickheaded at the sound of his calls at two in the morning.

After a week at home he shows no improvement.

Before he left the hospital the doctors brought up the possibility of hospice on more than one occasion. Each time I stiffened at the word, shook my head no.

My father isn't dying yet. He can't be. I just need to get him home.

He'll get better. They'll see.

After a week of this, though, a tiny thorn of doubt is beginning to twist inside me.

I'm so tired, Claire.

I know, Dad.

It's Sunday night and we're going through the nightly checklist, getting him ready for bed. He takes out his dentures, and I hold out a little dish for him to drop them into. He didn't want to get out of bed today, so we ate dinner in his bedroom, *Jeopardy!* on the television, a napkin tucked into the collar of his pajamas.

I walk into the bathroom and dump the dentures in the sink. I use two toothbrushes to scrub at them so I don't have to touch them. At one point I look up at myself in the mirror, and it's like I've forgotten what I look like.

I stare at my reflection and wonder how long I can keep this up. As determined as I am, I'm also deeply afraid of what's coming.

I'm scared that I'll disappear into this condominium in Southern California. I'm afraid that my friends will recede into the distance, that my budding career will vanish before my eyes. I'm afraid that I won't know myself by the end of it all.

I look away from my reflection and lock the dentures away in their case for the night.

Better get some sleep tonight, I call out. You've got physical therapy in the morning.

Honey?

I can hear it in his voice before he says another word. I already know what's coming next. I stand in the doorway looking at my father.

I don't want to do the physical therapy anymore.

I walk into his room and sit down on the edge of his bed, picking at the sheets like a little girl.

My dad takes my hand. Do you understand what I'm saying?

I can't think of a response. He squeezes my hand.

I've lived a good life, sweetie. You know that. I'm eighty-three years old.

My throat swells up.

Don't cry. Don't cry. Don't cry. I'm so fucking sick of crying.

It happens anyway.

You knew we didn't have much time left, honey. We've made the best of it though, haven't we? These last few years . . .

He trails off and I look up.

I nod at him.

He nods back at me, like we've just made a deal.

I MAKE THE CALL in the morning and a hospice nurse is sitting in our living room by early afternoon. She does a presentation that, years from now, I'll be trained to do myself. She explains the daily care my father will receive from the hospice team, and she tells us that he'll be able to stay at home now that he will have so much support caring for him.

I nod at her, but inwardly I'm weeping with gratitude. The social worker at the hospital was right. This job is too big for me to do on my own.

After signing on with hospice, my dad stops getting out of bed altogether.

A nurse comes every few days. She checks my father's vitals, goes over his medications, and schools me in the best ways to adjust his position in bed, how to empty his catheter bag, and where to check for bedsores.

For the next two weeks my half siblings take turns coming out from the East Coast. Mike comes first, then Candy, and Eric comes last.

They are solemn and careful with our dad. The joking, familiar pattern my father and I share seems startling in contrast, and I am reminded of the very different relationships we have with the same man.

I take advantage of their presence to revisit my old life. For the first time in over a week I drive up to Hollywood and stay the night at home with Colin. Before I leave, I go over my dad's medications with Mike, show him how to work the oxygen tank, explain the bedtime routine.

My father looks on from his new mechanical hospital bed. His eyes are wide like a child's.

I'll be back first thing in the morning, I remind him.

I speed along the freeway, streaming north. Driving is exhilarating. The sky is wide open, the world once again a fast place.

I exit onto Hollywood Boulevard. The city is surreal. It's somehow hard to believe that it's all still here.

Colin and I go to dinner at a Mexican restaurant. I drink margaritas until my limbs are heavy, until I don't care anymore that my father is dying. Until I don't care that I'm no longer in love with Colin.

Candy comes and goes and when my half brother Eric arrives to visit my dad, I stay in Hollywood for three days. I call the condo every few hours for an update but nothing changes. I don't know how to be away from my father. I don't know how to be at home.

On the third day I wake up early. My head is pounding from last night's alcohol and I sit on the edge of the bed until the room comes into focus. Colin is asleep next to me, breathing softly into his pillow.

I crawl out of bed and make my way outside to the back steps. I used to sit out here all the time when we first moved into this apartment. I sink down onto the top step, light a cigarette, and gaze down at Hollywood in the early morning. I let my eyes wander past the Capitol Records Building to where the city spreads out into a blanket of squat buildings, palm trees punctuating the landscape like pushpins on a map.

I think about my dad in his condo, in his bed. About how we are inextricably linked, even in this very moment.

This is it, I realize. This is the time in my life I've been moving toward all these years. I guess I thought I had longer, that maybe I wouldn't lose my father until I was thirty. But I know that's no longer true. He is going to die soon, and I am going to be alone.

It feels like a choice, even though I know it isn't.

Years later I will realize that maybe it really was a choice. Just as stopping at Christopher's that night in New Jersey was a choice, so was the one to arrive here, in this exact moment in my life.

Some part of me must know that even now, because of what I do next.

When I am finished with my cigarette, I stub it out and walk into the bedroom, where I nudge Colin until he opens his eyes.

I'm moving in with my dad, I say.

I know, he says, closing his eyes again.

No, I mean for good.

He opens his eyes again.

❖

ON MY WAY BACK to Garden Grove I replay the conversation with Colin. It was short and perfunctory. There wasn't much to say.

I'm shaking nonetheless. I've been trying to figure out how to leave Colin for years now, and I'm shocked by how easy it was to finally do so. He didn't fight me. Not once. Admitted that it was over for him too. His eyes were dead and he blew cigarette smoke at the ceiling.

We agreed that I would move my things out this week. We parted ways at the door and there was a wildness between us, something frightening and alive, fluttering like a bird.

I grip the wheel of the car with both hands and try to focus on my dad.

This is it. I'm really doing this, I think, as the car speeds south on the 101. Maybe when this is all over I'll just move somewhere where nobody knows who I am. I'll start over, pretend to be someone else, forget about all of this.

When I walk into the condo forty-five minutes later, I can immediately sense that something is wrong. Two days' worth of newspapers sits by the front door. Dishes are piled in the sink. The blinds are pulled shut against the noontime sun.

I see Eric's silhouette on the deck, the fine trail of smoke from the cigarette he holds between his fingers. My heart races as I make my way down the hallway to my father's room. The blinds are pulled in there as well and the room is dim. His six-foot-five frame looks somehow small beneath the sheets.

Dad, I say, taking one of his hands in mine.

His eyelids flicker but do not open. His breath comes in ragged shifts.

Dad?

I let go of his hand, placing it gently at his side and find Eric on the patio.

My voice is high, loud. What happened to Dad?

What do you mean? Eric's voice is flat.

He's completely out of it. He's hardly breathing!

Claire, he's dying.

I turn my back on him and go back to my father's side. I pull a rolling office chair up as close to the bed as I can and pick up his hand again.

After an hour his eyes focus, he flexes his feet. I squeeze his hand. I've decided not to tell him about me and Colin for the time being.

After a while he looks over, his face registering my presence. His voice is gravelly when he speaks.

I wish that I could just go to sleep and not wake up.

I pull my knees up to my chest and dig my chin into them, biting back the tears. I don't know how to respond.

Honey, you have to let me go. You have to.

Tears drip down into little translucent circles on my tank top.

You have to, honey.

Inside I'm screaming. But I know that he's right.

He closes his eyes and starts to slip into sleep again.

I choke out a sob but he doesn't seem to notice. There are things I need to say to him before he dies. I'm afraid to say them though. Saying them will mean that I'm letting go.

I think about that night with Michel, about my own night with my mother. Why do we feel like we have to say these things, these simple things that we spend our whole lives saying in one way or another?

Words. They are like living creatures. They must be honored.

Dad, I say, squeezing his hand until he opens his eyes and looks at me.

I love you so much.

He smiles at me, hinting at a nod.

I will miss you every day of my life.

He blinks, a slow heavy one, a nodding blink.

I manage to say to him, barely discernable through my closing throat, one last sentence.

If I ever do anything great in my life, it will be because of you and mom.

He nods at me and I try to memorize the color of his eyes. Gray like quarry stone.

That's it. Three sentences.

He falls asleep, and I remain at his side for hours, watching him breathe and listening to the sound of kids playing in the pool outside the window.

❖

OVER THE NEXT COUPLE of days my dad pulls through whatever cloud he'd been drifting into and returns to a familiar state, although one in which he can no longer hear. The hospice nurse explains that sudden deafness can be a symptom of dying patients.

I have to shout to be heard now, and hate the sound of my voice when I do. Sometimes I repeat the questions in my normal voice just so I can hear them the way I meant them to sound—soft and pliant. After a while I make up a series of flash cards that I can hold up instead.

Are you in pain? Are you hungry? Are you cold?

Before Eric leaves I spend one more day in Hollywood, packing up my belongings. Liz and Holly are living in LA now and they drop what they're doing to help me pack. Abby helps me drive it all down and unload it into my father's garage.

And that's it. I now live in a two-bedroom condo in Orange County. I soberly unpack my things into the dresser in the guest room, reluctantly place my toothbrush in the holder in the bathroom. Nobody can tell me how long my dad will live, how long I'll be doing this for.

It could be weeks or it could be months, the hospice nurse says.

That night my father wakes me up every three hours. I stand, slit-eyed against the brightness of the room, at the foot of his bed. I drop morphine onto his tongue and I lift his legs, which he can no longer lift himself, and reposition them.

The next day he is quiet. We sit together in the room, our reticence forced upon us. He reaches out his hand, and I lean forward to take it, my chin balanced on my knees, my eyes drifting to the corners.

He fusses with the bedsheets and flexes his feet.

I don't want him to die, but I also don't want it to go on like this.

Colin drives down from Hollywood that afternoon. We sit on the patio while my father sleeps and we say things that we needed to say a long time ago.

We talk about when we first met, about that first summer when we were both so young and so sad. He holds me for a long time after that, and I soak his shirt with tears, my breath hot and childlike on his neck.

When he leaves, I return to the chair at my father's bedside. He is still sleeping, so I take one of his hands in mine and close my eyes too.

I have never felt so alone in my life.

◆

A FEW DAYS GO BY. Liz comes over every day. She brings me lunch, and we sit on either side of my dad's bed while he sleeps. Several years from now Liz's beautiful sister will die of cancer, grief becoming an even deeper aspect of our friendship.

For now, I am impossibly grateful for her presence. Even though we are both twenty-five, I can't help but see us as teenagers still, a quality that makes it feel even more surreal to be the only ones here caring for my dad.

When she goes back to work, panic rises in my sternum. My father is still sleeping and the condo is silent. I pad along the carpet in the hallway and stand in the doorway to his room, watching his chest rise and fall. The oxygen machine hisses in a corner.

He only wakes once that night.

The next morning I wake him gently and then sit beside him while he looks around, getting his bearings. I offer him a sip of water but he shakes his head, motioning for me to give him paper and a pen.

Why? I shout. Can't you speak to me?

He insists. I pass him a pen and a small piece of paper, and then watch as he writes a series of numbers down in wobbly handwriting. They trail down the page in a seemingly meaningless order.

19

9

6

487

9

00

13

.98

0.6

19

088.7

I scan the numbers, trying to figure them out. I think about my father's engineering background, about when he used to help me with my math homework in middle school.

What are these?

Here, just write a number, he finally says, and thrusts the paper at me.

I write down the number three and hold it up for him to see.

Where do they come from? He has a look of awe on his face.

I laugh then and he does too. We both shrug at each other.

I leave the room after a while and place a call to hospice. Confusion in the last days is normal, says the nurse on the phone.

The last days?

Your father is actively dying, Claire.

◆

I AM AFRAID to leave the room now, so I take up residence in the chair beside my father's bed. I haven't showered in two days, but I am afraid to be away from him for longer than a minute or two at a time.

He passes in and out of lucidity, sleeping mostly, his eyes half-open, each breath few and far between.

My friends come over one by one. Holly sits in the living room reading magazines. Abby comes too, and I finally take a shower after she promises to alert me if anything changes with my father. The scalding water feels good and I stay there longer than I mean to. When I emerge, I find her sitting in the gloom, holding my father's hand and singing to him. She'd only met him once before, and I cannot fathom how large her heart must be to do what she is doing in this moment.

After Abby leaves I take up my post in the chair again, my father's hand in mine. I am determined to be here when he takes his last breath, determined to be holding his hand. I keep thinking about all the ways he's done this for me. All the things he did for others in his life. The least I can do is be here for him.

I watch as his mouth widens and each breath becomes deeper. His eyes are partly open, but I know that he is unconscious. The tendons in his fingers jerk, twitching in sleep. I stare at his face and wonder what is happening in his body, his mind.

I imagine that it's difficult for the body to stop functioning, for all these organs and nerves and synapses to just cease to do what they've done for eighty-three years.

After a while, I begin to kind of pray.

"Pray" isn't the right word because I don't think I really know how to do that. But I close my eyes and I think about my mother. I think about my father's parents too. I try to summon their presence.

Can you hear me?

Mom?

Grandma?

Please, please, please. Can you hear me?

Dad is here, I whisper to them. He's ready.

I picture my mother greeting him, see her pressing herself to him just to feel the warmth that my hands have left in his.

After a few minutes I open my eyes to find that his are open.

He leans forward suddenly and puts his hand on my face, my hair, my eyes. I close my eyes and let him. I don't think he's touched me like this since I was a kid. When he withdraws his hand, I look at him and see that there are tears in his eyes.

He talks then, for the first time in almost a day.

Life *is* worth living, he says suddenly, sounding more coherent than he has in days.

Years later, when I look down at the note card upon which I copied these words down, they will never cease to slay me.

Death and birth are such sweet sorrows, he continues. If there were no death, you would never know how sweet life really is. Somebody was smart enough to put that down in writing one day.

◆

THOSE WORDS WERE HIS LAST. The few things he utters over the next day are nonsensical, unintelligible. My father is all but gone.

Colin drives down from Hollywood again that night. We sit by my father's bedside, not talking, just watching his chest rise and fall and counting the seconds between each breath. The intervals grow longer and longer.

Past midnight Colin goes to bed, and I pull a blanket over myself in the chair. I am exhausted but I don't know how to let go of my father's hand.

I don't know how to let go of my father.

I want to scoop him up like a baby, to run away with him. I don't want to do this. I don't want to say good-bye.

But I know that I must. I know that in order to walk forward from here, I must. Everything about the last few years rises up through me. My mother and Vermont. Colin and New York. Los Angeles and all that is to come.

I stand and lean over the bed, laying my head down on my father's chest. I can hear his heart, distant and muddled within all the layers of him. I let my head rise and fall with each cadence of his breath. I want to stay here forever.

I close my eyes and sink into sleep.

A few hours later I wake up. Colin is next to me, his hand on my shoulder. I am back in the chair but still holding my father's hand, my wrist throbbing against the bedrail. My eyes flick to my father's face.

I watch him take in a breath.

I stand and stretch. I open the blinds on the other side of the bed and stand looking out at the sparkling California morning. There are a couple of kids playing in the pool, their shouts and splashes muffled through the glass that separates us.

I turn back to my dad and place a hand on his cheek.

Dad?

Dad?

Nothing. No twitches. No flutters. He does not respond, except to draw in another labored breath.

In the kitchen I call the hospice number and give them an update. They tell me to expect a nurse by evening.

Colin is readying himself to leave.

Do you want me to come back later?

I shrug. I am delirious. I am exhausted. All I know is that I can't do this for much longer.

When he is gone, I shuffle back down the hall and take up my perch in the office chair, holding my father's hand, counting his breaths.

Abby, Holly, and Liz all take turns coming to the condo. They sit in the living room, talking in hushed voices, jumping up the moment I enter the room, their eyes wide with concern.

It's almost seven in the evening when the hospice nurse finally arrives. Abby and Holly have gone. Colin has returned and is in the living room with Liz. I lead the nurse back to my dad's room.

I take his hand as she checks his vitals. She is quiet and kind, smiling at me with warm eyes. I don't know how she does this day in and day out. She wants to change his diaper, and so I stand to help her. We will have to turn my father on his side to do this.

I just want to warn you, she says, sometimes doing this—moving them when they're like this—causes them to go.

I stop what I'm doing and stand there, looking down at him. My entire being is flooding downward, pooling out around us on the floor.

It feels like a choice, even though it isn't.

I'm ready, I say, my voice a whisper.

Carefully we turn my father to one side and the nurse unclasps the diaper, pushing it to the side and placing a new one there. I stay on the side that my father is facing, my eyes glued to his, listening to the breath coming in and out of his mouth.

It's okay, Dad.

I can't tell if I'm saying this out loud or not.

It's okay, Dad.

It's okay, it's okay, it's okay.

We turn him and I go around to that side of the bed, taking one of his hands while the nurse finishes with the diaper. I look down at my father's hand, at the wrinkles and the thin threads of purple veins.

I am flooded with a thousand memories of him. In one split second I think about all the things he was in this life. The son and the brother and the father. The inventor and the pilot, the prisoner and the protector. I think about all the ways he held on to me after my mother died. The least I can do is hold on to him in return.

The nurse finishes, and we roll him back to the center of the bed. She pulls the sheet up, tucking it around his chest, and we both watch his face, watch him take in a breath. I cannot tell if I am relieved or not.

Then seconds go by and nothing happens.

More seconds. Too long. His eyelids are halfway closed, his mouth all the way open.

Dad?

He sucks in a breath.

The nurse's voice startles me.

Honey, I think this is it. Do you want me to get your friends?

I nod at her, my eyes never leaving his face.

I'm leaning over the bed, holding one of his hands with both of mine.

Dad, Dad, Dad, Dad, Dad, Dad, Dad, Dad.

My tears are dripping down onto the sheet that covers his chest.

Colin and Liz are there then. Liz is opposite me, holding my father's other hand. Colin is beside me, his arms tight around me.

I am squeezing my father's hands, still warm and pliant.

This is the moment. All of it swirling together. Me and my mother and father. The shared afternoons of puddled golden light. The future, the past, the present. All of it, all at once.

Right here, right now.

My father sucks in a breath and then it whooshes out again softly.

Dad, Dad, Dad, Dad, Dad, Dad, Dad, Dad.

He is gone.

Chapter Fifteen

2011, I'M THIRTY-TWO YEARS OLD.

I'M DRIVING IN frantic circles around Chicago's Lincoln Park neighborhood. I'm looking for a parking spot, but because of last week's blizzard piles of waist-deep snow obscure most of them. Story time at the zoo started ten minutes ago and my daughter, Veronica, is threatening certain death if I don't release her from the car seat soon.

Argh! I exclaim, finally cramming the car into a snow-filled parking space and twisting around to unbuckle Veronica's car seat.

Five minutes later we walk into story time, harried and frigid. As I remove our hats, scarves, and mittens I take a look around the room. A dozen moms and nannies are sitting on the floor with their toddlers, bopping their heads and clapping hands in time with the music.

We plunk ourselves down on the carpet and Vera promptly throws her arms around me in a desperate attempt to thwart the anxiety she is feeling around so many strangers. I rub her back and begin to sing along to "Old MacDonald Had a Farm." Although she keeps her arms around me, after a few minutes I feel her loosen her grip, craning her head to look around. I can't help but let a small smile creep across my face.

Right this moment I'm just another young mom at a playgroup with her daughter.

I'm not thinking about anything in the world but me and my daughter, about the feeling of her little body pressed to me, about her breath hot on my neck, about the bond between us.

It's only later that I am able to take note of how different I am from who I used to be.

I have spent the majority of my adult life thinking about what I don't have. For a long time, I could only look at my present and my future through the lens of my past. My parents' deaths colored everything I saw.

There's another side to grief though, and I'm on it.

◆

THE NEXT MORNING my cell phone rings as I'm getting ready for work. Veronica chirps from her high chair, where she's making messy attempts to spear a small pile of scrambled eggs with a fork. Greg sits in front of her, his hair still mussed from sleeping, and cajoles her playfully.

Mmm, can Daddy have some?

Veronica cackles and gleefully drops a handful of eggs onto the floor.

I finally locate my phone at the bottom of my workbag. My supervisor, Alex, is on the other end.

Claire, before you come in, can you to make a visit to the Hutchinsons? George is a phase 3 and his wife could really use some support.

Sure, I say, pulling on my heels and grabbing my bag off the coat hook in the kitchen.

I'm a bereavement counselor for a hospice, and George Hutchinson is one of the patients our team cares for. Phase 3 means he's actively dying and will likely be gone in a matter of days. I've talked to his wife, Judy, a few times on the phone but I've never met her in person.

When I moved to Chicago three years ago, I had just graduated from my master's program and wasn't sure exactly what kind of work I wanted to do. For weeks I scrolled through job listings online, going to various interviews and checking out the local mental-health clinics.

One night I saw an ad for a hospice grief counselor and something clicked. Of all the medical approaches my parents experienced, hospice was the only one with a positive outcome. Even though that outcome had been my father's death.

I first heard the word "hospice" a few months before my mother died. But instead of going that route, my mom went to that hospital in DC, where she had several more operations. I'll never stop wishing that she had chosen hospice instead.

Hospice provides care and comfort to dying patients. Sometimes hospice takes place in a hospital or a center, but more often hospice patients are in their own homes. The basic philosophy is to ensure that a person's dying experience is as peaceful as possible, for the patient as well as the family.

A hospice team is made up of doctors, nurses, health aids who bathe and clean the patient, a social worker, a chaplain, a volunteer team, and a bereavement counselor. Everyone works together to make sure that the patient and family are well cared for, not just physically, but emotionally and spiritually as well.

When my daughter was born, I experienced the opposite of death. I realized how much it takes to bring a person into this world and how the experience is rewarded with preparation and presence of mind.

Dying is the same.

My job as the bereavement counselor is to contact each family following the death of the patient. I check in to see how they're doing and I offer counseling and guidance. I facilitate grief groups and I also run workshops and conduct one-on-one counseling. Sometimes I meet with families or patients before the death.

Today, in George Hutchinson's case, I'm going to do my best to offer support to his wife.

I park in the driveway of the Hutchinsons' simple two-story house in a suburb near O'Hare airport. The neighborhood is quiet. Garbage cans are out, and a man walks his dog down the sidewalk.

I sit in my car for a moment and look at the house. You could drive down any neighborhood street and never know that inside one of the unassuming houses someone is taking their last breaths.

I ring the doorbell and wait a few minutes. I glance down the street again. The man walking his dog has disappeared. Finally a tired-looking woman comes to the door.

Judy?

She nods at me.

Hi, I'm Claire from hospice. We spoke on the phone a couple of times. I'm the bereavement counselor.

Her eyes well up with tears. She nods and opens the door wider for me to come in.

I follow her into a dimly lit living room. A man, whom I take to be Judy's son, is in the kitchen. He gives a little wave but doesn't introduce himself.

George is asleep, Judy says. That's Brian, our oldest.

I nod, taking a seat on the couch.

The nurse was just here, Judy says, her voice cracking. She takes a breath and continues. She said . . . She said . . . it's probably a matter of days, possibly hours.

I put my hand on hers. Her skin is warm.

She weeps silently for a few minutes, and we just sit together in the quiet room.

There is no solution for what Judy is going through. There is nothing I can say or do that will change anything. My presence is the only thing I can offer. But it's worth more than it may seem.

In all my years of grief, and in my years as a bereavement counselor, the single most powerful healing mechanism I've found is simple presence. The opportunity for a person to feel seen and heard in the middle of one of the loneliest experiences in their life can have a profound effect.

Next month we'll have been married for thirty-two years, she says. Judy exhales her sentences in halting breaths.

I always thought we had more time.

All of this happened so fast.

He was just diagnosed six months ago.

George was so full of life before he got sick.

Over the next hour she tells me about their life together. How she and George met, about their children and the places they traveled. She cries on and off and gets up twice to check on him while he sleeps. I never once see him.

When it's time for me to go, Judy stammers an apology.

I'm sorry I talked the whole time. I didn't mean to do that.

Please don't apologize, I say. That's what I came here for.

I know I'll see Judy again, likely as a member of my Saturday grief support group.

We embrace at the door, and then I get in my car, back out of the driveway, and drive away from the Hutchinson house.

A few hours later I hear from one of the nurses that George passed away.

◆

AFTER I LEAVE the Hutchinsons I drive to a nursing home in Arlington Heights to visit another patient.

Her name is Ethel James. Her son won't be there until three, but she is actively dying and he has requested that someone sit with her until he can get there.

I find her room at the end of a long hallway, on the second floor of the nursing home. I've never met Ethel and I've never spoken to her son. The lights are off and Ethel is lying in bed, under a blanket. Her eyes are closed. She is unconscious.

Her breaths come in rasps and they are few and far between. She seems peaceful though.

I pull a chair up to the bedside and carefully take one of Ethel's hands in mine. Her skin is warm but there is no response when I squeeze her fingers.

It's a strange thing to hold the hand of someone you've never met. I watch her chest rise and fall, and then my eyes travel up to her face, to the wrinkles around her mouth and the creases next to her eyes.

I wonder what she did in her life. Who she loved, who she lost. What her biggest dreams were. If they came true. I can't help feeling how connected we all are in life's simplest pursuits.

I settle back in the chair and close my eyes, Ethel's warm hand in mine.

◆

A FEW DAYS LATER I park my car in the underground garage at the hospital and grab my bag and a box of tissues from the backseat. It's Saturday morning, just after 10:00 a.m., and I'm about to lead my weekly grief support group. The click of my high heels echoes down the hallway as I walk toward the elevators, and I reflexively check to make sure that my short-sleeved shirt is covering the tattoo on my shoulder.

It's a dumb tattoo—it kind of looks like a Chinese throwing star—and it's right on the ball of my shoulder. I got it when I was eighteen, barely a week after my mother died. At first it was just a circle but a few months later, in Europe with Liz, I had the star tattooed over it. At the time the tattoo served no other purpose than to mark the occasion of the worst thing that had ever happened to me, but now the only thing it serves to do is ensure that I never wear sleeveless shirts.

The elevator dings and I step off and into a hallway on the tenth floor. I'm early—the group won't begin for another half hour—but I want to get set up before everyone arrives. I toss my bag in a corner, turn off my cell phone, and stand for a moment at the windows that look out over the flat, snowy Illinois landscape. I think for a moment about my intentions for the group, about what I hope to accomplish by being here today, and then I turn and place a sign-in sheet on the table, as well as two boxes of tissues.

Finally I take a seat at the head of the table and cross my hands in front of me, smiling as each member of the group enters the room. Marcy arrives first. She's in her early fifties, with short, stylish hair and a collection of fantastically chunky and eclectic jewelry. Her husband died six months ago and not one session has gone by when she hasn't hung her head and wept.

Sarah takes a seat next to Marcy. Sarah lost her father just two months ago. She cared for him at home, and now that he is gone she feels incredibly alone and directionless. James arrives after that. His elderly mother died in this very hospital, and he's confessed that he still finds himself wanting to walk through the familiar hallways to her room, hoping that she'll somehow still be there. Katie comes in right on time. Her husband died in a terrible car accident five years ago, leaving her to raise their children on her own. Katie has only now found herself able to face her grief. She revealed to me early on that she still pays the bill on her husband's cell phone so that she can call and listen to his voice on the outgoing message.

A woman named Trudy arrives and takes a seat next to Marcy. Trudy lost her boyfriend to a sudden heart attack just over a year ago. He died in her arms in the apartment they shared. A few weeks after he died she found an engagement ring he intended to give her, tucked away in his sock drawer. She wears it on her ring finger now and refers to him as her fiancé. She explains that it gives the loss more legitimacy.

When I say I lost my boyfriend, no one takes it seriously, she says. Calling him my fiancé changes everything. Only then do people think I actually lost something.

The rest of the group nods along in response to Trudy's statement.

Nobody gets it unless they've been through it, Sarah says.

And thus group has begun. We usually begin with a general check-in, unless a spontaneous discussion like this one starts things off.

It's true, Marcy chimes in. Did I tell you guys what the woman who sits next to me at work said last week? I'm still furious.

The group gives a collective head shake, and I settle deeper into my seat.

She told me that she thinks I'm being really negative, and that if I just focused on happier stuff then I wouldn't be so sad all the time. I lost my fucking husband, Marcy says.

I hope you said that to her. James looks expectantly at Marcy.

No, of course I didn't. I couldn't even speak. I just walked away.

I lean forward now. Marcy, tell us more about how you felt when she said that to you.

She begins to cry, and James pushes a box of tissues toward her.

I was so angry, she says, balling her hands into fists. But sad too. I felt so . . . so . . . lonely. Like no one understands what my world is like.

I can see other members of the group nodding their heads in agreement.

Marcy's voice grows stronger as she talks.

Coming here every week is a huge release. It's like you guys are the only ones in my life who get it. I can come here and cry and not have to explain anything.

I feel the same way, Sarah adds. I feel recharged after these meetings, like I can go back out and face the rest of the world.

Exactly, Marcy says.

Everyone is nodding now, the conversation unfolding on its own. I lean back in my chair again and steal a glance out the windows. The sun glints off little drifts of snow caught on the sill.

Even in the midst of all this pain and sadness I see something beautiful. I see a basic human connection. I see a bond created out of loss and love. I see what it means to move forward through life.

I see how fragile and how strong we all are.

◆

I DON'T KNOW what happens when we die.

I've spent over a decade thinking about it, and I still haven't come to a firm conclusion.

When I was growing up, my parents attended a bland amalgam of Presbyterian and Methodist churches. I went to Sunday school and attended youth groups, but none of it ever resonated. After learning about the role religion played in controlling populations, in my world history class in tenth grade, I came home and told my mother that I was no longer going to attend church.

Three years later, when she died, I realized I had no idea where she was. In those early years after her death, when I was full of sadness and fear, I decided that she was nowhere. It was easier to believe that she was simply gone, that life was pointless and bleak and that it could be over in an instant. The alternative—that she might really be somewhere else—was somehow more painful to accept.

As the years went on, my stance softened.

It happened in small moments.

I remember standing underneath the inky night sky one night in Wyoming, while driving across the country with my high school friend Laura. The night air was cool and the stars were brighter than I'd ever seen, and life suddenly seemed much bigger than I'd ever given it credit for.

In that moment I felt humbled—and foolish for thinking my life was so important that it might be all there is.

The night my father died I held one of his hands in mine as he took his last breaths. I watched his chest rise and fall for the very last time, and when I looked up at his face again, my father was gone.

He was gone.

My realization in that moment was swift and simple: we are not these bodies.

My daughter was born seven years later, on a cool June night in Chicago. I labored for nine hours without medication, and when her slick, hot body emerged from mine I felt every cadence of her arrival.

I also felt the undeniable presence of a force much bigger than me.

WHEN PEOPLE ASK ME what I do and I say that I work in hospice, they often recoil in a horror that ushers forth a series of well-meaning exclamations.

Oh, isn't that hard?

That seems so sad!

I couldn't do that.

The truth is that I don't find it sad at all. When I talk to grieving people, it's like looking at a negative image—the deeper the grief, the more evidence of love I see.

After my father died I let the follow-up calls from the hospice bereavement counselor go unanswered, and sought out my own coping methods. Sometimes these involved drinking and losing myself in the people around me, but I was also driven to learn as much about grief as I could.

I read everything from scientific texts to memoirs about loss. I found myself drawn to movies about death and to information specific to my particular parental loss. I read about trauma and its effects on development. I studied anxiety and how to overcome it. I read about attachment theory and tried to link it to my current relationships.

I couldn't help wondering if what I felt was normal. And each time I came across someone else's story, each time I found reassurance that I wasn't alone in my grief process, I relaxed a little more.

I see this happen all the time with the people I counsel. Whenever one of the members of the grief group relates to another, each time one of them registers recognition with another's loss, I see their shoulders drop just a little bit. I note the slightly audible sigh of relief. Just saying the words "it's okay to feel sad" can elicit an enormous release of emotions from a grieving person, and with that release comes a touch of peace.

The bottom line is that there is simply no one way to define grief, but the irony is that almost every grieving person I've met seems concerned about whether they're doing it right.

There just isn't a right way to grieve though. There's no easy way to heal, and certainly no time frame to adhere to. Yet without fail, the majority of people question the way they're going about it.

Almost all of them bring up Elisabeth Kübler-Ross's five stages of grief.

I think I'm in the anger stage, one will say.

I don't understand the bargaining process, another remarks.

I don't think I'm going through the grieving stages in the correct order.

Elisabeth Kübler-Ross herself says, in the opening paragraph of *On Grief and Grieving*, that "the stages have evolved since their introduction, and they have been very misunderstood over the past three decades. They were never meant to help tuck messy emotions into neat packages. They are responses to loss that many people have, but there is not a typical response to loss, as there is no typical loss. Our grief is as individual as our lives."

The stages are just there to give you a frame to work with, I tell them. You may never experience all of them. You may go through them out of order or sometimes find yourself in more than one of them at the same time.

More often than not judgments about how to grieve come not from the people who experienced the loss but from the people around them.

It's been six months, a friend might say.

After a year you have to move on, another might opine.

Even the *Diagnostic and Statistical Manual of Mental Disorders* allots only two months to grief in its current assessment of the process.

I know that I constantly considered myself a mess, but now that I'm no longer in the midst of grief, I can look back with understanding and sympathy at how I reacted to the loss of my parents.

It breaks my heart to see myself at age twenty-two in New York. How lonely I felt. How afraid I was of myself and the world around me. Of course I was lost in my relationship with Colin. Of course I drank too much. Of course I cried myself to sleep on a regular basis.

If I'd had someone, anyone, to guide me through those years, to tell me that what I felt was normal, that I wasn't alone, maybe it would have been different. But if you haven't been through a major loss, then the truth is that you just don't know what to say to someone who has.

I know now that grief is a process, and that to move through it you must give yourself over to it. I fought it for a long time, trying to fill up my life with as many people and distractions as possible. Years after my father's death, when I finally forced myself to sit through all those baths, I discovered that the grief had never really gone away. It had just been covered up.

I've had people show up to my group with decades of hidden grief in their hearts. One man lost his wife thirteen years before attending the group. Their daughter was six months old when his wife died, and he felt that, in the throes of taking care of an infant, he didn't have time to grieve.

Now that his daughter was entering high school he felt that he might have room in his life to attend to those lost emotions. The grief came hard and fast, as though it had never been hidden at all.

But isn't that like walking into pain? One of the members of my group asked this question recently when we were discussing how to sit with grief.

Why would anyone want to walk *into* pain?

I know I certainly didn't. But when I did, I found that it didn't hurt as much as I thought it would. And once I walked through it, I knew that doing so was much easier than what the effect would have been had I not.

I will always mourn the loss of my parents, and in the last few years, as I've become a wife and a mother, I've missed them more than ever. But I'm no longer actively grieving.

Losing someone you love is akin to a deep physical wound. It will eventually heal but there will always be a scar.

It's not that the loss goes away. It's just that you learn to live with it.

◆

AFTER THE GROUP CONCLUDES I gather up the boxes of tissues and the sign-in sheet and head back to my car in the garage. I turn off the CD player as I drive home, winding my way through the Chicago suburbs until the yards give way to sidewalks and buildings.

I live in a quiet neighborhood near Lincoln Square, on the north side of Chicago. Greg and I found this place three years ago, and I will always remember it as the place where I became a wife and a mother.

In the morning we wake to the sound of ducks quacking on the riverbanks, and if I time it right, every afternoon I can catch a glimpse of a rowing team powering north through the murky brown waters. The apartment itself is sun filled, with hardwood floors and an old art deco stove.

I park in the garage and climb the steps. I walk in through the back door, and I can hear Greg and Veronica before I see them. They are having an imaginary tea party by the living room windows.

It's early afternoon and sun floods the room, capturing them both in a golden light. My young, handsome husband and our beautiful, little daughter.

There is only a single breath before they become aware of my presence, and in that breath I wish desperately to stop time. I want to live in this moment forever.

But I know I can't.

I know that we will all keep marching forward. That Veronica will one day become a woman. That Greg and I will grow old.

That all three of us will die.

But I also think that somehow, somewhere, this moment will continue to exist. That it will spin out across the universe, the three of us, linked by love and by those who have loved us, encapsulated for the rest of time in a perfect bubble of golden afternoon light.

ACKNOWLEDGMENTS

It's hard to know where to begin thanking the people in my life for making this memoir possible. Creating this book wasn't just about writing, but about moving forward as an individual with the help of many, many others.

I'd like to first thank the esteemed group at Penguin, in particular Clare Ferraro and Caroline Sutton, and especially Denise Roy, who is more my idea of a soul mate than an editor. A generous heap of gratitude is due to my agent, Wendy Sherman, who believed in me when others didn't, and who is a model for the kind of savvy and confident woman that all females should aspire to be.

I am so appreciative of the team at Advocate Hospice in Chicago, and the members of my Saturday bereavement group. My time with all of you taught me more about life and love than you know.

I want to deeply thank two of my most influential writing teachers, Pearl McHaney and Joan Dulchin. Pearl, you flung open the door of literature for me, and Joan, you pulled me through it.

The amount of friends and family I want to acknowledge is vast. A big thank-you to writer friends Jillian Lauren, William Richter, and Brad Listi for helping me along the publishing path. Thank you to Jessica Herman, Emilie Zanger, Elizabeth Garrett, and especially Lien Ta for early reads and valuable criticism on these chapters, and for being the best kind of friends a girl could ask for. Speaking of girlfriends, Ashley Alexander, Laura Dawson, Channah Gray, Amber Hopper, Abigail Freeman, and Francesca McCaffery must also be thanked for their fierce love and support through the years. Holly Bond Farrell and Lucy Curtis, you both get a special shout-out for seeing me through some of the worst years, and loving me despite—we'll always have Bangkok. Liz Gillies, if I have a sister in this life, it is you.

Additionally, a hearty thanks must be sent out to all of my devoted blog readers. Your comments, e-mails, and support over the years have been astounding and have filled my life with a strange magic that only strangers over the Internet are capable of creating.

Finally, to my aunt and uncle, Pam and David Purdy, who have treated me like their own child, I will never be able to thank you enough for all that you have given me. Thank you to my brother Mike Smith—I'm always happy to tell you how much I love you. More gratitude to my aunt Penelope Chatterton and my cousins, Ron, Jessica, Kristen, Chris, Steffani, and Alex; I am honored to be part of this family. I also want to thank Bill and Rita and all of their children for folding me into your clan—I feel privileged to carry the Boose name.

Lastly to Greg and Veronica, you have healed me. I am so humbled to be your most important person.